Counseling
the
Depressed

RESOURCES FOR
CHRISTIAN COUNSELING

RESOURCES FOR CHRISTIAN COUNSELING

(*Other volumes forthcoming*)

VOLUME FIVE

Counseling the Depressed

ARCHIBALD D. HART, Ph.D.

RESOURCES FOR CHRISTIAN COUNSELING

General Editor

Gary R. Collins, Ph.D.

WORD PUBLISHING
Dallas · London · Sydney · Singapore

Scripture quotations in this volume are from the King James Version of the Holy Bible, unless otherwise indicated.

Library of Congress Cataloging-in-Publication Data

Hart, Archibald D.
  Counseling the depressed.

  (Resources for Christian counseling; v. 5)
  Bibliography: p.
  Includes index.
  1. Church work with the mentally ill.   2. Depression,
Mental—Religious aspects—Christianity.   I. Title.
II. Series.
BV4461.H37   1987   253.5   86-28940
ISBN 0–8499–0582–6

0 1 2 3 9 AGF 9 8 7 6 5

Printed in the United States of America

To Catherine, our eldest daughter, who has temporarily "returned to the nest" prior to her marriage. She has demonstrated that human love can be unconditional, not a duty, and that a parent's persistent prayers do not fall on deaf ears. As she soon makes her marriage vows, my prayer for her can be summed up in the one word I have come to associate with her—Shalom!

ACKNOWLEDGMENTS

BEHIND EVERY BOOK are numerous people who make it possible. This book is no exception.

I wish to express my deep and loving gratitude to my wife, Kathleen, for her continued support, encouragement, and honest criticism of the contents of this book.

In addition, I am thankful to two other women who helped me complete this writing assignment: Susan Nordin, my faithful and efficient secretary, helped me with research and then typed and retyped the manuscript with unfathomable patience, while Bertha Jacklitch, my administrative assistant, held the fort of my deanship role and protected me from unnecessary intrusions.

As always, my clients have contributed in many ways to this project. They have inspired me to believe that a Christian approach to psychotherapy provides a unique and effective resource for healing. They have also provided many of the illustrations and case material cited. While I talk freely about these clients throughout this book, let me hasten to add that I have taken the liberty of modifying their stories sufficiently to disguise their identities. I hope they derive much satisfaction from seeing that their painful experiences can help others.

CONTENTS

EDITOR'S PREFACE

HAVE YOU EVER BEEN DEPRESSED? Few, if any, of us would answer "no" to that question.

Depression has been called the "common cold" of psychological problems. It affects people of all ages (including children), it creates untold misery, it can come without warning, and it sometimes lasts for months or even years. Relatives often don't understand it, well-meaning Christians sometimes try to deny it, few of us can "snap out of it," many of its victims try to hide it, and every year there are thousands who end their own lives because of it.

I used to tell my students that depression is one of the most challenging problems for counselors. Often caused by a combination of physical and psychological influences, depression is like a snarled rope, difficult to untangle and holding thousands of people in a bind of despair and hopelessness. Who could guess how many articles and books, both popular and technical, have addressed the topic of depression and offered suggestions for its victims and their counselors?

As every counselor knows, we currently are living in the midst of a "counseling boom." Surely there has never been a time in history when so many people are aware of psychological issues such as depression, concerned about personal problems, interested in psychological writings, and willing to talk about their insecurities, inadequacies, and intimate concerns. Within only a few decades we have seen the birth of a great host of theories, degree programs, books, seminars, articles, new journals, radio programs, films, and tape presentations that deal with counseling-related issues. Numerous counselors have appeared, some with good training and great competence, but others with little sensitivity and not much awareness of what they are trying to accomplish.

Perhaps it is not surprising that the counseling field is confusing to many people, threatening to some, and often criticized both within the church and without. Nevertheless, people still struggle with psychological and spiritual problems, stress is both a personal and social issue, and many seek help from counselors.

And how does the counselor keep abreast of latest developments? Many turn to books, but it is difficult to know which of the many volumes on the market are of good quality and which are not. Nowhere is this more apparent than in the hundreds of books on depression.

The Resources for Christian Counseling series is an attempt to provide books that give clearly written, practical, up-to-date overviews of the issues faced by contemporary Christian counselors. Written by counseling experts, each of whom has a strong Christian commitment, the books are intended to be examples of accurate psychology and careful use of Scripture. Each is intended to have a clear evangelical perspective, careful documentation, a strong practical orientation, and freedom from the sweeping statements and undocumented rhetoric that sometimes characterize books in the counseling field. All of the Resources for Christian Counseling books will have similar bindings and together they will comprise a complete encyclopedia of Christian counseling.

In view of the complexity and confusion of the writings

on depression, my colleagues at Word Books agreed that we needed to find a clear writer, competent scholar, and skilled counselor to write a book on counseling the depressed. Dr. Archibald Hart came to mind almost immediately. Dean of the Graduate School of Psychology and Professor of Psychology at Fuller Theological Seminary, Arch Hart is a successful writer, a committed Christian, and a gracious gentleman who has skillfully and successfully helped many people untangle themselves from the grip of depression. Dr. Hart's previous work with the depressed qualifies him uniquely to deal with this crucial and common issue.

When he agreed to write the book I was delighted; when he sent the manuscript I was enthusiastic. In my opinion Dr. Hart has done a superb job of clarifying a complicated issue and giving practical counseling guidelines. His is a volume that avoids simplistic answers and combines the latest scientific knowledge about depression with realistic counseling guidelines. All of this is presented in an interesting and readable style.

I suspect you will find, as I have, that this book will be a valuable and frequently consulted addition to your counseling library.

Gary R. Collins, Ph.D.
Kildeer, Illinois

INTRODUCTION

ALMOST EVERYONE KNOWS what it means to be depressed. I certainly do.

But not everyone can counsel a depressed person because it takes a special kind of understanding to be helpful. Most lay people (and quite a few professionals) bungle their attempts to be therapeutic because they lack the courage to encounter depression. They may try to be helpful, but good intentions are not enough. Before you can successfully counsel anyone afflicted with this, the most painful of all emotional disorders, you need to be finely tuned to the intricate complexity of this multi-faceted malady; you need to know enough about your own propensity to depression to be inoculated against sympathetically picking it up from another. You cannot help when you don't understand!

Even experienced psychotherapists can be inept at helping depressed patients if the professionals do not understand the true nature of the malady. They are likely to lack the patience needed to walk through the dark valleys with the melancholic or they find that another's misery triggers reciprocal feelings in themselves. Their own depressive reactions are too easily set in motion by the pain of another's unhappiness. But don't disqualify yourself as a counselor of depressed persons too quickly. Effective depression counseling *can* be learned since the principles that underlie therapeutic help are well defined and quite easy to grasp. Almost anyone can be a more effective people helper if he or she will learn and apply these principles.

Sooner or later most of us will be confronted by depression. It's just a matter of time before a father, mother, brother, sister, child, or friend will become depressed. Whether we are mature and deeply spiritual persons or "babes in Christ," depression will hit us. Sometimes it is only a mild "downer"; sometimes it comes as the deepest blackness we can imagine.

In the work place, fellow workers will be overtaken with it for no apparent reason; in the parish, church members will not escape from it. In fact, according to my experience the average-sized church could have as many as 5 percent of its members experiencing a significant depression at any one time. Does this seem excessive? Perhaps it does, but this is only because so few people who are depressed ever ask for help. Depression does not get publicized; rather, it is the "hidden" illness. And at some seasons of the year, in winter, for example, the incidence of depression can be considerably higher. Most pastors recognize this and make provision for extra counseling time during these "depression seasons," or they set up special programs to give a lift to groups who are particularly vulnerable.

We cannot escape the reality of depression. We will either be a victim to it or called upon to support someone through it. This is a fact of human existence and the more we know about depression—its causes and progress and especially how we can help those afflicted by it—the more satisfying our ministries will be.

There is a further reality we cannot escape: A dramatic increase in the incidence of diagnosed depression can be expected in the next ten years—for reasons I will discuss in the first chapter. The Christian church has to face this challenge with understanding. We have to be willing to confront the challenge

16

because depression significantly impacts the spiritual dimensions of life, not just the physical and psychological. Much misunderstanding about depression has to be dispelled, and pastors and lay counselors need to be better equipped to deal with this insidious problem. Every minister ought to understand the basics of depression—what causes it, who is most susceptible, and what treatments are effective. Only then can spiritual problems be discussed and differentiated from the secondary consequences of depression. Only then will we be able to prevent the undue suffering of tortured and guilt-ridden people who unmercifully blame their pain on their lack of spiritual commitment or growth.

Are highly trained professionals the only ones equipped to help depressed people? Definitely not! While the more serious forms of the disorder *must* be referred to a trained specialist for evaluation and treatment, help can and must be provided at *many* levels. Some depressions need only caring and concerned lay counseling help. The normal expressions of depression: sadness, grief, and discouragement will often yield to the expression of care from understanding friends and loved ones. Others need more skilled help. This book is designed to provide the information needed to prepare counselors to help at all these levels.

It will be my goal to raise the level of helping skills of caring friends, lay counselors, pastors, people managers, and professionals, with or without a background in psychology. Obviously, sections of this book will speak to one level of helper while others will speak to a different level. I invite you to accept the level of help most suited to your background and interest.

Counseling
the
Depressed

RESOURCES FOR
CHRISTIAN COUNSELING

PART ONE

UNDERSTANDING DEPRESSION

DEPRESSION RANKS HIGHEST among the misunderstood emotions. It is seen as a destructive, negative, and even demonic condition, and Christians are encouraged to "do away with it." But is it always destructive? Is there not some healing element to depression? Should it always be avoided or are there times when depression should be welcomed, even encouraged, as a way of facilitating emotional healing?

These are important questions confronting the Christian counselor—professional, pastoral, or lay.

Effective counseling can only follow from a clear understanding of the nature and purpose of depression. Much depression experienced by normal people is functional; it serves an important purpose in the healing process. True, it can easily get out of hand, but the skilled counselor can turn the depression into a healthy and healing force. Distorted beliefs about the nature and function of depression can produce consequences more serious than the depression itself. In particular, they exacerbate the low feelings by feeding additional losses into the depression cycle, losses that cause further depression, even more difficult to eradicate.

The first section of this book is designed to provide the counselor with an in-depth understanding of the nature of depression. It is, because of space limitations, a rather brief treatment of a very complex topic. My goal is to show the counselor that depression should not always be condemned but sometimes welcomed and valued. It can often be used to bring healing to the total person.

CHAPTER ONE

POPULAR MISCONCEPTIONS ABOUT DEPRESSION

"THERE'S NO HOPE FOR ME." Those were Mary's first words to me.

As she walked in and sat down in my office, it was quite obvious that she was in a deep depression. I can usually read it in the eyes. Don't ask me how, I just know it when I see it. I've seen enough of those droopy and cloudy eyes to know that they spell *despair*. She had been deeply depressed for about eight months, she told me, and had tried everything—from herb tea to sleeping on her stomach—to get rid of it. She had prayed for many hours at a time, increased her tithing to the church, and attended regular prayer meetings—searching for relief. She had been counseled by three or four pastors and attended two healing services, but to no avail. Her depression would not go away. In fact, it seemed to be getting worse.

"Why is God doing this to me?" she wailed, tears streaming down her face. "Doesn't he know how much it hurts? My heart went out to her as I felt my own tears well up. She was desperate and had diligently tried every spiritual remedy anyone had offered her. Like so many other devout Christians, she was trapped between the pain of her suffering and the hope that a loving God would work a miracle.

"I've examined every aspect of my life," Mary continued. "I read my Bible as much as I can and I really do believe in God, but nothing changes."

Then one day, in utter desperation, she called the counseling line of a popular religious television program, thinking she might get some help. The counselor, without waiting to hear all of Mary's story, said to her, "It's quite obvious that you have displeased God and he is punishing you by sending depression. Otherwise you are demon possessed. I'll send you a pamphlet that will help." Then the counselor hung up.

Mary's heart sank even lower. If she had been in dark despair before she called, she was now in a black hole. The pamphlet she later received from the counselor made matters worse. It said that "the basic cause of depression is sin" and "anything less than faith in God is sin." It went on to admonish the reader to "recognize that depression was the result of sin and confess it to God." She brought the pamphlet to show me that she had proof she was "damned to go to hell."

FAULTY BELIEFS ABOUT DEPRESSION

Mary is not alone in having her depression intensified by the bombardment of insensitive and misinformed Christian counselors. I have encountered scores of "Marys" who have been damaged by this callous disregard for the many non-spiritual causes and consequences of depression. It so happens that one month later Mary was free from her depression and today lives a happy and peaceful life.

Erroneous beliefs about the nature and causes of depression abound. A recent newspaper advertisement for a "Christian psychologist" (this is what he called himself) announced that:

"Labels such as depression, paranoia, guilt . . . describe the condition of the unbeliever, not the Christian." He then went on to invite the reader to call his office for an appointment. While the advertisement might help the advertiser to pull in some troubled patients, it hardly helps to correct the many faulty ideas that are contributing to much unnecessary pain in our Christian communities.

Many Christian writers as well as influential preachers contribute to the perpetuation of these misleading ideas. "The cause of fear and depression is the breaking of God's spiritual laws," says a recent magazine article. "If you walk close to God, you'll never be depressed," said a prominent radio preacher. I shuddered when I heard his words. All over the country, troubled people must have had their pain aggravated.

Another Christian magazine article says, "Depression is not something you catch like a cold. It's something you bring upon yourself by free choice." It continues, "As children of God, we don't need to be depressed or defeated in life. God has already provided us with everything we need for life and godliness. . . ." To this second statement I say a loud amen! God *has* provided us with all we need for life, but one of his provisions is *also* the ability to mourn and grieve over our losses. This form of depression (mourning) is a healthy emotion and Jesus Himself said, "Blessed are they that mourn; for they shall be comforted" (Matt. 5:4). But to imply that *all* depression is contrary to the will of God, as the first statement quoted above does, is to distort the truth. This should become clear as we proceed.

The Consequences of Faulty Beliefs

What is the consequence of these ideas? Generally, they make depression worse. If you are depressed because of some natural event in your life, such beliefs can cause you to feel more of a failure than you really are and may even drive you away from God, rather than draw you towards him. While some depressions can respond to a severe scolding, most cannot. It is callous and almost cruel to punish those who cannot shake off or confess away their depressions, and that is what we do when we tell them that God doesn't want them to feel sad.

But aren't some depressions the consequence of sin? Could it not be that if we abandon God we get depressed? *Yes.* But only *some* depressions are like this. Most are the result of complex causes.

How are the beliefs I've described erroneous?

They are *simplistic* generalizations. These ideas usually begin with *all* instead of *some* and imply that solutions are easy. They also give the impression that there is only *one* type of depression with *one* cause.

They lump all feelings of "unhappiness" into the category of depression. Not all unhappiness or discontentment is depression. Depression is *not* synonymous with sadness, despair, or despondency. It is a unique clinical syndrome.

They tend to give one exclusive explanation for *every problem.* They leave no room for alternatives or variations. It's like saying that all pain is produced by a faulty brain. It's true that the brain is the organ that tells us there is pain, but the pain itself is the consequence of damage somewhere else in the body. All pain is not the same.

They spiritualize every human problem that cannot be understood or physically seen. This is a problem in the realm of the emotions. Because we cannot "see" the defect we tend to find spiritual causes.

They ignore honest and reliable scientifically derived information about the complex nature of depression and of the effective treatment so readily available today.

On this last point, I'm greatly concerned that those popular Christian writers and speakers who have spoken loudest about depression are those who have least explored the scientific literature on its nature and cause. This neglect, unfortunately, is not only obvious in the area of depression. It shows itself as a lack in the understanding of many other mental health problems as well.

Common Erroneous Ideas

I was at first tempted to do a very specific critique of the ideas of those popular Christian writers who have spoken out about depression—to point out the erroneous features of each of their teachings. On reflection, however, I doubt if this would be helpful. I have chosen, therefore, to present my point of view without directly criticizing anyone else and I leave it to the *reader* to weigh the facts and come to a personal conclusion. To help the reader see the contrast, I will attempt to provide a more general review of these erroneous ideas without pinpointing their specific origins. Most of the ideas don't really originate with these contemporary authors but have been around a long time.

Before presenting these erroneous ideas, let me make two preliminary comments. First, there are many forms as well as many causes of depression. Keeping this in mind will help you avoid the pitfall of looking for a single cause or general explanation. Ideally, we should have developed different labels for the different manifestations of depression. Since this hasn't been done, we are stuck with just one name for it. Second, some of the erroneous ideas I will discuss may seem (at least to some readers) to be very simplistic. They will seem like they have been resurrected out of the dark ages. Nevertheless, there are millions of people in our evangelical communities (and I suppose elsewhere also) who still cling to these ideas, no matter how archaic they may appear to the more sophisticated reader.

Here then, are the more common erroneous ideas about depression:

1. Depression is the result of sin. This is a common theme in the teachings of popular radio and television preachers, yet it's been around a long time. Job heard it when God tested him with affliction. His friends tried to comfort him by asking "Is not thy wickedness great? and thine iniquities infinite?" (Job 22:5). Job had already responded, "miserable comforters are ye all" (16:2). And he was right, because he had not sinned and God vindicated him in the end.

But is there any truth to this idea? Yes there is, but one must hasten to add a qualifying statement: Sin is *not* the only cause of depression, nor is all depression the consequence of sinful acts.

Scripturally, sin is seen as rebellion against God or the breaking of God's laws. Implied in the concept is the idea that we have set our will against that of God. There is no doubt in my mind that sin is a reality in our world. I know it all too well personally. And while provision has been made for sin to be forgiven, we still reap the consequences of our sinful acts.

Galatians 6:7 makes this clear: "Be not deceived; God is not mocked: for whatsoever a man soweth, that shall he also reap." This is not only a natural law, but a spiritual one also. Sinful behaviors can give rise to the necessary conditions that cause depression, but depression should never be seen as God's punishment for sin. Many people sin but never get depressed. And many people get depressed who have not sinned. As we will see in due course, the most common of all forms of depression is caused by the experience of loss. And in this regard there is *sometimes* a connection between sin and depression, as it is quite common for sin to set up the conditions for significant loss. What are just a few of the losses that can follow sin? A loss of confidence that you are in God's favor; a loss of the sense of God's presence; a loss of a sense of well-being; a loss of respect for yourself for violating your own values and moral standards; a loss of the inner assurance of God's Spirit.

These losses can cause significant depression, but note this significant point: The depression is a consequence of the losses, not the sin. Many don't feel these losses when they sin, and therefore experience no depression.

We should, as counselors, be careful to distinguish between the *cause* of depression (those acts or beliefs that create a sense of loss) and the consequence of the loss (depression). If the *cause* is sinful, then appropriate steps of personal confession and repentance are necessary. When we restore the lost relationship with God, the depression naturally abates since there is no longer a state of loss.

Separating the *cause* from the depression is extremely important for four reasons. First, if the *cause* is a natural loss, the element of guilt can and should be removed from the depression. This guilt often adds more loss and aggravates the depression further.

Second, if the *cause* of depression is sinful, the focus of spiritual counseling should be on the *cause*, not the depression per se.

Third, it helps to separate the pain from the disease. What doctor would only treat the pain and ignore the disease? In our analogy, the *cause* is the disease and the pain is the depression. We must constantly be searching for and treating the cause, not just the pain.

Fourth, separating the cause from the depression speeds up the healing process by clarifying for both the counselor and client the true nature of the depression. When we know what causes our depression, we more rapidly move to the place of healing.

2. Depression is caused by a lack of faith in God. Here the idea suggests that all depression is caused, kept alive, or perpetuated by a lack of faith in God. Simply stated, this implies that if you were "strong in faith" or "deeply spiritual" you would not get depressed or you would get over your depression quickly. If you don't, you are a spiritual failure.

Some years ago, a friend of mine had an interesting experience. His wife was going through a bout of significant depression which she could not control. She sought professional treatment but, because of the unique form of her disorder, she did not respond to treatment immediately. There was a delay of about three months between the time she started treatment and finally recovered. Both of them are deeply committed Christians and attend an adult Bible class regularly in their church.

Even though they were close friends of nearly everyone in the Bible class, they noticed that they were being shunned. And it wasn't just their imagination. Slowly, insidiously, but very definitely, friends kept their distance. It seemed that they were afraid of the depression or that they weren't quite sure how you should speak to a depressed person.

In telling of the experience, my friend said that he found out for the first time what it must be like to be a leper and be shunned by people. What was devastating, however, was to find out later that the reason for the shunning was that many of these basically caring and concerned friends believed that the depression would somehow "contaminate" their faith, not so much in an infectious sense but because it challenged the stability and validity of their faith. They feared facing up to the fact that depression could not be overcome that easily. A strong assertion of faith wasn't enough—and they didn't want to know about that!

Sometimes the cause of a depression *can* be clearly traced back to an inability to accept God's conditions for our lives or to adjust to situations in which God has placed us. This lack of

27

faith or trust in God's plan for us can both create and perpetuate depression—and is quite common. But so much depression is *not* tied to faith issues. We cannot generalize or make any statement that implies that whenever we are depressed it is a sign of weak faith. This is not true.

3. Depression is God's face turned against you. I actually heard a respectable television preacher say this to someone the other night. He implied that God had abandoned the listener and was waiting for repentance. As I recall, the preacher quoted some verses of Scripture to support this (they were taken out of context) and related it back to how his "mommy" used to turn her back on him as a little boy whenever he did something bad. "This," he said, "is what God does to us."

Poor preacher! If that was how his mother punished him for being bad, he is almost certainly doing the same thing to his own children. It is what psychologists call "punishment through conditional loving," and it is the cruelest form of punishment any child can experience. It means that if the child does good things, he or she gets love. If the child does bad things, he or she gets rejection. Often the child sets up a pattern of behavior that later tries to please others just to get their love. It is a major cause of neurosis in our age. Such children, when grown up, develop neurotic forms of guilt that cannot receive forgiveness. Their sense of "badness" is great and depression is a common emotion for them.

But is depression a form of God's abandonment? There are important theological questions here that we need to answer: Is God like a neurotic parent who will withdraw his love when he wants to punish his disobedient child? And even if God does do this, why should depression be the consequence?

It is true that if we reject Christ we will one day be judged (John 12:48). It is also true that God chastises his children (Rev. 3:19), but this is not the same as his punishment. How can God punish us now? If he did, then we wouldn't need his forgiveness. The idea that God punishes us now is very commonly held, but it is theological nonsense. This is the age in which we are called to repentance. God is patiently waiting for our response. There is no punishment now, because if there were then where would there be room for repentance? God

28

may be displeased with our sin, but his love for the sinner continues. Second Peter 3:9 assures us that "The Lord . . . is longsuffering to us-ward, not willing that any should perish, but that all should come to repentance." His punishment does not come now (in the form of depression) but later, on the day of judgment.

No, depression is *not* caused by God turning his back on us, but rather by our turning our backs on him. It is not God who is conditional in his love to us, but we who are conditional in our love to him. Unlike Job, we do charge God foolishly (Job 1:22) and withdraw *our* love when we don't get *our* way. This is a cause for depression, but we bring it on ourselves.

4. Healing from depression is a spiritual exercise. There are other prominent Christian leaders who concede that depression is often the natural consequence of normal life events and that it can have roots in biochemical and genetic causes. But that is as far as they go. "Healing," they insist, "is God's prerogative, and *only* God can cure depression, no matter how it is caused." I don't want to be too unkind, but I get the feeling that they also imply that this healing can only come through their specific ministries.

I fully acknowledge the power of God's interventions. Be thankful if God spontaneously heals your depression. Pray whenever you can for the sick. But please, please, please, don't take away from deeply hurting and pathetically pained individuals the wonderful relief that modern medicine and Christian counseling can provide.

God *never* intended that he should cure *all* our pain and suffering *all* the time. If this was his intention, why would he have encouraged us to "Bear . . . one another's burdens, and so fulfill the law of Christ" (Gal. 6:2)?

These same Christians who insist that only God can heal depression do not impose a moratorium on natural or medical treatment of more observable diseases. For instance, when confronted by a man who has had his leg badly crushed in an accident, they will quickly call for the paramedics and they will support surgical healing endeavors. Because they can clearly see the physical cause of the disease, they accept a physical cure as a God-given blessing. But when the cause of an emotional

29

problem cannot as readily be seen as physical (and many depressions are in this category), they push exclusively for a spiritual form of healing. My plea is for open-mindedness for *both* spiritual and physical forms of healing.

THE TENSION BETWEEN PSYCHOLOGICAL AND SPIRITUAL SOLUTIONS

At this point I would like to briefly discuss one of the most troublesome problems confronting the Christian counselor: the tension between psychological counseling and spiritual forms of help.

Since Sigmund Freud accused religion of creating neurotic dependency, there has been a tension between Christianity and psychology. Suspicion, fear, mistrust, and even outright rejection has been the church's response to psychology.

Some of this rejection has been appropriate. Psychology, like so many disciplines, has many "schools," and not every point of view is essentially true. But not all of it is false either, and much scientifically derived psychological understanding is not in conflict with our Christian beliefs. If anything, it complements our faith and serves as a tool of the gospel. For instance, when I come to see how my early upbringing influences my thinking and behavior, I help to release the power of God to help me change; I don't hinder it! Ignorance hinders the gospel (Eph. 4:18) and a fuller understanding of our human conditions drives us to God, not away from him (Hos. 14:9).

Carter and Narramore rightly argue that much conflict between Christianity and psychology is imagined.[1] Kirwan believes that Christian counselors can legitimately utilize the findings of psychology.[2] The issue for the Christian counselor or psychologist is not whether to use only spiritual or psychological forms of help, but how to use both in an integrated way, probably with a stronger bias towards the spiritual. After all, the ultimate meaning of life can only be determined spiritually.

LEVELS OF HEALING

As Christian counselors, we need to have a clear understanding of how healing can take place at many levels. Frequently we will be confronted with questions from depressed people: Why doesn't God heal me instantly? If he doesn't heal me, does it mean I am out of favor with him?

Depression, more than any other emotional disturbance, prompts questions such as these because the depression itself increases the sensitivity to guilt feelings and creates a hopeless outlook. An understanding of how God heals is a great challenge to the task of integrating theology and psychology. No matter what technique he or she uses, every counselor has to struggle with questions, such as Who does the healing? Is God's healing always instantaneous or does he heal gradually (as in "process" healing)? Do I leave it entirely up to God to heal or do I participate in some way? Is it appropriate to use a variety of healing methods, especially to mix psychological and spiritual methods?

The whole theology of healing is potentially divisive to the church. Without being partisan on the issue (I do not see myself as having the theological expertise to talk intelligently about the matter at a scholarly level) let me make a few basic assertions that I believe most Christians would accept. Then I will suggest a model by which various "levels" of healing can be understood and integrated.

First, I believe we cannot have a theology of healing without a theology of suffering. Sooner or later everybody dies, and in order to die you must get sick. Putting it another way, some sickness is the inevitable consequence of living and cannot be avoided. To live gracefully and peacefully, believers must learn how to suffer.

God is in the refining business. He wants to purify and cleanse. And suffering plays a role in this purifying; it helps us to become more like him. The apostle Paul demonstrates this clearly in 2 Corinthians 12:7–10. He found God's grace sufficient for his affliction and found that "when I am weak, then am I strong."

Second, God does not heal everybody. Why? This is a mystery hidden from us. Many have tried to explain it (often to excuse their own lack of power to heal "everybody"), but none satisfies me. Prayers for healing are not always answered. Perhaps our motives interfere, perhaps our fears. It is important that Christian counselors take God seriously on this matter, but that they not take themselves too seriously. It is necessary that you be free of the need to prove anything and of any personal desire to see dramatic results. If you are too caught up in instant cures, it is probably time to examine your motives. God's healing is a gift. And it is his prerogative to give it when he sees fit.

The healing of persons—whether in their spirits, emotions, or bodies—is central to the gospel. But are there not different levels of healing? Must God's healing always be in the form of a dramatic miracle? Can it not also be a gentle breeze blowing through a troubled body and mind, bringing newness of growth and freshness of spirit? In the latter case, healing may be less dramatic and more of a process.

I like to view the various understandings of healing as having several levels. This model has helped me to understand my role as a Christian psychologist better, and it may be helpful to you:

Level 1: God Heals through Miraculous Interventions

At this level, God clearly cuts across nature and performs a dramatic and supernatural (by our understanding) change in some diseased condition, moving it towards health. An example of this would be a person who clearly has a cancerous growth one minute, and no evidence of it the next. Or it could be a blatant schizophrenic, screaming and acting inappropriately one moment, who is totally calm and fully recovered the next. This is the healing advocated in James 5:14,15, ". . . and the prayer of faith shall save the sick."

I believe that this level of healing is provided as God's prerogative. He chooses when and where it is granted.

Level 2: God Heals through the Resources of the Gospel

Here, healing is provided through facilitation of natural processes by the use of supernatural resources. God, in a sense, cooperates with nature but the resources used by the Christian are supernatural.

In the Christian's life, the indwelling Christ works to heal memories, enable forgiveness, overcome fearfulness, and free us from cravings and strong desires. The resources of prayer, Scripture, and the power of the Holy Spirit enable a healing process to take place. James 5:16 suggests this. "Confess your faults one to another, and pray one for another, that ye may be healed. The effectual fervent prayer of a righteous man availeth much." Confession of faults to one another is closely akin to Christian counseling and we do this with prayer so as to be healed. *The Living Bible* translates verse 16 as "Admit your faults to one another and pray for each other so that you may be healed."

I believe that this level of healing is the prerogative of every Christian.

Level 3: Healing Is Effected through "Christianly" Living

Good, clean living, the avoidance of damaging substances, diet control, proper sleep, good stress management, and living at peace with God and others facilitates natural healing. Much "counseling" operates at this level of healing.

This is the prerogative of every person (not just Christians). It is merely the sensible application of God's rules for living. In a non-Christian, this level does not effect complete healing, but it does relieve much suffering.

Level 4: Healing through Human Interventions with Nature

This level of healing is primarily that provided by medical science. By supplementing body deficiencies, surgically removing clogged arteries or diseased organs, or using antibiotics to aid the body's immune system, we bring about healing by intervening or supplementing nature.

This level of healing is also available to all of God's creation.

As Christians, we ought to allow and be open to all four levels of healing. They are all appropriate and valid. While we pray for and trust God to intervene, we *also* utilize other levels. I like to think that level 2 is always available in Christian counseling as a birthright for all believers. Many of the techniques I will discuss fit in well here.

With a clearer understanding of the nature of many forms of depression and improved skill in diagnosing them, the counselor should be better able to select a level (or levels) of healing that is appropriate to the cause of a problem.

THE SPIRITUAL COUNSELING OF DEPRESSION

All depressions have spiritual components. One cannot be depressed, whatever the cause, and not experience some spiritual consequences. Usually these consequences are negative and destructive. In my book *Coping with Depression in the Ministry and Other Helping Professions*, I provide a complete discussion of the spiritual causes and consequences of psychological depression (chapter 3). Because it would be redundant to repeat all I have said there, I encourage you to read that chapter at this point.

The Relationship between Depression and Sin

In summary, I wish to emphasize that we must not condemn all depression as being sinful. There are, however, four conditions under which depression can clearly be related to sin:

1. When the cause of depression is sinful—as when we have committed sin and experience the consequence of this.

2. When we fail to take the necessary steps towards healing—as when we refuse treatment and perpetuate our misery (and that of those around us).

3. When depression is the consequence of giving power to others—as when we allow others to control our lives and deviate us from the plan and purpose to which God has called us.

4. When we fail to rise up from depression at the appropriate time—as when depression is so "dividend paying" and self-rewarding that we stay depressed when we should be shaking it off.[3]

The effect of depression on one's spiritual life can be quite devastating. Conversely, an inadequate spiritual life, with neglect of prayer and devotional exercises, can cause or aggravate depression. The sensitive counselor will explore the many alternative interplays between spiritual factors and depression.

To aid the counselor in counseling the spiritual aspects of depression, I would suggest the following guidelines:

Guidelines for the Spiritual Counseling of Depression

1. Assure your clients that depression makes spiritual problems seem worse. They should stop judging themselves until you

can explore the problem in more depth with them. If there is a problem, you will help them find a way back to God.

2. Assure your clients that God is still in control. He understands their pain and will help in the healing process. Pray with your clients to invoke God's healing.

3. Stop your clients from trying to figure out *why* God allows depression. The answer is "We don't know." Suffering is a great mystery, and blaming or trying to out-guess God is pointless.

4. Encourage your clients to exercise faith, even if doubts are overwhelming.

5. Create hope; convince your clients that they *will* come out of their depression sooner or later. Show your confidence that healing will take place and assure your clients that you will "be there" until it is over.

6. Point to spiritual resources. Encourage regular praying even if they feel God doesn't hear; encourage regular Scripture reading even if they can't concentrate.

CHAPTER TWO

THE PROBLEM OF DEPRESSION

DOWN IN THE DUMPS. Under the weather. The pits. The blahs. The blues. Lower than a snake's belly. The black pit. Everybody has a favorite expression to describe his or her experience of depression. And anyone, especially a pastor or counselor, who undertakes the care of others will soon realize that depression is an unavoidable part of life.

Depression is a complex emotion. While there is still much to be learned about it, a great deal is known already.

THE SCOPE OF THE PROBLEM

How common is depression? The answer depends on whom you ask. It is difficult to get an accurate estimate of how many people are depressed because criteria for diagnosis vary from study to study, and because so much depression goes unrecognized and untreated. Here are some sample reports:

Psychology Today reported that nine million adults in the United States are victims of depression every year.[1] Of this group, 15 percent eventually are driven to self-destruction. It stalks all ages and all walks of life. Whereas it used to inflict older adults, it is now as common in the young as the old.

At a symposium at Temple University School of Medicine in 1980, Dr. Robert Cancro reported that between ten and twelve million people experience a depressive episode in any one year.

Many people still "hide" their depression or see it as something they must live with or deny. "Put on a Happy Face" is not just a song title; it is a life philosophy for many, no matter what their mood. About seven million people are estimated to be clinically depressed at any one time and *not* seeking treatment.[2]

An extensive review of the literature reveals that the lifetime prevalence for depression is between 17 and 20 percent. This means that between 17 and 20 percent of the population can expect to become depressed in a lifetime.

High Risk Groups

What about risk factors that increase the likelihood of a person developing a disorder.

Various subgroups of the population are clearly at higher risk than others.[3] The following is a summary of these risk factors:

1. Sex. An overwhelming body of research shows a higher rate of depression in women than in men, with a ratio of two to one.[4] Why is this? The evidence is strong that the menstrual cycle with the associated hormonal and endocrine factors may be adding risk for depression in women. But women are also at risk because of the lower status many hold in our society.

2. Age. Recent community surveys report a higher prevalence of depressive symptoms in young adults (eighteen to forty-four years) than older adults. This is a change from earlier in this century when older adults were reported to be more depressed. The elderly are also becoming more depression prone as life-span is lengthened.

3. Marital status. Overall, separated and divorced persons show a higher incidence of depression than do those who have

never married or those who are currently married. Rates are clearly lower among married persons than among single persons.

4. Religion. No relationship between religion and depressive symptoms has been found, except in a few small religious groups that have inbred through closed marriages. Here, the more serious forms of depression are four times as common, presumably because of the strong genetic factor in its cause.

5. Social class. Whether defined by occupational, financial, or educational level, there is strong evidence that rates of depressive symptoms are significantly higher in persons of lower socioeconomic status.

6. Genetic factors. Over the past ten years, the understanding of genetic factors in causing depression has grown tremendously. There is compelling evidence that hereditary factors predispose one to the bipolar disorders—depressions that alternate with states of mania (previously called *manic–depressive disorders*). Hereditary factors are less clear in other forms of depression.

7. Biological factors. Almost monthly, research into the functioning of the brain and its connections with the body reveals some new complexity. There is a growing acceptance that clinical depression can be triggered in a number of different places in the body. The interactions are complex and still unclear. Physical illness almost certainly increases one's risk for depression, but so does having a certain "high risk" physiology. These will be explored in more detail later in this book.

Prospects for the Future

As we look into the decade ahead it is the considered opinion of many experts that we will not be seeing a decline in the incidence of serious depression, but rather an *increase*.[5]

There are many reasons for this. Here are some of the more important:

1. Aging population. More and more people are living longer and depression proneness increases with age.

2. Children and teenagers are becoming more depressed. Depression in these groups is becoming easier to diagnose. Many teenage problems are now better understood as problems of depression rather than as "adjustment reactions."

3. Increased stress. As we become more technologically sophisticated, we don't become less stress prone, but more. The pace of life has and is increasing all the time, and the resulting strain pushes our bodies to the limits.

4. Increased disillusionment. Our culture in general is changing its values and tending to become less certain of what it believes in and stands for. People are increasingly questioning whether or not we have all the answers for right living in a complex world. This disillusionment impacts all of us, even when we feel we have a right relationship to God. Depression is the inevitable consequence of this diminished hope.

5. Age of melancholy. The earlier part of this century was characterized by what many psychologists and sociologists called an *age of anxiety*. Most of Freud's preoccupations with psychological illness focused on anxiety and how we defended against it. Since the Second World War, this age of anxiety seems to have given way to an age of melancholy.

Only a return to the values of a sound Christian-based set of beliefs can restore us to wholeness and heal us from such a mass melancholy. Clearly, our hope should be in God, not in our material success or national achievements. Somewhere along the way we've become derailed and need to get back "on track" again. In the meantime, we can expect people to become more depressed. It is our responsibility, or perhaps obligation, to help them cope with this pain in an effective and life-restoring way.

AN OVERVIEW OF TREATMENT

Depression has been with us since the beginning of human existence. It is built into our minds and bodies just as thinking and feeling.

Historical Perspectives

It is helpful for the counselor to have a historical perspective on the understanding of depression. This prevents us from repeating the mistakes of the past.

In ancient times the "slough of despond" was fought with whipping, blood letting, exorcism, and the soothing ministrations of music, baths, and "gentle words." Some sections of our modern world haven't moved much beyond this and still condemn depression as evil, a sign of the devil's domination over a life, and obvious evidence that one is failing to appropriate God's blessings. Nothing could be further from the truth. Unfortunately, many hold to this archaic view of depression and are kept in a state of unnecessary guilt and self-punishment by these notions. The sense of failure it creates only causes more depression.

The introduction of electro–convulsive therapy (ECT) in the 1930s opened the door on our modern understanding of the disorder. For the first time in human history, the possibility of effective treatment for severe depression was opened and, even though it may have been abused at times, this form of treatment released many from their black holes of misery. But the treatment required hospitalization and didn't work with all serious depressions. It was not the cure-all for everybody.

Finally, and only as recently as the 1950s, did we discover effective antidepressant drugs. Miraculously, the rate of hospitalization for severe depression began to drop. Newer psychotherapeutic techniques that supplemented and aided the medication have also been introduced.

The Current Status of Treatment

While the advent of antidepressant medication in the 1950s revolutionized the treatment of depression, its effectiveness is still only confined to that group of depressions we refer to as *endogenous,* meaning "from within the body." It appears that only those depressions that have some biological (probably biochemical) cause, can be treated effectively this way. Of course, this group of depressions does not account for all depression. If anything, it probably accounts for less than a third.

Electro–convulsive therapy (ECT) has been and continues to be a help to many sufferers. However, the current antiECT opinions run strong and the stigma that is so often attached to this form of treatment prevents many from seeking this help. It is used only in extreme cases or where there is a high risk of suicide and urgent improvement is needed.

This leaves psychotherapy (or counseling) as the remaining form of treatment. Surprisingly, it is proving to be very beneficial and, in combination with antidepressant medication, has been shown to help even those depressions that are purely bio-logical in origin. The medication helps to deal with the acute symptoms and the counseling reorders the long-standing char-acterological or behavioral problems that either precipitate or aggravate the depression.

Considering all types of depression, counseling (or psycho-therapy) is probably the most universally used treatment. But there are many approaches to counseling, and the big question facing all newcomers to the counseling field is: Which form of counseling is most effective?

There is no simple answer to this question, because it really depends on the cause and nature of the depression. Psychody-namic types of psychotherapy, based on Freudian theories, emphasize the understanding of unconscious motivations and childhood origins of adult problems. For some depressives, this approach may be most beneficial. At the other extreme, behav-iorists emphasize the here and now, and see depression as a state of deprivation, particularly of insufficient rewards. They attempt to change the behavior of the depressed so as to in-crease rewards and thus try to remove the cause of the depres-sion. Perhaps for some, this is the appropriate approach.

The point to be grasped is this: All types of therapy have been shown to contribute some help. Given the complexity of the depression problem, a counselor or therapist must avoid what some have called *the tyranny of therapeutic exclusiveness* or the tendency to stick only with one type of counseling approach.[6] The challenge of depression counseling is best met with versatil-ity and flexibility and a well developed armamentarium of many approaches. This is called an eclectic approach, and in it one tries to adapt the therapy to the problem, and not the problem to the therapy. In this book I will attempt to be eclectic, but with a strong emphasis on the cognitive approaches and a recog-nition of the important contributions of the biological, psycho-logical, *and* spiritual causes of depressions. It is this latter point of consideration that is so tragically missing from secular ap-proaches to counseling.

While I believe that different types of depression respond more quickly to a "tailored" therapeutic approach, the general effectiveness of some approaches are not as well established in the research as others. For instance, psychodynamic approaches have not shown as encouraging results as highly structured shorter-term therapy. Recent research with the cognitive and/or behavioral approaches seem to indicate that they produce more rapid results, but whether or not they are more long-lasting is not clear. Group therapies, where a lot of peer support (and pressure) is exerted, is giving very encouraging results.[7]

The most promising approach to the treatment of depression in recent years has come from a combination of the cognitive and behavioral schools of therapy. One of its proponents is Dr. Aaron Beck, of the University of Pennsylvania, who has designed a twelve-week treatment program to correct three major thought distortions characteristic of depressives: seeing themselves as deficient and unworthy; seeing the world as frustrating and unfulfilling; and seeing the future as hopeless.[8]

Another short-term approach that has been successful has come out of Interpersonal Psychotherapy (IPT). Based on the theories of Adolf Meyer and Harry Stack Sullivan, IPT is designed to help patients understand their current interpersonal problems and to teach them to relate better to those people who are special to them. Sounds like Christian love, doesn't it? Perhaps the apostle John's three epistles are being rediscovered by contemporary psychotherapists! In any event, this approach is based on the assumption that since depression can arise out of and lead into interpersonal problems, better social functioning can ameliorate depression proneness.

The results of both these approaches, cognitive therapy and IPT, are viewed to be so encouraging that an extremely rigorous study is being sponsored by the National Institute of Mental Health to test their relative effectiveness in treating moderate to severe depressions with and without antidepressant medication. Pastors and other counselors should pay close attention to these approaches because they offer treatment techniques very compatible to a Christian world view.

THE DEPRESSION SPECTRUM

In providing an overview of our current understanding of depression I would be remiss if I did not strongly emphasize just how complex a problem we are dealing with. Depression comes in many colors. Sometimes it is a "light blue"; at other times it can take the form of the "blackest despair." Some mood variations are normal, others are not.

Adding to the confusion is also the realization by many researchers that depression is not only a coat of many colors, but it is also "many coats." There are many *types* of depression, each with its own specific cause and each producing variations of intensity. It is more correct, therefore, to think of depression as a "spectrum" disorder.

Despite this complexity, it is helpful to see depression as being one of three things (or even a combination of these):

1. It can be a *symptom* of something. For example, if you have influenza or a serious disease, depression will be one of the side effects.

2. It can be a *reaction* to life events, as in bereavement or being fired. We call this *reactive depression* because it is, in essence, a response to some aspect of human existence.

3. Or it can be a *disease* in and of itself, such as when the body is suffering from some disorder of the bio–chemistry that keeps it in psychic equilibrium. Even here, the spectrum of biochemical disorders is vast and difficult to categorize in any simplistic way.

Since depression is a very complex disorder, with many manifestations as well as a vast array of causes, it is inappropriate for us to categorize it in simplistic terms and label it as evil, demonic, or a sign of spiritual failure. Those who are depressed have enough pain to bear without being burdened with additional guilt.

As I seek to unravel some of this complexity, it is my prayer that readers will come to a clear understanding of the problem and find in this understanding greater effectiveness in guiding their suffering parishioners, clients, friends, and perhaps even themselves back to full joy in living.

CHAPTER THREE

WHAT IS CLINICAL DEPRESSION?

WHAT MOST PEOPLE CALL *depression* is actually a whole group of mood disorders with differences in symptoms and degrees of severity. But whatever type of depression one may be confronted with, there is an important differentiation to be made between normal depressions and those that are abnormal.

We all occasionally experience gloomy moods and often say that we are depressed, but the differences between normal unhappy experiences and what would be labeled *clinical depression* are many—and sometimes confusing.

Short periods of discouragement, sadness, and even wishing oneself dead are a part of normal living. These unhappy feelings may last a few hours, a few days, or perhaps even weeks, but

44

they are generally not severe enough to interrupt the business of living and they hardly need any professional help.

On the other hand, there are people who either prolong their normal sadness unnecessarily or whose depressions get in the way of effective living. Here the sadness must clearly be considered abnormal. Where is the boundary? When is a bout of sadness out of control and when does someone in such a state need counseling or professional help? These are the questions to be considered in this chapter.

NORMAL AND CLINICAL DEPRESSIONS

Many depressions are normal in the sense that they are tied to everyday problems of existence. We take these normal depressions in our stride. We are not overwhelmed by them nor do they make a lasting impression. On the other hand, there are bouts of sadness that are significantly more impactful; they jar our systems with enough force to cause emotional whiplashes. They may create much misery and may even remove our ability to manage our own affairs. These we refer to as *clinical depressions.*

Where do normal depressions end and clinical depressions begin? This is not an easy boundary to define. The word *depression* has so many different meanings that it is not easy to pin it down by itself—say nothing of the word *clinical.* Sometimes the boundary is determined solely by duration of the depression. At other times, the severity of the symptoms will be the determining factors. A general rule of thumb is to reckon that symptoms that interfere with normal functioning—including sleep, appetite, and capacity for work and social relationships—require treatment. When these symptoms occur the depression has clearly crossed the boundary from normal to abnormal.

The Case of Mary and Tom

To illustrate the essential differences between clinical and normal depressions, let us examine two brief case histories.

Mary is a young mother of two small boys. Most of the time she is overworked, overwrought, and overwrangled. Her children are healthy, robust, and rambunctious, and a day in her life is one hectic round of dressing, feeding, wiping, washing, watching, running, shouting, and collapsing. She loves her children, but almost every day they stretch her patience and strength to the limit.

Her husband, Tom, works for a research company as a chemist. He loves his job, often comes home late from work, and makes excuses to go back to his laboratory over weekends. Tom doesn't fully comprehend the complexity of raising two small children. While he loves to play with his kids each day, he can take only about a half hour of their liveliness. Then he sends them back to mother to be put to bed.

One morning Tom gets up, takes his shower, dries, and dresses. He assumes his wife is getting the kids dressed, making breakfast, and feeding the cat. When he steps out of the bathroom, he sees that his wife is still in bed. When he goes to wake her, she shouts, "Leave me alone," and bursts out crying. He can't understand what is wrong. He tries to comfort her, but she passively resists him. He has no alternative but to take care of the kids and cancel his day at the office. He doesn't know it yet, but Mary has just entered a clinical depression. Her exhausted, overstressed body and mind have just "given up." Tom is about to discover the painfulness of the deep unhappiness that depression can cause.

The Case of Alex

Alex is a supermarket manager. Still single at thirty-two, he has never met the woman who could capture his heart. He finds that he quickly becomes bored with the girls he dates. They don't "excite" him or, if they do, they don't show any interest in the activities he enjoys. He is a regular churchgoer, a habit his parents had modeled for him, and, one Sunday, sitting across the aisle, he sees his "dream girl." He stares at her all through the service. She is obviously new in the church because she fumbles at times, not knowing the right liturgy. He likes everything he sees. While she could not be described as "stunning," she has all the qualities and characteristics he has always found attractive: a few freckles, slightly upturned nose, and very petite.

At the end of the service he follows her out, intending to introduce himself and offer to "show her around." She walks out of church, down the side pathway to the street. He darts between a few churchgoers, steps up his walking pace, and then the blow strikes. His dream girl goes to a car with two small children in the back and a handsome chunk of a man behind the driving wheel. "She's married," he gasps. The idea had never even occurred to him.

He is stopped in his tracks. He walks away dejected. A depression is coming over him. He thought he had found a dream, now it was shattered. *Life will never again be worth living,* he thinks. He makes his way back to the front of the church where a group of singles usually meet before going to lunch together. He wonders if he could ever eat a meal again. An hour later, he is tucking into a juicy steak with gusto, engrossed in a conversation with Elizabeth, the girl he has known since he learned to walk and whom he'll probably marry anyway.

Alex has experienced a brief normal depression. It came, lingered—and went. It left no permanent trace nor did it interrupt his happiness for more than a brief hour.

Differences Between Clinical and Normal Depressions

The boundary between clinical and normal depression is not always easy to define or identify. There is much subjectivity to these judgments. When we examine well-developed forms of both depressions, however, some differences clearly stand out. Here are some of them:

Clinical depression is a more severe form of depression than normal.

Clinical depression is clearly a "problem" for the sufferer, normal depression isn't.

It is not easy and often impossible for the sufferer of a clinical depression to recover by him- or herself.

Clinical depressions last significantly longer than normal depressions.

Clinical depressions are qualitatively different from normal depressions in the depth of the despair encountered, as well as the impact that the disorder has on the whole personality.

Normal depressions can be "shaken off" without too much effort. It is impossible to shake off a clinical depression.

Normal depressions often are "healed" by the passage of a brief period of time or by distraction.

Normal depressions are often nothing more than brief periods of general unhappiness.

Clinical depressions clearly give evidence that something is seriously wrong.

I will be focusing in this book primarily on clinical depressions. Normal depressions cure themselves and hardly warrant any intervention. They teach us more effective ways of living and coping. When a normal depression doesn't remit within a reasonable period of time (at the longest two weeks) then it becomes a clinical depression and should be treated along the lines I will describe.

One last thought about the distinction between clinical and normal depressions. The differences must not be thought of as being synonymous with the differences between biological (endogenous) and psychological (exogenous) depressions. This latter distinction is a very useful one, as we will see later, but it is possible for a psychologically triggered depression to be just as painful and serious in its symptoms as any biologically based depression. The mind and body act as a whole and psychological forces can be as powerful as biological forces, if not more so.

Who Gets Depressed?

Everybody! Depression afflicts us all: rich and poor, old and young, bright and dull. It is important that the counselor realizes this so as not to communicate that depression is not a strange and rare disorder. From the descriptions given in Scripture, we can clearly see that many biblical characters suffered at times from depression. King Saul, Job, and Elijah are just a few of the many in the Bible whose depressions are clearly recorded. Historical as well as modern day servants of God have suffered from depression, John Calvin, Martin Luther, and John Wesley knew depression intimately. Kierkegaard was obviously a deep sufferer of depression, and Charles Spurgeon, the great English preacher and teacher of the last century, believed that depression was the natural companion of every minister. In a lecture, "The Minister's Fainting Fits," he clearly outlined the many reasons why ministers must inevitably suffer from bouts of depression.[1]

Great national leaders have suffered from depression. Abraham Lincoln was a sufferer, as was Winston Churchill. With chilling accuracy, Churchill called his periodic depression "the black dog." Novelists, poets, and playwrights have endured it. If anything, it has helped them to understand the human condition better. Poe, Dostoyevsky, Milton, and Eugene O'Neill, to name just a few, were all the better at their craft because they knew and could describe the pain of human depression.

But not everyone has benefited from depression. The bleakness of discouragement and despair has caused many to end their lives prematurely. Probably suffering is caused by depression more than from any other single disease affecting mankind. It is inevitable, therefore, that every pastor and counselor will be confronted by scores of sufferers who will see their sadness, apathy and lack of energy, as reasons for not wanting to go on. Hopelessness and pessimism will move many to want to end their marriages or turn to alcohol and drugs. The far-reaching consequences of untreated depression are mind boggling and I'm convinced that much of this human suffering and devastation can be prevented by better informed preaching and more skillful counseling of pastors and counselors.

CONTEMPORARY MODELS OF DEPRESSION

There are probably as many ideas about what causes depression as there are theories about personality and psychotherapy. Each makes its contribution to the total truth and no single theory can adequately account for all depression. As I have already shown, depression is a spectrum disorder, having many causes. People who insist that they know what causes depression, without qualifying what form they are talking about, are misleading their listeners.

Without examining the specific techniques for treating depression that might arise from different schools of thought, let me briefly outline how each attempts to explain the causes of depression. With this overview you should be able to come to some conclusion about what model of depression you would like to adopt or, better still, how you would like to combine these into a more eclectic approach that recognizes the strengths and weaknesses of each.

Six dominant schools of thought, reflecting ten models of depression, are generally recognized by those knowledgeable in the field of depression. Table 1 summarizes these as well as the

Schools of Thought	Models of Depression	Mechanism Causing Depression
1. Psycho-analytic	(i) Object loss	Separation: disruption of an attachment bond
	(ii) Aggression turned inward	Conversion of aggressive instinct into depression feelings
	(iii) Loss of self-esteem	Helplessness in attaining goals of ego ideal
2. Cognitive	(iv) Negative cognitive set	Hopelessness
3. Behavioral	(v) Loss of reinforce-ment	Deprived of adequate re-inforcers
	(vi) Learned helpless-ness	Uncontrollable life circumstances and painful outcomes
4. Sociological	(vii) Sociological	Loss of role status
5. Existential	(viii) Existential	Loss of the meaning of existence
6. Biological	(ix) Biogenic amine	Impaired neurotransmitters (chemical messengers)
	(x) Neurophysiological	Cholinergic dominance

Table 1
Ten Models of Depression

mechanisms that cause depression. I will take each in turn and comment on them briefly so that the reader will have a general overview of how various schools see the problem.

A more detailed discussion of the various theories of depression is contained in the book *Clinical Handbook of Depression* by Janice Wood Wetzel.

Psychoanalytic Models of Depression.

The early work of Freud has and continues to influence our understanding of depression. Modern psychoanalysis, however, has not remained static but has continued to develop beyond the theories of Freud. Classical psychoanalytic theory has given birth to other systems, such as object–relations and ego psychology theories. Each has developed its own views on the nature of depression.

Object loss: According to classical psychoanalytic theory, depression results from the imagined or real loss of love "objects" in childhood. These objects are persons who are significant in a child's life, such as parents or most often the mother. (The term *object* has been borrowed from philosophy where one's self is seen as subject and others are object.)

A further elaboration of the "object loss" idea is that when an individual is fearful that rage felt in reaction to threatened or real abandonment will create rejection, the anger toward the love object is turned back on the self and directed inward. The result is depression. Early Freudians, in fact, viewed depression as a restitution and reparative punishment. In this way it was "dividend paying" for the sufferer.

Loss of self-esteem: Ego psychologists, while accepting basic Freudian ideas, focus more on helplessness and lowered self-esteem. Their focus is on the ego, and they see depression as being triggered by an intolerable breach between one's actual ego state (who one is), and one's ideal ego state (who one would like to be). This results in lowered self-esteem. Proneness to depression reflects an excessive dependence on others in order to maintain a fragile self-esteem.[3]

Cognitive Models of Depression

A further extension of these theories has led to systems of therapy generally embraced as "cognitive therapy."

Negative cognitive act: Freudians see depressed persons as being torn between the rage of not being given a "fair deal" and fear of expressing their rage at the lost object. Unable to respond, their self-esteem is diminished and a mind-set is established that includes feelings of worthlessness, hopelessness, inferiority, and dependency. Cognitive psychologists, such as Aaron Beck, see this negative cognitive mind-set as primary (a cause of the depression) and not a consequence of the depression.

For them, the depressed person develops a constellation of negative perceptions of the self, the world, and the future. These errors in thinking cause a depressed person to interpret events within a schema of self-depreciation and self-blame.

I believe that this cognitive model of therapy is extremely valuable, and I will comment on it further throughout this book. As a system of therapy, it is consistently proving to be an effective way of helping depressed people cope with their depression, even when the depression is of biological origin. It doesn't always "cure" depression, but it certainly helps the sufferer cope with it better.

Behavioral Models of Depression

The cognitive model I have just described is often included in the behavioral school (as a cognitive–behavioral theory) because so many therapists have combined behavioral techniques of reinforcement with strategies for changing how a person thinks.

More basically, the behavioral model is concerned with the relationship between behavior and the events that occur immediately before or after the behavior. The emphasis here is an observable and measurable action. Subjective feelings are set aside and all behavior is considered to be governed by the law of reinforcement. Behaviors that are positively rewarded are strengthened; behaviors that are negatively rewarded (punished) are weakened.

Loss of reinforcement: For the behaviorists, depression is a learned response and the result of inadequate or loss of reinforcement. Insufficient personal gratification or appreciation can precipitate depression; rewards have been deprived. A state of deprivation can cause depression, but the depression can also remove someone from social and other reinforcing situations, so the environment becomes the reinforcer of the depression itself.

This is an interesting and very helpful point of view. The depressed person is seen as having diminished personal and environmental resources to "self-reinforce." Because the depressed person is withdrawn, few effective coping skills are available. All this can lead to a prolongation of depression.

Learned helplessness: The experimentation of Martin Seligman has led to a further extension of this approach. With both animals and humans, he was able to demonstrate that uncontrollable traumatic events can be very debilitating. He called this *learned helplessness* and used the concept to describe how a person could become depressed when, in the face of emotional stress, he or she could not learn how to control or remove the stress. In short, the person believed he or she was helpless. For self-esteem and a sense of competence, one must feel in control of one's own environment. In states of helplessness, these feelings are removed.

While the model does not precisely describe the mechanism that causes depression, the most obvious explanation is that the depressed person is experiencing a loss, a loss of control. This loss causes the person to react by retreating into depression.[3]

Sociological Models of Depression

Clinical psychologists are not the only ones who have tried to explain depression. Sociologists and social psychologists have examined group processes and cultural factors and have tried to show how traits interact with the environment to cause depression.

I will not attempt to discuss the various theoretical subgroups but will focus on the essential feature of the model—that social factors are the primary causes of depression. Here the external situation, or the people with whom an individual lives, works, plays, worships, is emphasized more than the individual's internal mechanisms.

From birth, the human is entirely dependent on others to meet his or her needs. To become independent one must learn to balance one's own needs against those of others. For this, support from various social groups is needed. Loss of this support, as well as loss of role status (the position one seeks to fill in life) can give rise to depression.[4]

Existential Models of Depression

For the existentialists, depression results when the individual discovers that the world has lost meaning and purpose. It is not so much a single school of thought as it is a philosophical focus on the meaning of existence. It embraces a wide range of theorists from those with a strictly spiritual focus to those who are purely secular. The secular theorists tend towards humanistic values.

Soren Kierkegaard was the earliest and most thorough existential theorist. Others include Sartre, Heidegger, and Binswanger. In more recent times, Rollo May has made many aspects of existentialism understandable. Many of the concepts of existential psychology, including its views on alienation, authenticity, loneliness, nonattachment, and surrender, are very helpful to the Christian counselor. These concepts all have biblical counterparts and therefore lend themselves readily to a Christian interpretation of healing.[5]

Biological Models of Depression

The evidence for biological roots in *some* depressions is overwhelming. There is no doubt that much depression (how much we don't clearly know) has its roots from within the body and brain in disturbed or imbalanced biochemistry.

Biogenic amine theories: One group sees depression as the symptomatic output of a genetically vulnerable central nervous system. The system is depleted from biogenic amines (chemicals that help nerve impulses) and becomes hyper- or hypo-aroused. In effect, there is a disturbance in the production, absorption, or balance of the neurotransmitter in the nervous system. This model will be explored more fully in a later chapter. It is especially important because tests are available to measure this defect and antidepressant medication is an effective treatment for it.

Neurophysiological theories: This is a more recent group of theories that sees some depressions as resulting from cholinergic dominance—mechanisms of arousal and suppression. These might account for the cause of the most serious of all forms of depression, the bipolar form (previously known as *manic–depressive psychosis.*)[6]

Which Model Is Right?

I think there is only one correct answer to this question: They are all right, to some extent. No single theory can account for *all* depression, this is clear.[7] Some of the theories overlap with, or are merely variations of, others. For instance, the theme of "loss" is clearly central to a number of these theories: loss of love objects, loss of self-esteem, loss of control, loss of life's meaning, and loss of reinforcement. This accords with Freud's basic tenant that depression is a response to loss, that differences in the object of the loss (concrete and real or abstract and imagined) is of little consequence to the depression. The depression is, therefore, a process by which the mind and body comes to terms with the loss it has suffered. In this sense I see depression as a grieving process, and it is the same process whether the loss is minor, as when I cannot find my favorite book, or major, as when the loss is the death of a loved one.[8] The difference is only in the meaning of the lost object: the greater the loss, the greater the depression.

This is the understanding I will adopt in this book: Depression can be a response to loss. Of course, not all depressions are responses of this sort. Some result from illness, where the depression is merely a symptom of the disease, and some from biochemical disturbances. What is important for counselors is that they do not get locked into any one model or theory. This will spell disaster. No acceptable unified hypothesis has yet been devised so that, as I have already emphasized, one should be open to an eclectic understanding of the problem and adopt a multi-faceted approach to its treatment. We must take into account the psychological, environmental, spiritual, intrapersonal, interpersonal, as well as biological factors in an integrated way. Pastors and Christian counselors, because of their sensitivity to spiritual issues, are uniquely placed to be at the forefront of healing for those whose lives are being destroyed by depression.

CHAPTER FOUR

DIAGNOSING DEPRESSION

THE IMPORTANCE OF ACCURATE diagnosis in treating depression cannot be over stressed. A lot of unnecessary pain can be avoided if you can quickly pinpoint the precise nature of a depression and identify its causes. While the average pastor or counselor cannot be expected to have all the knowledge necessary to diagnose all forms of depression, you should know enough about the various disorders to be able to decide whether or not a particular depression is within your range of skills. If you do decide to counsel a depressed client yourself, you should have the confidence to know that it is a type of depression with which you can effectively work.

THE IMPORTANCE OF ACCURATE DIAGNOSIS

Even experienced psychologists and psychiatrists can misdiagnose depression, with serious consequences. I recently counseled a man in his early forties who had been placed on disability leave because he could not do his work. The company's psychiatrist had evaluated him and diagnosed him as having a "personality disorder." Furthermore, the psychiatrist stated that Jim would never be effective in performing the duties assigned to him and recommended that he be dismissed. Jim was convinced that there was something else wrong with himself. Ever since he could remember, he had had bouts of depression. While they never incapacitated him, he would lie around feeling listless and lazy, and he would often become extremely irritable. It was during one of these moods that he verbally attacked one of his work colleagues. He was quick-tempered, short-fused, and intolerant of frustration. No one could work with him.

After six months of disability leave, Jim finally decided (with some prompting by his wife) to seek another opinion and get some help, and that was when he came to see me. After administering a battery of tests, his physician agreed to my recommendation that Jim be placed on antidepressant medication while he continued in psychotherapy. Two months later Jim was ready for work. He described his newfound mental state as "clear headed, balanced, and free from moodiness—for the first time since I was born." His problem was clearly one of those depressions that responded well to antidepressants.

Not all depressions are this easy to diagnose or cure—but many are, and it behooves the counselor to do the best he or she can to get to the bottom of the problem.

There are many benefits to be derived from arriving at an accurate diagnosis:

It ensures correct physical treatment, when this is appropriate.

It helps to build client–counselor rapport by demonstrating that the counselor is competent.

It aids the counselor in conceptualizing the nature of the problem more completely.

It gives direction to the counseling process and avoids unnecessary time being spent exploring irrelevant issues.

It helps to mobilize "special" forms of treatment, such as when the client has a mixed depressive and anxiety problem.

It helps free the counselor from the guilt that comes with not being able to help a depressed client who has a form of depression that is incurable.

Let me underscore the importance of this last point. We all feel like failures when we cannot help someone who comes to us. This is one of the irrational hang-ups of people helpers. We do not readily accept our limitations and we engage in unnecessary guilt-talk because we feel we failed. Competent counselors develop an understanding and acceptance of their limitations. They know when they have reached their limit and either stop wasting further time on unnecessary and ineffective interventions, or they make a referral to a more specialized professional. It is sad, but true, that some depressed people simply don't want to get better. Accurate diagnosis can help you develop the courage to say "This person's problem is beyond me" and let the case go.

SYMPTOMS OF DEPRESSION

There are basically two ways to diagnose a condition. The first is to describe its symptoms without regard to its causes. The second is to determine the cause (or "etiology") and give second place to a description of the symptoms.

For example, appendicitis could be described as a sharp pain in the right lower abdomen with feelings of nausea, shivers, and fear. Or it can be described as inflammation of the appendix with involvement of adjoining tissue. The first describes the symptoms of the disorder, the second the cause.

Overview of Symptoms

Before exploring in greater detail the different categories of depression, let me provide an overview of the major symptoms of depression. These symptoms are common to all forms of depression so the counselor needs to be familiar with them:

1. Mood. The mood is sad, unhappy, and "blue"; crying may be present in some forms of depression, but not all.

2. Thought. Thinking is negative, with pessimism about the future; ideas of guilt and self-denigration are frequently present; there is loss of interest and motivation; there is a decrease in efficiency and concentration, even with some

memory disturbance; suicidal thoughts are common in the more severe depressions.

3. Behavior. Energy is depleted; there is sluggishness, retardation, or agitation; personal appearance can be neglected.

4. Physical. Many physical symptoms can be present, including loss of appetite, loss of weight, constipation, poor or excessive sleep, loss of sexual drive.

5. Anxiety. Although sadness is the central mood disturbance, many depressed persons complain of fears, anxiety, tension, uncertainty, and indecisiveness.

The DSM–III Classification

A really effective diagnostic system should be able to both describe the symptoms of a disorder as well as point to its cause. This has been easier for physical disorders. Unfortunately, in the realm of emotional disorders (especially the depressions) it has been much harder, and the major system of classification available to us today does not give us a clear picture of the *causes* of depression, only its symptoms. This does handicap us somewhat, in that widely differing forms of depression can give rise to identical sets of symptoms.

The latest *Diagnostic and Statistical Manual of Mental Disorders of the American Psychiatric Association* (known simply as *DSM–III*) sets out the "official" classification system for depression. It uses the term *affective disorders* to cover both depression and its opposite, mania, or extreme excitement.[1] The word *affective* comes from the Latin *affectus,* which means "the disposition of the mind." It relates to all disturbances of mood, no matter what the cause.

The greatest weakness of DSM–III is its tendency to categorize disorders like depression according to their symptoms rather than their causes. Presumably this is because the panel of experts who put it together could only agree on the former.

To be useful, therefore, we need to develop, in addition to an understanding of this official system of classification, a system that describes the disorders of depression according to their etiology or assignment of causes. Only if we are able to identify the *cause* of a depression will we be able to facilitate its cure. Or, to put it another way, accurately describing the symptoms of a depression will be of little help in pointing to a method of treatment—unless we can also identify the cause.

I will first present and discuss the DSM–III categories of depression, so that the counselor will know the official classification system, then I will provide an overview of the important causes of depression. Accurate diagnosis requires that we understand both the symptoms and the causes of depression.

In the diagnostic manual, the class "Affective Disorders" is divided into the following categories: 1. Major affective disorders (a full affective syndrome); 2. Other specific affective disorders (only a partial affective syndrome of at least two years duration); 3. Atypical affective disorders (those disorders that cannot be classified in either of the previous two categories).[2]

Hardly an adequate classification, is it? It ignores distinctions between biological and psychological causes of depression, and says nothing about personality contributions.

Each of the above three categories is further divided into subclasses, again with primary emphasis on symptoms and not causes:

1. Major Affective Disorders.

Manic episode. Here there is an elevation of mood, euphoria, and extreme excitement. This must not be confused with just a normal "high" or overexcitement. The disorder is clearly marked by excessive hyperactivity, grandiosity, and lack of judgment. Activities (like spending sprees, reckless driving, and unusual sexual behavior) are flamboyant and bizarre. Sleep need is decreased with the manic person who either does not go to sleep or is wakened many hours before the usual time, full of energy. The term *bipolar* is used to describe alternations between mania and depression.

The disorder must last at least one week before it can be diagnosed as mania. Treatment is with a drug, lithium, which is also used in some forms of depression.

Major depressive episode. The essential feature is depression, but it is a severe depression that is prominent, relatively persistent, with a loss of interest or pleasure in all usual activities. There is also loss of energy, sleep disturbance, feelings of worthlessness or guilt, difficulty thinking or concentrating, and thoughts of death or suicide.

To make this diagnosis, one must exclude obvious physical causes such as influenza, underactive thyroid gland (hypothyroidism), and certain drugs or medications such as reserpine. Even antibiotics, antihypertensives, and contraceptive pills can cause these depressive reactions.

The manic and depressive episodes are divided as follows: *Bipolar disorder, mixed*—here the mania and depression alternate rapidly every few days; *bipolar disorder, manic*—the patient is in a current manic episode; *bipolar disorder, depressed*—there has been one or more manic episodes, but the patient is now in a major depressive episode; *Major depression, single episode; Major depression, recurrent.*

A few further points to remember about this classification of depression:

The first manic episode of a bipolar disorder usually occurs *before* age thirty, but may reoccur at any time thereafter.

Major depression may begin at any age, including infancy, and the age of onset is fairly evenly distributed throughout adult life.

Manic episodes typically begin suddenly, and symptoms escalate over just a few days. It could last from a few days to months. They are briefer and end more abruptly than typical depressive episodes.

Most people who have one or more manic episode will eventually have a major depressive episode.

The onset of major depression is variable. It develops over days or weeks, with or without severe stress or illness serving as a "trigger."[3]

2. Other specific affective disorders.

Cyclothymic disorder. This is a "lesser" form of depression of at least two years duration, with a number of periods of normal or elevated feelings. Life is not disrupted, but feelings of inadequacy, social withdrawal, and diminished productivity are common, alternating with periods of hypomania (a mild form of mania). The cyclical nature of the moods is what gives it its name. It must *not* be confused with the bipolar disorders, although some researchers think it is a mild form of the more severe disorder. I believe that personality factors may contribute to the variations of mood seen in this category.

The disorder usually starts in early adult life and becomes a part of the individual's lifestyle. Such a person is always swinging between extremes of mood.

Dysthymic Disorder. This category used to be called *depressive neurosis.* Here there is a chronic disturbance of mood (depression) with loss of interests and energy, but not of sufficient severity to be a major depression.[4]

The person may feel sad, blue, down in the dumps, but can be distracted or it passes off in a few days.

3. Atypical Affective Disorders. This is the catch-all for those depressions that don't fit anywhere else. There are two subcategories.

Atypical bipolar disorder. Here there is a pattern alternation not fitting the other categories.[5]

Atypical depression. Here the depression doesn't fit the other categories. Sometimes this is because there is another illness superimposed on the depression, such as schizophrenia.[6]

THE CAUSES OF DEPRESSION

While it is important for the counselor to have a basic grasp of the categories of depression just described, it is more important to have an understanding of various causes.

Unfortunately, no universally accepted system has yet been devised. I will present the system that I use because it seems to be true to both the research data as well as my clinical experience. This etiological classification is presented in Table 2, and in the discussion that follows I will attempt to elaborate these categories further.

Primary Depression

This category includes those depressions that were previously called *psychotic* as well as *manic–depressive psychosis.* It embraces the more serious and mostly genetically determined depressions, where the melancholia is very deep and incapacitating. This form of depression is of two types:

1. *Unipolar depression.* Here there is a history or evidence only of depression. The victim may be agitated (restless, hand wringing, pacing) or retarded (sluggish, slow, and inactive). Sometimes the depression alternates between agitation and retardation.

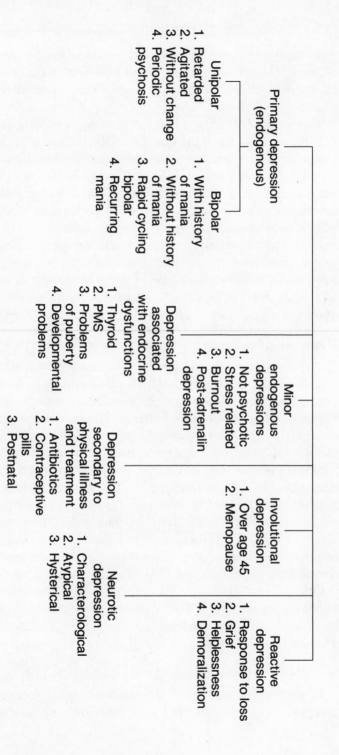

Primary depression (endogenous)

Unipolar
1. Retarded
2. Agitated
3. Without change
4. Periodic psychosis

Bipolar
1. With history of mania
2. Without history of mania
3. Rapid cycling bipolar
4. Recurring mania

Minor endogenous depressions
1. Not psychotic
2. Stress related
3. Burnout
4. Post-adrenalin depression

Depression associated with endocrine dysfunctions
1. Thyroid
2. PMS
3. Problems of puberty
4. Developmental problems

Depression secondary to physical illness and treatment
1. Antibiotics
2. Contraceptive pills
3. Postnatal

Involutional depression
1. Over age 45
2. Menopause

Reactive depression
1. Response to loss
2. Grief
3. Helplessness
4. Demoralization

Neurotic depression
1. Characterological
2. Atypical
3. Hysterical

Table 2
Diagnostic Classification of Depression by Etiology

2. *Bipolar depression.* Here there is a history or evidence of mania (hyperexcited and active). Sometimes a history of cyclothymia (milder alternating mood swings) can justify this diagnosis.

The treatment of these two forms of depression is quite different, because they are presumably different types of depression. Unipolar depression is treated with antidepressant medication such as the tricyclics whereas bipolar depression with antimanic medication such as lithium. Unfortunately antidepressant medications may take two to three weeks before they are effective (some new drugs are more rapid), and lithium takes five days to two weeks before it works, so there is some continued discomfort while treatment is becoming established. Counseling is *essential* while waiting for the treatment to take effect, as well as during the drug treatment. Combined drug therapy *and* counseling is the most effective treatment in these cases.[7]

Depression Associated with Endocrine Dysfunctions

The endocrine system deeply affects our emotional state. Disorders of the critical glands like the pituitary, adrenal, and especially the thyroid can cause mild to severe depressions. Clinically, hypothyroidism (a thyroid that is underactive) can be confused with a depressive disorder.[8] Lithium treatment of a bipolar disorder can also profoundly affect thyroid function. Medical evaluation is, of course, essential if thyroid dysfunction is suspected. The tests ordered by the physician should include a measure of thyroid reserve such as elevated thyroid stimulating hormone (TSH), as well as the standard T4 (thyroxine). Very often, only the T4 is measured and this may not be adequate to evaluate the thyroid gland. Treatment is focused on correcting the underlying deficiency.

Other depressions in this category would include the premenstrual syndrome (PMS) and certain depressions of development such as those experienced during the adolescent period. These will be discussed more fully in a later chapter.

Minor Endogenous Depressions

In recent years a lot of attention has been focused on this category of depression. It bears some relation to the primary depression in that antidepressant medication is very effective in reducing the symptoms. As its name implies, it is "from within" or due to biological causes, but relatively minor in severity. Not only are these depressions much less severe, they are not psychotic, and are often related to periods of stress. They differ from psychological depressions in that there are no obvious precipitating events (except perhaps too much stress) and the person reports many episodes of low-grade depression, sometimes saying that he or she has "always felt this way."

Counseling alone only brings mild improvement, whereas the addition of an antidepressant drug (often at quite low dosage) brings marked improvement. Since this type of depression is quite common, it will be discussed in more detail in chapter 6.

Depression Secondary to Physical Illness and Treatment

I always become depressed when I have influenza. So do most other people. Illness often creates depression because the body needs to rest for the healing process to take place. The depression serves to disengage us from our environment and to slow us down. Without it we would self-destruct.

But many other illnesses also cause depression: cancer, chronic pain, and diabetes are just a few of the common causes.

Treatment of illness can also be a cause of depression. Antibiotics produce depression, as do the antihypertensive drugs (used for treating high blood pressure) and contraceptive pills.

The treatment of these depressions is not always easy and involves either the removal of the drug producing it or the curing of the underlying disease.

Involutional Depression

This category is reserved for depressions that begin in middle to late life. It was originally thought to be due to biological changes occurring during menopause, but little evidence has been forthcoming to prove this.[9] The problems of aging appear to be more complex than this, and the unique problems of getting old will be discussed later.

Neurotic Depression

This is the same as the dysthymic disorder discussed under the DSM–III categories. This type of depression serves to protect the individual from anxiety and is more a personality characteristic than it is a distinct type of depression. The person "uses" depression to avoid responsibility or escape trouble.

Treatment is *only* with counseling and psychotherapy. Medication is of no help and may only serve to reinforce the neurotic depression by giving the impression that the illness is legitimate. The individual must learn new and more effective ways for coping with anxiety and responsibility. It takes long and persistent counseling to effect a change.

Reactive Depression

I have left this category to last because it is the most common and important of all from a counselor's perspective. The majority of depressions suffered by normal people are of this sort. They are called *reactive depressions* for two reasons: 1. They are a "response" to something going on in a person's life. 2. They are purely psychologically triggered.

The reaction is usually to some loss or rejection that has been perceived. The body and mind is designed to respond to loss with depression. I believe it to be a variation of the grieving response. While the "trigger" may be purely psychological, the chain of events that follow includes not only changes in the mind (the sense of a loss) but also changes in the body. These changes are not yet fully recognized or understood, but we know they are there. I can feel them in my body and, even when the loss is restored, I may not immediately return to normal because the biological changes underlying psychological depression take a little while to "burn off."

Since the treatment of reactive depression is solely through counseling and psychotherapy, it will be the major focus of this book and discussed in more detail in chapters 5 and 9. The astute counselor, however, will need to be on the alert for complicating biological factors and indications that medication may be helpful in supplementing the treatment of a depression.

DIAGNOSTIC POINTERS

Are there helpful diagnostic pointers that can aid the counselor in determining more precisely the nature of a given depression? Fortunately there are, and I have presented these in summary form in Table 3 (see pages 68–72) so they can easily be assimilated. Because of space limitations I have omitted reference to depressions due to physical illness and involutional depression. Diagnosis of these depressions should be left to a physician. The inexperienced counselor should be cautious in using this table since it is easy to over- or underinterpret the descriptions given. Wherever possible, try to get someone more experienced to supervise your use of the diagnostic table at the end of this chapter.

A variety of depression rating scales have been developed, and the counselor may find these useful in determining how severe a given depression is. The book *Concepts of Depression* by Joseph Mendels provides a brief summary of the more important scales.[10] Perhaps the most widely used is the "Beck Depression Inventory," a full description of which is provided in *Cognitive Therapy of Depression.*[11]

Table 3

The Symptoms of Different Types of Depression

A. General Factors

Symptom	PRIMARY DEPRESSION		Minor Endogenous	Neurotic Depression	Reactive Depression
	Unipolar	Bipolar			
Cause	Disturbance in structure and function of brain	Disturbance in structure and function of brain	Minor disturbance in function of depression system; exhaustion of adaptation	Anxiety and chronic emotional stress	Response to real or threatened loss; helplessness; displacement
History of depression in family	Yes	Yes. High incidence of family mania	Often. One or other parent "depressive"	Can be "modeled" by parents	No connection
Precipitating event	Not necessary—but may aggravate	Not necessary	May follow stress	A lifestyle	Always present
Nature of onset	Fairly rapid (one to six weeks)	Fairly sudden (days) or rapid	Sudden or gradual	Gradual, but chronic	Sudden—related to perception of loss
Age at onset	Any age (most after ten)	First attack before thirty	Any age	After early adulthood	Any age
Nature of depression	Very deep	Very deep	Mild to severe	Variable	Mild to severe

	Months to years	Weeks to many months	Months to years—even chronic	Lifetime	Days to months
Duration of depression	Months to years	Weeks to many months	Months to years—even chronic	Lifetime	Days to months
High risk groups	Females Older males Family History	Both sexes Family history	All ages Both sexes	Both sexes Childhood anxiety	Females Divorced or single Older males
Tendency for depression to recur	The older the first attack, the sooner will be recurrence	The earlier in age of onset the longer is interval between recurrences	Tends to be chronic or episodic	Chronic	Depends on life circumstances

B. Emotional Symptoms

Mood	Dysphoric, sad, hopeless; mood is persistent	Dysphoric, sad, hopeless; mood is persistent	Dysphoric or mostly normal; relatively persistent	Variable, often exaggerated; depressed in evening or when anxious	Sad, hopeless, discouraged; can be distracted
Self-feelings	Very negative, self-rejecting	Very negative, self-rejecting	Variable, usually unchanged	Not affected	Minor change
Crying	Intense, spontaneous, agitated	Intense, spontaneous, agitated	Not common	"If I could cry I'd feel better," but seldom cries	Tearfulness, quiet, and associated with ruminations
Humor appreciation	Absent	Absent	Slightly diminished	Unchanged	Diminished but distractible

Symptom	PRIMARY DEPRESSION Unipolar	Bipolar	Minor Endogenous	Neurotic Depression	Reactive Depression
Gratification	Can't experience pleasure	Can't experience pleasure	Diminished pleasure	Variable "self-sacrificing"	Diminished but distractible
Self-blame	Excessive; self-reproaching	Excessive; self-reproaching	Mild	Variable	Unchanged
Motivation	Totally lacking	Totally lacking	Variable	Variable	Not usually affected
Interest in normal activities	Totally disrupted; unable to experience pleasure	Totally disrupted; unable to experience pleasure	Variable but temporary	Unchanged	Diminished interests but distractible
Suicidal or death wish	Severe, preoccupied with death	Severe	Mild death wishes	Uses threats to manipulate	None
Concentration	Impossible to concentrate	Impossible to concentrate	Unchanged	Variable; chooses not to concentrate	Mildly affected
Memory	Marked disruption of short-term memory	Marked disruption of short-term memory	Unchanged	Unchanged	Unchanged
Contact with reality	Can vary from good to poor	Can vary from good to very poor	Good	Good (denial may be common)	Good
Hallucinations	Mood congruent (not common)	Usually mood congruent (less common)	Absent	Absent	Absent

Fear	Yes—delusional	Yes	Not necessary	Variable	No connection
Fluctuations in mood	Worse in A.M. Better in evening	Worse in A.M.	Variable; adrenalin arousal improves mood	Variable	Better in A.M. Worse in evening
Guilt	Intense and irrational; delusional	Intense and irrational; delusional	No connection with depression, as a rule	Variable	Rational guilt—can be severe
Variability of mood	Shifts are slow, mood is stable and unchanging	Very marked; rapid shifts to anger or depression	Slow shifts—mood stable	Variable	Variable

C. Cognitive Symptoms

Self-image	Grossly distorted	Grossly distorted	Mildly distorted	Variable	Unchanged
Self-esteem	Depreciated	Depreciated	Variable	Variable	Unchanged

D. Physical Symptoms

Sleep	Early morning insomnia, but day-time lethargy	Early morning insomnia, but day-time lethargy	General insomnia or hypersomnia	"Escapes" through sleeping	Hypersomnia
Dreaming	Falls asleep quickly and dreams early in cycle	Reduced dreaming; total sleep may be less	No change	No change	Reduced dream sleep

| Symptom | PRIMARY DEPRESSION | | Minor Endogenous | Neurotic Depression | Reactive Depression |
	Unipolar	Bipolar			
Eating habits	Appetite change—usually diminished	Appetite change—usually diminished	Appetite change—Variable	"Binging" sprees	Loss of appetite
Fatigue	Chronically tired	Varies from person to person	Very marked periods of fatigue	Variable	Moderate change—"weary"
Sexual interest	Completely absent	Completely absent	Variable	Fluctuates	Fluctuates—but arousal is possible
Retardation	Reduction in spontaneous activity; slow and deliberate	As with unipolar, except when agitated or manic	Mild change	Not affected	Little change
Speech	Slowed and output reduced; pitch may lower; Monotone	As with unipolar	Mild change	Not affected	Little change

CHAPTER FIVE

UNDERSTANDING
REACTIVE DEPRESSION

ALL OF LIFE IS LOSS. From the day we are born we begin to lose something. We grow older and lose time. We graduate from kindergarten school and leave behind safe places and special friends. We go from adolescence to adulthood and lose a degree of freedom and carefreeness. We make investments and lose money, we make bad decisions and lose self-confidence. Later in life we begin to lose our faculties, teeth, and hair. Finally we give up life altogether.

One of the major psychological skills we must all master in life is to cope with loss. When we fail to adjust to loss we experience the most common of all depressions—reactive depression. It is called *reactive* because it is just that—a reaction to loss. The loss can be many things: loss of a love object, loss of self-esteem, an ego ideal, a role, a favorite pet, energy, control, or respect of others. Sometimes no actual loss has taken place, only an imagined one. But it makes no difference to the mind and body; depression will still be the end result. Whether or not the depressive reaction becomes a clinical depression or not depends on our coping skills, the severity of the loss, and the speed with which we can adjust to its absence. We adjust quickly to some losses and hardly notice the passing of a rapid depression. Other losses are not so easy to accept, either because they have come on top of previous losses or because we feel that the loss was not warranted. A significant clinical depression may ensue.

THE EXPERIENCE OF REACTIVE DEPRESSION

To illustrate the experience of reactive depression, let me outline the case of Martha who is not a Christian. She married when she was about eighteen and soon realized she had made a mistake. She had been desperate to get out of her childhood home, where a stepfather had been quite rejecting of her, and her mother had been indifferent toward Martha since the birth of two sons by Martha's stepfather. When Martha met a dashing thirty-five-year-old divorced man who said he loved her, she jumped at the opportunity to get away and start her own life, even though she didn't really love her suitor.

By the time she was thirty-five, Martha had two teenage sons and her husband had had several affairs. Martha couldn't stand living with an unfaithful husband, so she moved out with her two sons. To avoid having her husband cause trouble with her boys, she moved from the East to California and settled down to build a new life for herself.

But it wasn't easy. Despite the fact that she was relieved to get out of an unhappy marriage, she grew deeply depressed. She had no energy, and going to work was a painful chore. Even though she had fantasized how wonderful it would be when she was "free," she found herself having no interest in life. She went to work, came home, attended to the bare essential needs of her two boys, then collapsed on her bed, often sleeping the whole night without changing out of her work clothes.

Instead of being relieved when her divorce proceedings were finalized, she became more depressed and just sobbed and sobbed. Nothing was pleasurable anymore. Even though she knew that her ex-husband's unfaithfulness was impossible for her to control, she kept blaming herself for the breakup of the marriage.

Martha's depression was reactive, in that it was the direct consequence of her life circumstance and a chain of losses. She was on a downhill spiral with the depression becoming self-perpetuating.

Fortunately, through the insistence and help of a Christian she met at work, Martha sought help for her problem. It took six months of intensive counseling and a further period of supportive help, but today, one year later, Martha is once again fully functioning, a vital Christian who is finding life to be a rich and meaningful experience. With those who never seek help for their depression, this is not always the outcome. Emergency treatment centers are inundated at certain times of the year with those who try to take the only way out they know— suicide. For them there seemed to be no hope for a happy life. Sadly, some succeed!

What does the depression of a significant loss feel like?

"When I wake up in the morning I'm too scared to get out of bed," one client told me.

"I have an awful, sickening feeling. Sinking, sinking, like I'm going to fall into an abyss," said another.

You feel as if you are damned, but your friends won't hear of it; they tell you that you are a good person and that God won't harm you. You feel terribly frightened, but your friends keep insisting everything is going to be okay. Fear permeates your life, undermining your confidence. You can't make the smallest decisions. What will I wear? What shall I eat for lunch? What do I do today? They all become huge questions.

You feel guilty a lot. Every action, every thought is a cause for guilt. You feel like a failure and you beg for forgiveness. You want to keep punishing yourself, hoping you will get rid of the terrible feelings inside. You remember bad things you did when you were a child and wish you could go back and make amends.

The loss may have happened a long time ago—when your

father abandoned you and deserted your family, when a special friend moved away. You felt so small and helpless—and no one understood. You cried then, but even now as you remember you want to cry again. You keep wondering if it was your fault, if you did something wrong.

The loss might be more recent. You depended on a person. You loved and protected him and now he has left you. You feel deserted, dejected, desolate. You feel all alone and abandoned. You are convinced that there is no way out of this blackness. Everything seems so hopeless.

Such is the experience of reactive depression. Scores of people in every city, every day, have these feelings. For some it is mild and moves on rapidly. For others it is a deep pain that never seems to let up.

GRIEVING THE LOSS

Reactive depression is the *most common* form of depression. It is the "common cold" of the emotions.

To be effective, the counselor must be able to help the depressed person identify the root loss, comprehend the full meaning of the loss, then place it in some perspective. In many respects, recovering from such a depression is best understood as being a grieving process—and very much the same whether the loss is the death of a loved one or dismissal from a job. The difference lies only in the significance of the loss; most of us value loved ones more than jobs.

The similarities between mourning and depression have been observed for centuries.[1] In recent times Sigmund Freud noted both the similarities and the differences, although for many other psychologists the similarities continue to be controversial. Obviously one cannot relate grief to every form of depression— at least not directly. Also, many losses remain elusive to depressed people, so that the grieving process as such never even begins, let alone completes itself.

There is no doubt in my mind that reactive depression is an integral component of the grief experience, but the reverse is also true: The grief experience is what reactive depression is all about. If grieving is the pathway through the depression of loss, then it is the process of grieving that provides the counselor with the key to effective help. Whether the loss is real, symbolic, imagined, or anticipated, depression will be the consequence and grief work must be done before the depression can be resolved.

Grief Work

According to Freud, when the work of mourning is completed, depression is relieved.[2] I believe that this is true for *reactive* depressions.

What is the process of grief? Essentially it is a process of letting go, but we understand its stages better than we do its process. It can be helpful to the counselor to understand both of these.

First of all, let us differentiate mourning from grief. Both are essential to resolving the experience of loss. Here are some helpful definitions: *mourning* is the *process* of withdrawing emotional attachment or investment from the lost object or person. It takes place whether the loss is tangible or simply an idea.

Grief is the *emotion* experienced in mourning. It is a longing for something that is lost.

Grieving involves allowing yourself to have the feelings of grief. It is generally believed that one cannot complete the mourning process without allowing oneself to *feel* the emotions of grief. These feelings are essential to the cognitive adjustments that must be made to the loss.

What are the *stages* of grieving? Four stages central to recovery from a significant loss are generally accepted.

1. Denial. This is a refusal to accept the loss and see what is clearly true. The recognition of reality is too painful to bear. Attempts are repeatedly made to recover the lost person, object, or idea.

2. Anger. When the reality of the loss finally dawns, a feeling of "unfairness" emerges. This gives rise to anger and resentment. It can be directed at the self, the lost object, or others, including the counselor.

3. Depression. Despair over the loss sets in and hopelessness pervades the emotions. Self-rejection, lowered self-esteem, and guilt feelings are experienced. During this period the cognitive

process of adjustment to the loss begins to take place, and this leads to stage 4.

4. Acceptance. Understanding, tolerance, and acceptance of the loss finally emerge with the realization that one can survive and flourish in spite of the loss. The loss is placed in perspective.[3]

When working with clients with a reactive depression, I've seen that it's extremely helpful for me to recognize these stages. They inform me as to what is going on, where the client is in the process, and what further help is needed. It is the counselor's task to facilitate the process of grieving as much as possible.

A Christian Perspective on Loss

Christian counselors are uniquely equipped to help people deal with reactive depression. Not only do they have the resources of God the Holy Spirit to aid them and the client, but the Christian gospel addresses itself very specially to one of life's major problems: loss.

From a theological point of view, the loss is *not* the central issue in reactive depression. The real problem lies not with the absence of the lost object but with the *attachment* to it. In other words, depression continues because we will not let go of the loved object; we will not free it to be dead, lost, removed, or not materialized. This distinction between the *loss* and the *attachment* is crucial to depression counseling. We all suffer loss. We do not all need to be so attached! We can accept our losses with less pain and depression if we will learn how to let go of our attachments.

We humans are remarkably tenacious. For reasons of security or just plain simple hoarding, we do not let go very easily. When we love, we also want to possess; when we want something we desire, it becomes an obsession. Powerful forces attract us to what we own. Because we cling to possessions, ideas, reputations, and people, we experience losses very deeply and the ensuing depression is unnecessarily painful and prolonged. I repeat: The problem of depression is not the loss; it is the attachment to the lost object. We simply *won't let it go!*

The pain of this is easily understood for non-Christians. What do they have to live for? God might as well be dead. They are "trapped in existence," living in a completely meaningless world, looking forward to a meaningless eternity. Their pattern of life is due entirely to arbitrary ways of living and any form of existence will do. It leads, at best, to what Jean Paul Sartre called the "nausea of existence." This is the best they can hope for. It is no wonder that they must cling tenaciously to every morsel and object of life.

But what about Christians? Those who must lose their life for Christ? Are we not called to let go of everything that gives us security and cling to our Savior? I believe so, but too often I am as frightened as you are to let go. Like the child first learning to swim, I want to grip the safe rail on the side of the pool and not venture out to the waiting arms of a father who is coaxing me to trust him.

This is one of the painful aspects of human existence: We become too attached to life and its benefits. We become overly attached to our spouses, parents, children, cameras, reputation, ambitions, and ideas. Giving them up voluntarily is painful enough, but their being taken away is unbearable. What if we were not so attached to them? We fear we might become callous, unfeeling. Yet the central call of the gospel is that we are to let go of all we cling to and find our security in an eternal Savior.

Matthew 16:25, 26 set out powerfully the conditions of discipleship. They are also very sound conditions for mental health:

> For whosoever will save his life shall lose it: and whosoever will lose his life for my sake shall find it. For what is a man profited, if he shall gain the whole world, and lose his own soul? or what shall a man give in exchange for his soul?

Paul Tournier points out that the word *life* as it appears in verse 25 is used to translate two distinct Greek words: *psyche* and *zoe*.[4] The *psyche* is what animates our individual lives to action. *Zoe* is universal life, life in God—the life that triumphs over death and blossoms into eternal life. The person who loses his or her life for Jesus Christ is *not* only the martyr who must be thrown to the lions, but is *also* the person who revises his or her values, who is prepared to let go all accumulated treasure and security, if need be, in order to be attached to Jesus Christ. Tournier then goes on to stress that there must be a "necessary progressive detachment from the world." This means a closer fellowship with God. With Paul Tournier, I believe that as we let go of the world we become *less* prone to depression because there are *fewer* things that can be taken away and represent loss to us. This is the gospel's answer to the problem of depression!

The apostle Paul understood this perfectly. In Philippians 4:11 he writes, "I have learned in whatsoever state I am, therewith to be content." How did he achieve this contentment? Philippians 3:7 gives the key: "But what things were *gain* to me those, I counted loss for Christ." He then goes on to say that he counts "all things but loss" for Christ. They are only "dung" in his eyes (v. 8).

If there is one essential ingredient in neurosis, it has got to be a problem of overattachment. The neurotic is overattached to security, to things, and to people. What Paul is calling us to do is become "underattached." I don't think that total detachment is the goal since the notion of detachment seems too harsh and unrealistic. It implies that there is nothing more to live for and we might as well give up and die. This is not the Christian's position. We have a task to fulfill, and life must go on. But to become underattached or even nonattached, as some would describe it, is healthy. Christian maturity (which facilitates mental health) is a process of becoming *less* attached to life's objects. It is a process of slowly letting go, of taking our fingers off, and freeing ourselves to be wholly Christ's possessions.

Paul never claimed to have attained this totally (Phil. 3:13), but he made this "prize of the high calling of God in Christ Jesus," his life goal (v. 14). So, too, must it be ours. It helps us come to terms with life's many losses and frees us from unnecessary depression and from perpetuating those depressions that are quite legitimate.

DEPRESSION RESPONSES

A person faced with a loss can respond in several ways. First, let's look at the most ideal grieving process.

The Ideal Depression Response

If we were to be perfectly healthy, spiritually and psychologically, how would we deal with our significant losses? I call this the "normal" depression response and it goes like this:

Shortly after becoming aware of the loss, the reaction of depression sets in (see Figure 1). The loss is processed both consciously and unconsciously by the brain and influenced by previous experiences of loss. A state of depression sets in and the depression gradually deepens. The depth of the depression depends on the meaning and value of the loss so that each of us will experience the depression of a given loss differently. Eventually the depression levels out and recovery begins. This point of change generally occurs at the time we begin to let go of the lost object.

Recovery continues and the depression lifts as we return to our previous normal state.

The time for the whole cycle depends on the severity of the loss (the greater the loss, the longer the depression) and the way we process the loss in our thinking. It should be a normal process

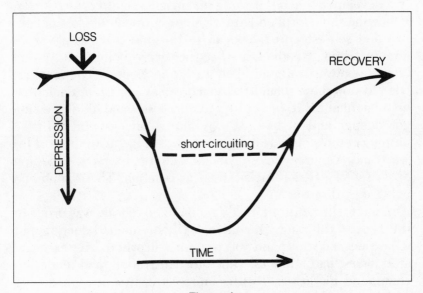

Figure 1
The Ideal Depression Response

that rapidly resolves itself. Some ways of thinking, however, prolong the depression because they refuse to let go or they continuously re-create the loss. Since this is very important to grasp, let me illustrate this point with the following case history:

A young minister once consulted me because he frequently became depressed. After preaching at two worship services on a Sunday, Bill generally felt exhilarated. He believed he was a good preacher and his people responded by showing appropriate evidence of growth and change.

One Sunday, however, as he got up to preach during his second morning service he felt faint. He had not been feeling well all week, but dismissed it as a mild case of the flu. He started to preach but everything began to spin around him. The next thing he remembers is lying on a couch in the church office with a bunch of concerned parishioners hovering over him.

Bill quickly recovered from the flu and in a few days was back at his work. However, a depression began to settle on him. Two weeks later he was feeling so bad that he decided to get some help.

As we explored his thinking pattern it became clear that he had developed a habit of using his imagination to create losses. Following the fateful collapse (which represented a loss of control and self-esteem) he began to imagine that people were afraid of him. He thought that they were being overly kind because he was frail and likely to "go to pieces." The more he tried to stop these thoughts, the more they persisted. Each time he thought about it, he created further losses and his depression got deeper and deeper. It was like a runaway bush fire— nothing could stop it as it fed on itself. All the assurances of his wife, and even a few close friends, didn't help; he was feeding his losses like fission fuels a nuclear reaction. There is no end point, only disaster.

In counseling Bill, I quickly recognized that he was prone to this type of thinking. During his early life he had been taught to "expect the worse and you won't be surprised." He exaggerated losses, had a low tolerance for frustration, and tended to compound his losses. By the end of the first session during which we explored these tendencies, he was already starting to recover from his depression. We continued in the next few sessions to work on his general thinking style so as to prevent future runaway depressions, and he quickly recovered from his despondency.

The Depression Spiral

This runaway depression, or a "depression spiral," is a common complication of reactive depression. It starts out small, but deteriorates into a self-perpetuating abnormal depression. What happens is best illustrated in Figure 2.

Here, the perception of the loss triggers the depressive reaction. As the person starts to become depressed, further reactions are produced, usually by a style of thinking that creates further imagined losses. The reaction may first be one of disgust or self-blame. It may be a feeling of disappointment and guilt. One feeling links to another, and each reaction represents a further loss. It could also be that one anticipates further losses that are to follow the first. For example, if I do not get a raise in salary at the time I expected it, I have to contend with the loss of the raise (which could make me depressed) *and* I

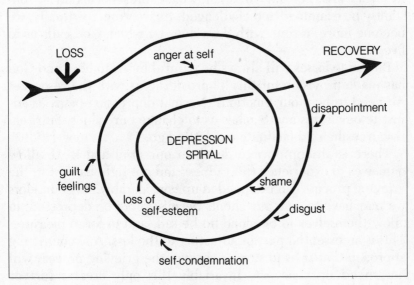

Figure 2
The Depression Spiral

begin to imagine all sorts of other losses ("perhaps it means I am to be fired" or "perhaps someone else is being promoted over me").

These additional losses are mostly figments of our imagination, but they are enough to add extra spurts to the depressive response, sending it into an ever deepening spiral. This is how a depression can become self-perpetuating, feeding off the negative thinking that depression naturally produces, creating further losses. The bottom of this spiral can often be so black that the risk of suicide is very great. For a few, fortunately, the spiral just burns out with time, loses momentum, and spontaneous recovery eventually occurs.

It is important for the counselor to be able to recognize such spiraling depressions and know how to intervene. Recovery is accomplished primarily through challenging and changing the thinking patterns that constantly feed the existing depression.

Don't Short-Circuit Normal Depression

The most important point for every counselor to grasp is that there is an appropriate amount of grieving that should be done for every loss. For the Christian, what represents loss must constantly be examined and challenged. As we grow spiritually, we become more in tune with the values by which God calls us to live.

But some losses will always be painful for us to bear and God has made provision for this by providing us with the resources we need to heal our emotions. Normal depression helps us adjust to our losses and teaches us to change our values. Spiritual resources help to facilitate our letting go.

There is an appropriate depth to our grief and if we allow ourselves to experience this sadness and not fight against it, the grieving process can be speeded up considerably. As counselors we may have to give our clients permission to be depressed, to allow themselves to be alone, to be sad, and to forgo pleasure. This is an essential part of adjusting to the loss. Any counseling approach that tries to stop or shorten the grieving process will not speed up recovery. Invariably this only creates further guilt. *You cannot "short-circuit" the grieving process.* Telling someone to "snap out of it" or that "God is not pleased with your depression" only creates further loss—and depression. It is callous advice and only reflects our own discomfort with another's pain. Often, we feel so guilty when someone else suffers that we desire their suffering to go away so *we* can feel better. If this is how you respond to suffering, you'd better not try to be a counselor. Both you and the sufferer will be worse off!

MIND-BIOCHEMICAL CONNECTIONS

In closing this chapter on understanding reactive depression there is one further point counselors should understand. While reactive depressions are primarily psychological reactions, the resulting depression is *not* solely a psychological state. Biological changes accompany *all* depressions, even when they are triggered psychologically. This means that there is a chain of events following the awareness of a loss that starts the mind–body chain of events that leads to depression. While the mind can resolve the loss, the body still needs time to recover. The biochemical changes accompanying the depression take time to return to normal. One may continue to feel depressed long after the problem seems to be resolved.

Recently I experienced this phenomenon quite vividly. Needing a little break from our hectic schedules, my wife and I decided to spend a few days at a beach-front hotel. On the last day of our stay we checked out of the hotel and went to have lunch at a marina restaurant. While we were eating, my wife looked at her ring finger and gasped, "I don't have my diamond on." Panic! We quickly reviewed the morning activities and concluded that she had left the ring in the hotel bedroom. We remembered that the hotel maids were cleaning adjacent rooms as we left. We envisioned that the ring had been stolen. It was our engagement commitment of thirty-three years ago. It was a symbol of our long and happy marriage. How could we ever replace it? Besides, it is a diamond ring and they don't come cheaply! We both become depressed.

Hurriedly we called to alert the housekeeper to our dilemma and rushed back to the hotel. My wife headed for the housekeeper's office and I rushed directly to the bedroom that had been ours. The room was open but the beds were still unmade. I began to search. I turned out the trashbasket, checked all the drawers and closets. The longer I looked, the more depressed I grew. What would Kath say? That ring was her most-loved object. She had promised it to one of our daughters. My imagination ran away with me. I could visualize the days, even weeks, of painful mourning ahead, not just for Kath but for myself as well.

Just then, she came through the doorway with the housekeeper. Thoroughly dejected, she started her own search. She walked to her bed, pulled back the bedcovers, and there it was. Apparently she had taken it off to put cream on her hands and placed it on the bed next to her.

Now the point of the story is this: Even though our loss had been restored, we continued to feel depressed for a while. Sure there was a sense of relief and our loss did not get any larger, but we were still sad. For some hours afterwards our bodies continued to feel the loss. Eventually our body chemistry was reset and our depression was gone.

This is important to remember because many people who experience such temporary losses do not allow time for the body's chemistry to heal. They are likely to interpret their continued low mood as a sign of failure, reject themselves, and create further loss and depression. Many depressions are perpetuated this way.

The healthiest way to deal with sadness following restoration of the loss is simply to *accept it.* Give the body time to heal after the mind is recovered.

CONCLUSION

As we will see in chapter 9, there are effective techniques we can use to speed up the grieving process and recovery from depression without short-cutting any part of it. We can do this without pushing a person to get better quicker. Recovery is aided when everyone—parents, spouses, children, pastor, and counselor—*believes* that the depressed individual needs an *attitude of acceptance.* Lots of Christian love can help to stop the creation of further losses. Self-rejection and self-blame must be cut off by showing the sufferer that reactive depression is a normal response to loss, and that usually the loss is not sinful but only a sign that we have cared very much for someone or something. God understands this—so should we!

CHAPTER SIX

UNDERSTANDING BIOLOGICALLY CAUSED DEPRESSION

MANY COUNSELORS RESIST the notion that *some* depression can have a biological origin. They prefer to believe that *all* depression is psychological (or even spiritual) because, for one reason, this makes their job less complicated. It also means that the client is dependent on them alone for treatment.

Understanding the biological causes of depression also takes a lot of time for those who do not readily understand biochemistry and who find scientific terms to be confusing. This keeps them clinging to simplistic explanations and leaves them in their more comfortable and less complicated belief systems.

The treatment of the biologically caused, or endogenous, depressions is a *team effort*, and this demands that the counselor be open to cooperating with other healing disciplines. Historically, the medical profession is a lot more team minded than psychologists or counselors, who tend to practice in isolation. Physicians acknowledge the need for specialist expertise more often and utilize consultation with a wide variety of disciplines in their treatment efforts. We counselors tend to "go it alone" and feel threatened if a problem we are working with requires cooperative treatment.

Again and again I have encountered resistance on the part of my psychologist colleagues to appropriate medical treatment of some depressions. Just this last week I experienced such a situation. A minister I have seen in therapy for about three months was showing no progress in relieving his depression. I became increasingly convinced that his problem was biologically based.

I consulted his physician, who ran some routine checks on his thyroid, sugar metabolism, and other endocrine function, and we discovered that adrenalin production was very low. This needed further investigation, but the physician and I agreed that we should, nevertheless, start the client on antidepressant medication. The client happened to mention this to a friend who was a counselor. The counselor friend was horrified that we should even consider drugs, let alone medical tests, and expressed this openly to my client. This was confusing to him, and it took me a whole session to undo this negative advice and convince him that nothing would be lost by the treatment but everything was to be gained. We were following a "diagnosis by trial medication" procedure, and I explained that his counselor friend simply did not have the background and training to pass judgment on the wisdom of this approach. As it turned out, the next round of testing produced evidence of a tumor in the endocrine system, so that the extra diagnostic effort was well justified. Counselors with little training in biological matters should not rely on their own judgment in these matters!

Such encounters with inadequately trained and biased counselors is quite common. The purpose of this chapter, therefore, is to provide a basic understanding of our current understanding of biologically caused depressions. In it I will try to show how essential it is to begin appropriate treatment as early as possible. The increasing tendency for the public to take legal action for negligence makes it imperative that the counselor be able to take appropriate steps when obvious signs of physically caused depressions are present.

I do not intend to provide a detailed account of how to treat a biologically based depression. This is beyond the scope of a counselor's responsibility, and cases suspected of having biological involvement should be referred to an appropriate professional. This is not to say that psychotherapy has no part to play in treatment. It very much does. But its role is supportive to and can only follow the primary treatment that must be focused on the removal of the biological cause.

How common are biological depressions? We do not have a clear answer to this question. From my own experience, biologically caused depressions are far more common than most of us would expect. A simple diagnostic pointer is that the more serious the depression is in the absence of a recent significant loss, the more likely it is that the cause is biological.

Biological factors can contribute to the cause of depression in several ways. They create conditions that could increase an individual's vulnerability to depression; reduce a person's resistance to depression; set up "deficits" in development that may make someone depression prone; increase vulnerability to stress induced depressions; shape the personality to be more depression prone; modify the functioning of the nervous system to create biochemical deficits or surpluses for depression; slow down recovery mechanisms.

Unfortunately, even though remarkable progress has been made in our understanding of the biology of depression in recent years, the roles of the various contributing biological factors, and their relationships to social and psychological factors, are still not fully understood. We certainly don't have treatment methods for all of the possible biological factors that have been identified, but we *do* have effective treatments for some. It is the responsibility of the counselor to point a depressed person towards those treatments that are available.

BIOLOGICAL MECHANISMS IN DEPRESSION

Any cogent theory of depression must integrate information from various levels of understanding. Only an integrated theory will stand the test of time and truthfulness. What are the biological mechanisms that cause some depressions?

An excellent publication put out by the National Institute of Mental Health, summarizes our most recent understanding of biological causes. This report emphasizes that at a fundamental level, all behavioral responses to our world are dependent on electrical and neurochemical transmission in the brain. Nerve impulses trigger the release of neurotransmitters, or special chemical messengers. Every nerve pathway has special gaps (synapses) and the purpose of the neurotransmitter is to help the nerve signal jump across this gap.[1] An understanding of this mechanism will help the counselor to know how and why antidepressant drugs are helpful.

Figure 3 shows a simplified drawing of such a synapse. The nerve impulse, arriving from the left, must release the neurotransmitter from the "sending" (or transmitter) side, which then rapidly travels across the gap to the "receiving" (or receptor) side. The neurotransmitter is absorbed by the receptor and then sent back to the sending side in a very complex manner. Alterations in the amount of neurotransmitter being produced or being destroyed and defects in the whole balance of the process, whereby the signal is transmitted across the gap of the synapse, are what cause the major type of biological depression with which we are confronted. There are also other types of biological depression, but I will come to these later in the chapter.

While, for some time now, one special class of neurotransmitter has been implicated in depression, the focus of attention has settled recently on two important culprit substances: The first is *norepinephrine* or (*noradrenalin*) and the second, *serotonin*. At first it was thought that too much of either of these neurotransmitters was responsible for mania and depletion was what caused depression, but it is now understood to be more complex than this. For one thing, some synapses are norepinephrine dominated while others are serotonin dominated. This has important implications for antidepressant medication because

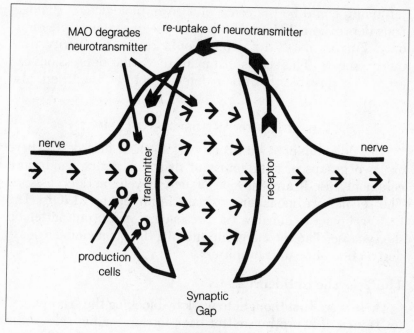

Figure 3
Simplified Diagram of Synapse

some drugs are known to act specifically on norepinephrine while others act only on serotonin. Some act on both, and since there is no known reliable test to determine which substance is deficient, these dual acting antidepressants may be the better ones to use initially.

A number of things can go wrong with the neurotransmitter and the synapse, thus causing depression. There can be 1. insufficient production of neurotransmitter; 2. insufficient release of neurotransmitter at the sending side; 3. insufficient receiving of neurotransmitter at the receptor side; 4. degradation of neurotransmitter during transmission; 5. insufficient return of neurotransmitter from the receiving to the transmitting side; 6. excessive removal of neurotransmitter from the synapse by monamine oxidase, a chemical which is supposed to help regulate the balance of the neurotransmitter.

Each of these six defects, separately for norepinephrine and serotonin, could be the cause of a given biological or endogenous depression. This makes for at least twelve possible disorders. Furthermore, the defect could range in severity from mild to severe. This shows that many dissimilar depressions can arise. It is possible that other defects, not yet identified, also exist.

THE ACTION OF ANTIDEPRESSANT DRUGS

How do antidepressant drugs work in these disorders? There are two groups of antidepressant drugs. The first (and more commonly used) are tricyclic or heterocyclic antidepressants. The second are monamine oxidase inhibitors or MAOIs. The first group act to enhance the presence of neurotransmitters in the synapse. The second group inhibits the monoamine oxidase destruction of neurotransmitters.

The Tricyclic Antidepressants

These were first thought to work by blocking the "re-uptake" (or return of neurotransmitter back to the sending side of the synapse) of either norepinephrine or serotonin. By blocking the return of neurotransmitter to the sending neurons, more neurotransmitter was thought to be available to carry the nerve impulse across the synapse. However, recent findings say it is more complicated than this.[2]

The big question that plagues scientists is: Why is there a delay in the onset of action of antidepressant drugs? Almost immediately after a patient starts the medication, the drugs act to block the return of neurotransmitters. But despite this immediate action, it takes two to three weeks before the therapeutic effect shows itself in a reduction of depression.

Why this delay? Why do some drugs have a more rapid therapeutic onset than others, but end up being about the same in effectiveness? These questions remain unanswered at the present time. Some believe that the time lag has something to do with adjustment of the receptor side; others think that changes in sensitivity to receiving the neurotransmitter takes place. Most feel that antidepressants act in various complicated ways to restabilize an unbalanced system. Correcting the basic problem starts a process of healing that takes time to accomplish. We will probably never find one single reason. The important point is, these drugs do work!

Monoamine Oxidase Inhibitors (MAOIs)

After a period of diminished use, this group of drugs has re-emerged as useful agents for treating some forms of biological depression. They are generally used only after a trial on some of the tricyclics for two reasons: First, the biological defect they correct is less common. Second, their undesirable side effects are a little more difficult to manage. In particular, caution has to be exercised in eating certain foods. Foods with high tyramine content (produced by fermentation of protein) must be avoided. These foods include cheeses, pickled herrings, certain alcoholic drinks, and certain drugs. Without close supervision, reactions between the drug and these foods can be dangerous.

The MAOIs do just what their name suggests: They inhibit the action of monoamine oxidase which degrades the neurotransmitter excessively. One form of the drug takes about ten days to be effective, the other three to four weeks. The longer onset drug (hydrazines) have a lower incidence of unwanted side effects than the quicker acting drugs (nonhydrazines).

Lithium

There is one further drug I should mention that is often used in disorders that alternate between depression and mania (bipolar depressions), and recurrent unipolar depressions. Lithium is used to control the manic phase, but is often helpful also during the depression phase, although it is not strictly an antidepressant. Despite its effectiveness, its mechanism of action remains unclear.

Manic–depressive illness and the recurring unipolar depressions are among the most common and treatable depression disorders. In most sufferers, the illness recurs with episodes becoming more severe and frequent with age. Seventy to 90 percent of patients respond to lithium.[3]

DIAGNOSING BIOLOGICAL DEPRESSIONS

In chapter 4, I provided an overview of diagnostic pointers to the various types of depression. These pointers were primarily descriptive of psychological symptoms. Are there biochemical tests that can be used to determine the presence of biological depression of the sort just described?

Investigators have identified two biochemical markers that can be used to identify severely depressed patients who respond well to medication. While some uncertainty still surrounds both procedures, they are often used in clinical settings to aid diagnosis. They are known as: 1. the dexamethasone suppression test (DST), and 2. MHPG level (*MHPG* stands for "three-methoxy-four-hydroxyphenylglycol").

An extensive review of these tests is not appropriate here. It is rightly the domain of psychiatry and should only be evaluated by a physician. Let me provide a brief description of the purpose and effectiveness of these two tests just so that the counselor can have a basic understanding of how they are used and interpreted.

The DST

The majority of severe endogenous depressives secrete increased amounts of cortisol, a hormone produced by the adrenal glands. This defect is related in some complex way to the mechanisms described earlier in the chapter. A drug, dexamethasone, suppresses circulating cortisol. But it has been found that up to a half of endogenously depressed individuals do *not* suppress cortisol at some time during the twenty-four hours following the administration of dexamethasone. These nonsuppressors respond very well to antidepressant medication. Because of this, the test has been proposed as helpful in choosing patients who should be placed on antidepressants and monitored for progress during therapy.

Referral to a physician with a request for a DST is not sufficient for our purposes here, because this test is also used for purposes other than evaluation for depression.

For depression evaluation, guidelines for using the DST are as follows:

1. Reserve the DST for depressed clients in whom the diagnosis is in doubt or there is symptomatic evidence of endogenous depression.

2. After taking a blood sample to measure baseline cortisol,

the physician prescribes one milligram of dexamethasone to be taken at 11:00 P.M.

3. The next day, blood is taken at 8:00 A.M. and 4:00 P.M. for cortisol measurement.

4. Any evidence that the cortisol level stays above five milligrams per one hundred milliliters at either of these times is taken as a "positive" finding.[4]

The paradox of the test is that whereas a high percentage of those with "positive" results will respond to antidepressant medication, many with a "negative" finding will still find antidepressant medication helpful.[5] The value of the test is in being able to predict a definite response without having to wait three weeks to see if medication will help. A knowledgeable physician or psychiatrist should be able to advise you on the use of this test and when to continue with an antidepressant despite a negative finding.

Whenever I have found a positive finding on this test, I have seen a definite response to antidepressant medication. In about a third of the negative findings, I have still seen a positive response to medication, especially when the results are borderline. While this is a useful test, it is by no means perfect, and clinical judgment may still have to be used.

MHPG Levels

MHPG is a substance found in the urine and is a breakdown product of a neurotransmitter. Sometimes, and I want to emphasize *sometimes,* patients with *bipolar* depressions have lowered MHPG (i.e. less than one thousand milligrams per twenty-four hours) in their urine. Some experts have noted that patients with *unipolar* depression fall into two groups: one with lowered MHPG and one with elevated MHPG. They have proposed that low MHPG patients have a norepinephrine deficit and will respond to the desipramine group of antidepressants (trade names such as Norpramine and Pertofrane) which selectively block the re-uptake of norepinephrine, whereas patients with high MHPG levels have a serotonin deficit and respond to the[6] amitriptyline group (Elavil) that block serotonin re-uptake.

Difficulty surrounds the problem of how to collect urine over twenty-four hours, and results can be contaminated by caffeine, diet, and exercise. The test, therefore, is usually reserved for hospitalized patients where extraneous factors can be controlled.

OTHER FORMS OF BIOLOGICAL DEPRESSION

To this point, my discussion has focused on the more common endogenous depressions. There are other forms of biological depression to which the counselor needs to be alert. These include depression following adrenalin exhaustion (post-stress depression), depression accompanying diseases of the endocrine system, depression in the premenstrual period, seasonal depressions, and depressions associated with drug usage.

Depression Accompanying Adrenalin Exhaustion

The "postadrenalin depression" is frequently experienced by those who have just had a "high." Whenever the body has experienced a period of high adrenalin demand, such as coping with an emergency, public speaking, or meeting a deadline, the adrenal system becomes exhausted and switches off when the demand is over. It is like the calm following a storm, except that the calm is more like a total switch-off. Most of us feel it as depression. It is the body's way of demanding rest; it turns you off to all interests and saps you of energy so that you are forced into a period of recovery. During this time the adrenal glands and other important systems are rejuvenated. The longer your system has been in a state of demand or emergency, the longer it will take for it to rejuvenate.[7]

A vivid biblical illustration of this type of depression occurs in 1 Kings 18 and 19. During his encounter with the prophets of Baal, Elijah challenged the Israelites to follow God—or Baal.

Elijah alone was God's prophet, whereas Baal had 450. Elijah took charge and commanded that two bullocks be sacrificed and placed on two separate wood piles with no fire. The prophets of Baal were to go first, call on their gods to light the wood, and then Elijah would call on his.

The challenge to Baal lasted four or five hours and the false prophets cut themselves and gushed blood to please their gods—but to no avail. Elijah mocked them all the time, then built an altar in the name of his Lord, poured twelve barrels of water over it until it was totally saturated, prayed, and the fire of the Lord consumed the offering. It even "licked up the water that was in the trench" (18:38). He then slew the 450 false prophets and, having received Jezebel's threat on his life, flees into the wilderness where he rests under a juniper tree and asks to die.

Why did he run away? Had he not just had a glorious victory and demonstrated that God could take care of him? Of course! But he was still human and the most obvious explanation is that he was experiencing a classic "post-adrenalin depression." This is clear in the pattern of his black mood (19:4) and the need for sleep (19:5–7). In fact, his model for recovery is as modern as any I know: He rested and slept until his system was rejuvenated. For Elijah, that rest fortified him for another forty days (v. 8).

Modern prophets also experience the "Elijah syndrome." Ministers frequently report that the day following their preaching and other stressful activities is full of depression. Their "wilderness" experience occurs on Mondays, and for quite a few clergy it is a miserable and debilitating twelve to twenty-four hours. The older we get, the less resilient is our adrenal system and the more depressed we become after an adrenalin high.

Other people often experience the adrenal letdown on weekends, when the heavy demands of the work week are over. Saturdays or Sundays can often be very depressing for a busy executive. Others experience the low after examinations, vacations (especially those with lots of travel), and holiday seasons.

What can the counselor do to help? Here are some suggestions:

1. Make sure depressed clients understand the body's need for rest and recovery, and why depression is necessary for healing. (It removes us from our environment so that we don't self-destruct.)

2. Help them to monitor their mood fluctuations and see the connection between their high demand activity and the ensuing depression. Keeping a "mood log" is helpful.

3. Teach them how to "manage their adrenalin" and not be so high strung.

4. Help them to cooperate with their low mood, engage in

low demand activity, and rest. Suggest that they increase their sleep period and encourage them to sleep more when anticipating a period of heavy demand.

5. Prevent them from overpsychologizing or spiritualizing their low feelings. It is not sinful to feel this way. It is not some psychological defect—merely the body's natural recovery system at work.

Disorders of the Endocrine System

Depression can easily be mistaken for a disorder of the endocrine system, especially hypothyroidism.[8] The counselor should be on the alert for any possibility of such disease. All cases of depression that do not respond to counseling within a reasonable amount of time should be referred for medical evaluation.

The glands of the endocrine system (thyroid, parathyroid, thymus, pancreas, pituitary, adrenal, ovaries, and gonads) produce hormones that are released into the bloodstream to perform many functions including growth, sexual development, and emergency responding. Lowered function on most of them can produce depression. I will briefly discuss only two: lowered thyroid production (hypothyroidism) and lowered adrenalin production.

Hypothyroidism (its severe form is called *myxedema*) produces a sluggish metabolic state. Caused by iodine deficiency or inadequate stimulation, the symptoms include depression, mental sluggishness, suspiciousness, and self-accusatory ruminations.[9] Often there is a family history of thyroid dysfunction. A tendency to be overweight is also often found.

Lowered adrenalin production can be caused by defects anywhere in the pituitary/adrenal chain. It is the pituitary gland in the brain that produces ACTH to stimulate the adrenal glands. Partial inadequacy can follow pregnancy, severe influenza, infectious diseases, or prolonged stress. Symptoms include lethargy, weakness, and episodes of hypoglycemia.[10] One is easily fatigued, drowsy, and seclusive. There is decreased sex drive and loss of appetite.

Medical tests for both these conditions are routine and a referral to a physician should discover them if they are present.

Disorders of Metabolism

Certain disorders of metabolism can also produce depression. The body is constantly assimilating food, breaking it into simpler substances that can be stored and used, releasing energy for vital processes, then discarding it as waste. When things go wrong here, depression can sometimes result.

The metabolism of sugar is especially important. Abnormally low blood sugar levels (hypoglycemia) can produce restlessness, negativism, emotional instability, apprehensiveness, dizziness, and depression.[11] Sometimes it also stimulates anxiety attacks.

Depression and the Physiology of the Female

While Chapter 13 discusses in more detail the depressions unique to women, a brief mention here of the many depressions of a biological nature affecting the female would be appropriate.

The reproductive organs of the female are extremely prone to creating mood swings. The depression at the onset of menstruation, the premenstrual syndrome (PMS), the use of contraceptive pills, pregnancy, postpartum reactions, and menopause all revolve around the female's reproductive system. And as we currently understand it, the system is fraught with depression pitfalls.

In his book *What Wives Wish Their Husbands Knew about Women,* Dr. James Dobson has an excellent chapter that reviews the menstrual and physiologic problems of the female.[12] The variation in estrogen levels markedly influences the moods of women. This in turn affects self-esteem, productivity, and interpersonal relations.

Fortunately, in recent years there has been a greater awareness and acceptance of the sensitivity of the reproductive system. Effective treatment is readily available to deal with these problems, often in a Christian context.

PART TWO

COUNSELING A DEPRESSED PERSON

So YOU ARE CONFRONTED with someone who is deeply depressed. All the signs of the mood disorder are present and a careful review of the history and presenting symptoms rules out obvious physical causes of the depression. How do you now proceed? Are there special precautions or preparations that are unique to depression counseling? I believe there are, and this section will try to clarify them.

Counseling the depressed is a very demanding enterprise and not all people helpers are capable of doing it. Of course, the more you understand depression, the greater will be your effectiveness. But sometimes a counselor who has experienced too much hurt or loss may find it difficult to be helpful because he or she cannot keep personal dynamics on the sideline. Personal issues keep intruding or the pain of the melancholic client is too much to bear. I understand this! I've been training clinical psychologists for a long time and I have seen what devastation a depressed patient can work on a novice counselor, especially one who has not taken the time or trouble to prepare for the special demands of the task.

If you intend to work regularly with depressed people, you will need to develop a "stomach" for the melancholic's pain. With careful attention to a few important principles, especially separating sympathy from empathy, you can greatly increase both the satisfaction of the counseling task and your tolerance for the depressed client.

CHAPTER SEVEN

PREPARING TO COUNSEL
A DEPRESSED PERSON

THERE IS ABUNDANT EVIDENCE that structured counseling helps many depressions, even when they are primarily biological in origin.[1] If anything, counseling has been shown to be equal to or better than medication in most depressions. The combined treatment of counseling and medication is clearly the most effective for endogenous depressions.

But is all counseling equally effective? Clearly not. Some counselors do better than others when it comes to working with depression. The reason is, I believe, that the unique pain of the melancholic calls for a special kind of understanding.

When I first started practicing psychotherapy, I hated working with depressed patients. Their depression depressed me;

their pain rubbed off on me; to top it all off, none of them got better. I quickly learned that I was making a number of fundamental mistakes and as I began to modify my approach, lo and behold, my effectiveness increased. Then one day I realized that I had begun to enjoy working with depressed patients. I felt that I understood them and could point them to a way out of their dark abyss. Now I love depressed people! As I share some of the insights I have gained over the years, perhaps you will come to love them too!

WHAT DOES IT TAKE?

If I were to summarize three personal characteristics essential to effective depression counseling, they would be compassion, determination, and an ability to listen effectively.

Jesus was a model counselor. He knew how to heal in the miraculous sense, but he also knew how to heal through his presence and influence—and that is what counseling is: influencing others towards wholeness, through your influence, and presence.

The most beautiful example of Jesus' counseling ability occurs in Luke 24:13–35. It is the story of how Christ appears, after his crucifixion, to two disciples traveling on the road to Emmaus. Please read this portion of Scripture again to refresh your memory of the encounter. As you do so, think about how Jesus counsels the couple. He performs no miraculous healing but just talks to them and allows them to talk to him. In the process he brings healing.

The two travelers were clearly depressed. This is obvious to Jesus at the outset because he asks them why they are sad (v. 17). Then he models all the characteristics of a good counselor, as modern research has been able to identify them:

He invites them to speak about their hurt. Even though he knows all that has happened, he asks them to tell him "what things" had transpired (v. 19). This clearly is not for his benefit but theirs, because he knows all about the events of the past few days. He understood that they needed to recount the details.

He listens without condemning or short-circuiting. They must have walked quite a few miles as they described all the details.

Not once is he impatient. Even though he reproves them (v. 25) for being fools for not grasping the full message, he does not offend them for they invite him to stay the evening (v. 29). Later they even remark: "Did not our heart burn within us, while he talked with us by the way?" (v. 32).

He instructs them from the Scriptures (v. 27) and points them to the larger scheme in God's eternal plan. He helps them to pull back and place all their apparent catastrophe in proper perspective. This was no failure, but a glorious victory; this wasn't time to be cowering, but to get ready to herald in a new age, for a New Covenant between God and people had been made.

He heals their depression. Verse 31 tells us "and their eyes were opened, and they knew him." But they also saw God's plan unfolding and knew he was in control. That's why they immediately returned to Jerusalem to tell the disciples. Let me emphasize again: The healing of their depression was *not* a special miraculous work. Jesus made himself known and allowed the natural process of recovery to take its course. This is a "healing" that comes from cooperating with the risen Christ. It is still powerfully available to all of us today.

THE CHARACTERISTICS OF AN EFFECTIVE COUNSELOR

As mentioned in the previous section, there are three special characteristics that can make someone an effective depression counselor. These personal qualities can be nurtured, if they are understood. I will discuss each briefly and offer suggestions on how you might enhance these within yourself. In each case, think of how Jesus demonstrated these qualities. Set him up as a model for how you would like to be as a counselor.

Compassion

This is the first ingredient of good counseling, but it is very often misunderstood. *Webster's New Twentieth Century Dictionary* defines *compassion* as feeling "pity" or "sorrow for the sufferings or trouble of another." This is misleading because the compassion of a counselor is not just a "feeling of pity." Pity often connotes a slight contempt because the person pitied can easily be regarded as weak or inferior. Your compassion should always be felt as denoting a deep respect for the one who is hurting, and your urge to help should be tempered with the realization that "But for the grace of God, there go I." In no way is the counselor superior to the sufferer.

Your compassion should also not be dominated by sympathy, which is sentimental. When you use sympathy in counseling you try to understand the pain of another by using the sympathy as a frame of reference or by feeling the same pain. For instance, sympathy says: "I know how you feel because I've been through it myself." This shows a callous disregard for how unique each one of us feels our pain. No other person can feel exactly what and how we feel. Our pain is unique. And, in any case, the last thing anyone who is hurting wants is someone else to feel their pain also. This only compounds their suffering by suggesting that they are causing hurt to another.

The compassion of the effective counselor must be characterized by empathy. Over and over again, research has shown that empathy heals people, whereas sympathy doesn't.[2] *Webster's New Twentieth Century Dictionary* defines *empathy* as "the projection of one's own personality into the personality of another in order to understand him or her better." The key word is *understand.* Compassion that doesn't try to understand another's pain is nothing more than pity. Empathy is different from sympathy in that its focus is on *understanding* the pain of another person, not feeling it with them. In fact, if you actually get caught up feeling the pain of another person, (which often happens and is quite natural), you need to pull back to a more neutral position because the focus of the counseling can too easily shift away from the pain of the client onto yourself. You'll find yourself talking too much about your own problems.

More important, the empathic compassion of the counselor is effective because it helps the hurting person feel more understood and accepted than he or she could without that compassion. How can you improve this quality of compassion in yourself? Here are some suggestions:

1. Practice being *warm* to people. This presupposes that you understand your own problems and weaknesses enough that you don't mind being vulnerable or exposing your real nature to others. If you don't have these qualities, maybe you

need some counseling yourself. Practice being friendly. Walk up to strangers and greet them openly. Be interested in others. Show respect for their opinions. Be considerate of their needs. Be sincere in your manner of speaking and listening.

2. Practice being *honest.* Counseling cannot be a masquerade. There is a quality of communication that separates ordinary social conversation from "counseling talk": There are no secrets in counseling. Don't be blunt, but work at being straightforwardly honest. Don't be devious, but direct. Be honest about your own errors and openly willing to admit them. People will be more open to trusting you if you are this way.

Determination

What was striking about Jesus' counseling with the couple on the road to Emmaus? His determination to get *them* to talk about *their* experience. When Jesus first asked them to explain why they were sad, the couple responded, "Art thou only a stranger in Jerusalem, and hast thou not known the things which are come to pass there in these days?" (Luke 24:18).

Jesus must have known that they had already talked themselves out over the events of the past few days. Verse 14 says that before he joined them "they talked together of all these things." Why not just pick up where they left off? It would have saved time and he could have moved on to his next appearance. Why not be efficient and reveal himself there and then, and get on to the next task? But even though they had already "communed together and reasoned" (v. 15), Jesus, with determination and a willingness to stop and listen, asks, "What things?" (v. 19). In effect he was saying, "Go on, even though I may know all the details, tell it to me again."

This is a beautiful model for the counselor who must enter the frame of reference of the one who is hurting and say, "Even though I know where and why you are hurting, tell me about it."

The determination of the effective counselor must be characterized by faithfulness. It must be persistent in seeking the cause of the depression and communicating hope. You may dislike the client. You may be disappointed in his or her shallowness and disregard for your advice. But determination will carry you through.

Listen Effectively

Different people counsel differently. I doubt if any two counselors anywhere do exactly the same thing. There are also many different "schools" of counseling. Yet despite these varied approaches within greatly differing personal styles, most counselors are helpful to people who hurt. Why? I think it's because they all have at least *one* thing in common: They have learned the art of *listening*.

Isn't it sad that so few people listen anymore? I mean really listen. Little children can tell their secrets only to a doll or a pet, because parents don't have time to listen. Pastors can't listen because they clutter up their job descriptions with a multitude of petty responsibilities. Others won't listen because they desperately need to talk themselves. So, many end up having to pay a psychologist or psychiatrist to listen to them. Professionals have become the only ones to whom we can tell our secrets—and know they will listen and not punish us for what we have shared.

In his book *Clinical Theology*, Frank Lake, the British psychiatrist, provided a powerful apologetic for listening. He quoted Bonhoeffer as saying that of all the services which all Christians must give to one another, listening is the greatest.[3] Lake cited a biographical novel of Saint Luke (*The Man Who Listens* by Taylor Caldwell), as it explores the transformations that occur in human personalities in the presence of an active listener. The story is about the way people with all sorts of problems speak to a man behind a curtain, whom they cannot see. In their telling of their stories, they talk themselves into complaining against God and the universe. Finally, when the curtain opens, they see their listener: not a complacent human, but Christ on the Cross. What a relief! Jesus Christ goes on listening even when dolls, pets, and psychologists have shut their ears.

Now I don't think that good listening skills come naturally. I believe it is a behavior that we all must, and can, learn. Years of experience in training counselors has convinced me of these simple truths: Good listening is at the foundation of good counseling; most of us have to learn how to listen therapeutically. Jesus epitomized this ability in his counseling, not only with the couple on the road to Emmaus but with everyone he encountered.

The tools of counseling are *talking* and *listening*. Most of us prefer talking and dislike listening. For counselors, listening is the preferred mode.

This is why preachers and lecturers, generally speaking, are not naturally good counselors. Their communicating roles (preaching and teaching) train them to be good talkers. It takes a lot of retraining for them to learn how to change their mode of relating to listening.

Every year I teach a course that helps pastors to become better counselors. Every year there is a lot of resistance to changing advice-giving habits. And every year these ministers go away converted to the realization that listening invites people to open up at a deep psychological level—whereas advice giving blocks the healing process.

Listening to others and encouraging them to tell what for years has been hidden is a humbling experience. But it can also be threatening and a burden. Not everyone can tolerate it.

Let us look at some reasons why therapeutic listening to others is not easy:

Our culture teaches us to conceal our inner thoughts and feelings. When we hear others talk about them, we feel threatened.

Listening takes time. Most of us are too impatient to be bothered by the slowness of the process. We think we have answers and want to present them too quickly.

We have a built-in tendency not to want to be confronted by the pain of others.

Listening to the disclosure of hidden facts and feelings requires a "genuine" response. We don't like this responsibility.

The pain of others often creates anxiety within us—anxiety that we might also one day suffer this way. If we don't know about it, we can't fear it.

How should we listen? This is not intended to be a treatise on listening skills and I would refer the reader to any one of the many excellent texts on developing listening skills, including *The Skilled Helper*, which has an excellent companion training manual.[4] I would say, however, that it is absolutely essential that we "reflect" to the client what he or she is saying. In other words, it is important to be able to repeat *in fresh words* the essential attitudes and feelings of the client. This shows the client that he or she is being understood at a deep level.

GENERAL RULES FOR THE COUNSELOR

Whatever the source of the depression, the first task of the counselor is clear-cut: Get the client to talk so *you can listen.* This provides the information for understanding the cause and dynamics of the depression.

Some Important Don'ts

1. Don't give the client unqualified reassurance that "everything is okay" or that "there is nothing to be depressed about." Such statements are seen as evidence that you don't understand the problem.

2. Don't exhort the client to "snap out of it" or "pull yourself together." This is ineffective and you will be seen as callous.

3. Don't spiritualize the problem before you have evidence that it is a spiritual problem. Overzealous (and often overanxious) counselors quickly jump to spiritual solutions because they *seem* so much easier to deal with. But often they are harder, and you can easily intensify neurotic guilt by making the client feel like a failure.

4. Don't probe and ask petty questions just to fill up the silent moments. Depression is a serious business and depressed people are not interested in the weather, your family, or the church budget. Stick with the painful stuff, even if it means a lot of silence. It will pay off in due course.

5. Don't jump to or make premature interpretations about the depression. For example, don't say, "You're depressed because you lost your job," or "You're depressed because your husband says he doesn't love you anymore." These are too global and can be viewed as offensive, harsh, and superficial. They can easily miss the subtleties of complex depressions.

On the last point, I once saw a patient whose wife had recently died. He was in a deep depression and I assumed that the cause was obvious, so I said, "You're depressed because you've lost your wife." He was offended and said so. This was what every friend had said to him and he didn't need me to repeat their analysis. I retreated and stopped assuming. As I probed his pain, the picture that emerged was quite different. He had not been close to his wife; they had been alienated for many years even though they lived together. While he was sad about her death, this was not the cause of his depression. As we probed further, the real cause emerged: Ten years earlier, there had been an alienation from a son who had rejected his father and blamed him for many of his personal problems. The father was only now, after the death of his estranged wife, beginning to get in touch with this alienation.

Some Important Do's

1. Do take advantage of the probability that the depressed person is interested in his or her current feelings and wants to explore them. Show that you want to understand how sad, hurt, dejected, or forlorn it feels. You may have to describe the feelings to the client, and the closer you come to characterizing how he or she feels, the more you will win the belief that at least here there is hope that someone understands.

2. Do place a high priority on listening and not talking. Your comments and interjections should be designed to help the client talk. Ask open-ended questions. A question like "Do you feel sad?" can only have a single-word answer. If the question were "When do you most feel sad?" or "How does the sadness affect your thinking?" you encourage the client to explore the deeper issues of how he or she feels.

3. Do accept the depressed client's dependency needs. He or she will lean heavily on you. Depression takes away all self-sufficiency and leaves the sufferer frustrated, deprived, and lost. Be supportive and definite. If the client asks, "Should I tell you about my hobby?" don't say, "If you think it is pertinent." Instead, say yes. If he or she asks, "Do I need to come back again?" don't say, "That's up to you" (as some schools of therapy encourage), but say, "I'll see you next Friday at 10 A.M."

4. Do emphasize that the feelings you are talking about are the client's feelings, not yours or anyone else's. They are feelings and not facts. Don't reinforce the notion that the dejection is an objective reality. It is merely a subjective experience. I tell my depressed patients, "The world seems black because *you* are

wearing emotionally tinted glasses. It is the depression that distorts your world. The world is not how you see it."

Some Important Musts

With every moderate to severely depressed client, the counselor must do the following:

1. Look for life-threatening symptoms (i.e. suicidal or homicidal impulses, evidence of self-neglect or poor self-care).

2. If there is a suicidal threat, take appropriate steps to preserve life (warn the family, report to police, or refer the client to an intensive care facility).

3. Inquire about a history of a previous depressive bout. Recurring depressions are common and may indicate an endogenous component. This will give you some idea of the course the illness is likely to run. It will also help to determine the precise nature of the depression. Explore previous treatment strategies. Find out what treatment has been effective in the past, because it is most likely to work now. For instance, if the client has had a previous successful response to a particular antidepressant drug, that should be the first treatment used.

4. Inquire about a family history of previous depressive episodes and other illnesses. Endogenous depressions tend to run in families and if there is a family history of a particular type of disorder, this should first be checked out in the client.

5. Determine the client's attitude to the depression, understanding of the severity of the disorder, and expectations for help. If the client downplays the severity, you may need to confront with some reality. If the client exaggerates the severity (which is more often the case), you may need to give lots of reassurance and create an atmosphere of hope that help is on the way. Be positive and constructive in all that you say, both to the client and the family.

6. Define the client's strengths, coping mechanisms, and environmental supports. Find out how the client copes in normal circumstances. A history of successful coping will be an asset and provide you with resources on which you can build. Knowing that a client enjoys certain hobbies or activities will help in "prescribing" distractions. Getting friends or family members to be supportive is essential.

7. Obtain an appropriate consultation (either for psychological and/or medical factors) that might help you understand what is causing depression. This is especially important if you feel out of your depth or if the client does not respond to your efforts to build rapport. It is better to be safe and request a consultation that may be nonproductive, than sorry because you failed to do so.

The Dangers of Advice Giving

Depression, more than any other clinical problem, tends to bring out the advice-giving impulse in me, and possibly in you too. Partly it's because the pain can be so intense that I want to get some healing going quickly. Partly it's because I tend to be problem-solving oriented. I have to restrain myself from giving advice too early in the counseling process. Chances are, you will have to also.

To the layperson, counseling is synonymous with advice giving. Offering "common sense advice" in a friendly setting is the oldest form of therapy. And in many life situations, that is exactly what we need, but in clinical depression it is the least helpful approach, especially in the early stages of counseling.

The giving of advice is most appropriate when the contact is short and where the consequences are not major. The greatest limitation of advice giving is the temptation to use it indiscriminately and profusely.[5] Whenever you give advice, you run the risk of triggering "resistance."

By *resistance* I mean a special form of conscious or unconscious defense that opposes the purposes of counseling. Psychoanalysts first used the term to describe the unconscious opposition toward bringing unconscious material into consciousness. It can vary from rejection of counseling to overt antagonism. It comes out as "Yes—but. . . ." Everything you suggest is countered with many reasons why it won't work, and the counseling process degenerates into a battle of wills. Alternatively, a strong dependency occurs. People come to expect, even demand, that you make their major (and many minor) life decisions for them.

Early in my career I had a client who tricked me into giving her advice. It started with one simple question about which she wanted my opinion. Then it became a few, and later she would come in with a long list of issues on which she needed advice. All of it was a mask for her real pain and a tactic to avoid confronting deep issues. One day she complained that my advice on a particular matter hadn't turned out right, and she asked me how I was going to get her out of the predicament she found herself in. Only then did I wake up to see the trap into which I had fallen. Advice giving should be avoided as much as possible. Teach people *how* to make decisions, don't make their decisions for them.

A counselor cannot know enough about a person or that person's situation to decide his or her major life issues. The best you can do is listen and try to move the client to a place where he or she can make a decision, given a complete understanding of all the facts. Occasionally issues of morality and values will enter into counseling and you may need to express an opinion about a weighty issue. By all means, state your opinion, but do so in a way that leaves the counselee free to make his or her own decision.

PLANNING THE COUNSELING PROCESS

In closing this chapter on how to prepare yourself to counsel a depressed person, a few thoughts on how to plan the counseling process are appropriate.

Counseling will go in whatever direction you intend, whether the intention is overt or covert. You might as well make it overt and take control of where you want it to go. Nothing is more confusing to a client than having no idea of what is going on.

Structuring the Process

It is very useful to "structure" the counseling process for the client. What this means is that you outline very clearly what it is you are doing and why. This aids the building of rapport by demonstrating to the depressed client that you are in control.

Some therapeutic approaches have de-emphasized any formal attempt at structuring (e.g. Carl Rogers), but I strongly advocate it.

In structuring you let the client know what you believe is the nature of the problem; what the limits of your ability to help are; whether or not you will use other resources (such as a psychologist or physician) for consultation; and the general stages the counseling will follow.

On this latter point, you might explain that you will need two or three sessions at the beginning just to explore the nature and background of the problem, before you start on any "therapy." This helps the client not to expect miracles in the early stages. When you have formulated a clear plan, then this should be shared in a general way with the client. Use appropriate language but try not to be too technical.

Just recently I began seeing a depressed patient who had been in therapy for six months with another clinical psychologist. The patient told me that her biggest frustration was not having any sense of what the psychologist was doing. "Every week I would go there, sit down, and talk for an hour. Then I was told that the hour "was up," and I'd go home and ask myself what I was doing. When she pressed the psychologist for an explanation, his only response was: "Trust me." She didn't and changed psychologists.

On a practical level, you need to structure your counseling by setting time limits. Inform the client how long and how often each session will be. If these limits are not communicated, the client's confusion can be aggravated.

Setting Goals

Before you can plan a counseling process, you need a clear idea of your goals and purposes. *Immediate* goals might include elimination of symptoms (this could require medication), mobilization of support to improve morale (this may require other family members to become involved), or merely the building of rapport and trust (the client may be excessively suspicious). *Ultimate* objectives may include the removal of causes (such as changing a job or being more honest with a spouse), the development of insight (a better understanding of how childhood traumas influence present functioning), or growth in social skills (better communication, stress management or assertiveness skills).

It is helpful with depressed clients to prepare an inventory of *unchangeables*. Certain life situations—marital status, race, sex, intellectual abilities, and job opportunities—are invincible. Fighting them is like being a Don Quixote. Nothing will conquer or change the windmills we charge. They need to be accepted and adjustments made to accommodate them.

Then prepare a list of *changeables*. So much in life can be changed. Learned forms of helplessness would have us believe that we must accept every inconvenience as invincible, or that we cannot affect the outcome of any circumstance. Much depression is relieved as soon as a sufferer feels in control again and can see that there are options open for action.

Finally, assure the client that just as there is no stigma attached to repeated visits to a physician because "cures" don't happen all of a sudden, so repeated visits to a counselor are necessary and no cause for alarm. Assure the client that in the realm of personality and emotional problems, healing is a *slow process*. This message is as much for your benefit as the client's, because counselors, unwarrantedly, expect more from their clients than do physicians.

Counselees are more unreasonable in demands on their psyches than on their bodies. We always expect more from our complexes than our biochemistry! The erroneous belief, especially in Christian circles, that the will should be able to overcome all pain and suffering at a moment's notice creates the illusion that an individual should always be able to rise above his or her problems. Just correcting this mistaken belief can go a long way toward helping a sufferer out of depression.

CHAPTER EIGHT

THE PSYCHODYNAMICS OF DEPRESSION

THE STORY OF DEPRESSION is usually told in terms of symptomatology, etiology, and treatment. But crucial to our understanding of this painful human emotion and sickness is also an appreciation of the underlying *experience* of depression and the way psychological forces operate to produce and sustain a depression.

It is not sufficient for a counselor to know the symptoms of the various types of depression nor to be able to accurately diagnose a sufferer as having a reactive, neurotic, or any other type of depression. Pinpointing the cause of a depression is only the beginning of the helping process. If it points to a biological cause, then correcting the biological defect will bring about a cure. But what about psychological causes of depression? No pill will cure them. A deeper understanding of the "psycho-dynamics" of depression is a necessary condition for effective counseling.

The term *dynamics* is borrowed from physics and is usually used to describe those forces that tend toward producing or changing an activity. It explains how motion takes place under the action of forces. In psychological usage, it refers to the way psychological forces act to produce a certain state of mind. We assume that various forces—physical, moral, social, and histori-cal—all operate to move us toward our present mental state. These forces may shift from time to time, producing a constant state of change. Some understanding of these forces can be helpful in determining why a person feels a certain way and in helping to change it.

In depressions that are triggered by psychological causes, and even in some of the biological depressions, identifiable mecha-nisms produce the depression. While each depression is experi-enced as unique, the mood is in fact controlled by consistent patterns of response that are, to some extent, universal. While some of us may exaggerate specific aspects of this response over others, there is enough consistency for us to be able to speak of the dynamics of depression and to infer that we are all subject to a certain set of universal laws. If these laws were not consis-tent and generally the same for everyone, we would never be able to help anyone through counseling. It is because we can generalize and predict how someone will feel when a given set of circumstances (or forces) arises that we can be helpful as counselors.

THE IMPORTANCE OF UNDERSTANDING

Understanding people and the problems of living is quite a complicated business. Sometimes, the closer we come to under-standing a problem, the more we discover how little we know. In truth, we can never know *exactly* how someone else feels. Each person is unique. Each experience is unique. Each depres-sion is like no other. We intuitively feel this and squirm and become irritated when someone remarks, "I know *exactly* how you feel." There is no way someone else can know. We compare our feelings with the feelings of others to see if they are the same, but we can never really know how we would feel in the same circumstances. This truth is important for counselors of depressed people to grasp. You can never completely under-stand another's feelings; you can only come as close as guessing, based on how you would feel in similar circumstances. God may know us from top to toe and be able to count the hairs on our head—but people can only guess.

But depressed people do need to be understood. Not judged, not evaluated, not lectured, not pushed, not punished, not de-preciated, and certainly not patronized, but genuinely under-stood. This brings healing by opening the person to the grieving process and by providing the insights needed to become de-tached from lost objects.

Now while we can never know exactly how another feels, we can help someone to discover how they feel themselves. This is the task of the counselor—a very challenging task. Each de-pressed person has his or her own world of conflicts, values, attitudes, and behaviors that are the forces giving rise to how he or she feels. Our task is to help clients discover these forces for themselves. The more effective we are in facilitating this discov-ery, the more our hurting clients will feel understood and be able to cooperate with the healing process.

Depressed persons are often confused about *how* they feel and *why* they are as they are. They are also noncommunicative because this is partly the function of depression: to remove us from our environment. The first task of the counselor is to induce the client to talk. Whatever the dynamics of the depres-sion are, these can only be determined in dialog with the suf-ferer. The source of the pain and the subjective reasons for the discouragement, negative thinking, and obstinate behavior can only be explored through verbal communication. This helps the grieving process by conveying understanding and empathy, by showing the depressed person that there are reasons why he or she feels sad. This is a form of reassurance that every depressed person desires. He or she doesn't want to be told that there is nothing wrong. On the contrary, depressed people *do* want to know how badly they feel. But at the same time they also want reassurance that there are others around who don't reject them for the way they feel and that their pain is deeply understood as being *their unique suffering.*

Whether a depression is caused by biochemical disruptions or psychological interruptions, the sufferer *experiences* something very painful. The counselor should develop a deep appreciation for this experience so that he or she can communicate this depth of understanding to the sufferer. It may well be that ultimate relief will come from some medication, but this does not absolve the depressed person from the experience of psychological pain. There is always a dark valley to be traversed no matter what the cause of the depression and the astute counselor can guide the journeying sufferer safely through this darkness. For the sufferer of a psychologically triggered depression there is no relief from medication. The experience of the depression is all there is and the valley is often deep and very dark. It must be faced with courage and determination.

David knew this valley well and the Book of Psalms is full of his experience of it. This is why the Book of Psalms has been such a great source of comfort to those who are depressed through many centuries. The feelings David describes are universal and eternal (at least in this life). They describe the experience of depression with so much depth that all people everywhere can recognize their own emotions—and find the reassurance and comfort they crave.

Psalm 69:1–3 is just such a description.

> Save me, O God; for the waters are come in unto my soul. I sink in deep mire, where there is no standing: I am come into deep waters, where the floods overflow me. I am weary of my crying: my throat is dried: mine eyes fail while I wait for my God.

For the normal person these words might be very gloomy. But for the painfully depressed they are life. They reflect understanding; they resonate with deep feelings that long to be brought into the open that seek for a way out of the abyss of anonymity. Whenever I have read Psalm 69 to a depressed patient as a way of describing how he or she feels, I hear, "That's it. That's how I feel," and then I usually sense a relief, which comes from two realizations:

1. The sufferer sees that his or her pain is a part of the larger pain of human existence; the sufferer is not alone in suffering nor the target of special punishment.

2. The sufferer sees a glimmer of hope that if others have experienced this same pain and survived, then he or she will also.

FORCES THAT INFLUENCE THE DEPRESSION PROCESS

Why are some people more depression prone than others? Why do some experience depression while others do not? Why do some feel their depression more intensely than others?

If we set aside the biologically produced depressions, depression is neither mysterious nor unexplainable. True, at the present stage of our knowledge we cannot always accurately diagnose or treat a particular depression, but the psychological forces that influence depression proneness are quite recognizable.

Depression is essentially a healing process, a response to specific life circumstances. But for many this reparative process cannot take place because the person is not psychologically equipped to cooperate with it. Depression will occur more often in such an individual, and it will last considerably longer than it needs to. Life has just not prepared this person for the adjustments that must be made to deal with loss.

What are some of the life experiences, especially of early life, that can predispose one to depression? There are many, but I will confine my discussion to the following: early sadness, early losses, and early anxieties.

Before I proceed, however, allow me to point out the crucial importance of early life experiences in setting the stage for later depression. Every human comes into the world with a fundamental state of receptivity and with a demand to integrate all that is received. In other words, most learning starts after birth, and everything we learn at later stages of life has to be integrated into what was there before. Each day's learning must be fit into that which was learned the day before. This is an ongoing process. But what was previously learned will also have an influence on future learning; it will determine how we learn what we are now experiencing. Nothing we now do or learn is free from the past, and this is both good news and bad news. It is good news because I don't have to keep learning the same thing over and over again. It is bad news because learning new things often means unlearning something from the past. Much of what we do when we counsel someone who is depressed, therefore, is helping them unlearn past experiences so that *new* learning can take place.

Mark's Story

I can illustrate this by citing an interesting case of depression I treated some years ago. A minister in his early thirties consulted me because of an unexplainable depression he experienced three or four times a week. Mark felt he could not control it and feared that he was going crazy. Mark appeared to be a robust and healthy individual. As I explored his history, I could find no evidence of familial patterns of depression or significant life traumas. He was happily married and successful in his ministry. No significant losses were evident. He was physically healthy and a recent check-up had eliminated thyroid or other endocrine problems. So why did he get depressed periodically?

His pattern of depression went like this: He would awaken refreshed and energetic from a good night's sleep, go to his church office after spending time with his wife and preschool daughter, and be productive all day. Because he frequently had evening meetings, he would come home around 4 P.M. for a break, and that was when the depression invariably hit. A black cloud would come over him. He would lie on his couch in his home study for two or three hours feeling despondent and irritable. When his wife returned from her work around 5 P.M., after having picked up their daughter at the day-care center, he would continue being despondent. If anything, he would get angry and explode over some petty thing as soon as she came through the door! Slowly the depression would pass as the evening wore on, so that by 8 or 9 P.M. he was over it.

As we explored his problem together, it quickly became obvious that there was a connection between what Mark was experiencing and his early childhood. The connection had eluded

Mark, but, as he talked about his experience, it became clearer to him and it went like this:

When he was a child, his mother had to work. She divorced her husband when Mark was quite young and buried her life in her career as an accountant. The nature of her work was such that she never quite knew when she was going to get home in the evenings, so Mark had to spend the period between returning from school—around 3:30 to 6 or 7 P.M.—alone. This bothered him greatly in his early childhood but subsided when he finally got to high school. He had developed the habit of just not returning home until early evening, when he knew his mother was home. He'd spend time with friends or go to a movie, but he always avoided being alone at home.

He recounted quite vividly how much he detested being alone at home. The emptiness and quietness of the place; the loneliness of the experience, the feelings of abandonment, were often unbearable. Without knowing it, Mark had established a pattern of depression in his early childhood that was to dog him the rest of his life.

He had never seen the connection between his wife not being home when he arrived from work and his mother's pattern of not being there to comfort him as a child. For the next few weeks we kept a careful record of his moods. It clearly established that his depression occurred whenever his wife was not home when he arrived from work. Whenever she was, his mood was one of elation.

Knowing the cause of his depression relieved some of Mark's low mood almost right away. We followed with some conjoint therapy in which we recruited his wife to help in providing clear messages about her intended time of returning home after work. We systematically desensitized Mark to his wife's absence. By restoring his confidence that he was not being abandoned (an unconscious fear that had developed in childhood) the problem rapidly abated and he remains free of it to this day.

Early Sadness

The personality of many depression prone individuals has been shaped by the experience of much sadness early in life.[1] The sadness can be caused by inadequate love, even when the parents are willing to accept the care of the child. The caring, however, often is perceived as being "duty bound."

In many cases, sudden "change" because of unexpected events may produce early sadness. The events range from abandonment by a parent through illness or death to displacement by a newly born sibling. As a rule, the childhoods of many depression sufferers have not been as traumatic as the childhoods of people who later become schizophrenic or even seriously neurotic.

Now, while I distinguish between sadness or unhappiness and true clinical depression throughout this book, it must be stressed that unresolved sadness or unhappiness *can* become transformed into the more intense feelings of depression.[2] Or, to put it another way, if we stay sad for a while, the whole mind–body system will become depressed.

Sadness is specifically a human phenomenon. I doubt if other forms of life can experience it as we do. Animals may experience depression (where certain biochemical changes similar to those in humans are taking place) but the experience of "sadness" requires a sensitive intellect that can weigh life events and pass judgment on them. It is because we know what is happening to us and don't like it, that we become sad. And while most depression also shows sadness as one of its symptoms, not all sadness gives way to depression. I can be sad over the pain others are suffering, but this does not necessarily make me depressed. However, when sadness persists, and especially when the painful thoughts accompanying it are allowed to dominate thinking, the switch to depression may finally occur.

A lot of sadness, especially that experienced in early childhood when the skills for adjustment are minimal, can predispose someone psychologically to more depression. It is a learned response that conditions the total system to give up hope and slide into despair.

In a sense, in the presence of repeated sadness, our cognitions or thought systems are taught to be negative and pessimistic. The child who is sad all the time, retards his or her mental processes and adopts a very negative mindset. This makes it easy to interpret unhappiness in a way that quickly moves it to depression. They just do not have the ability to say to themselves, *I am sad now because such-and-such has happened; it will soon pass and then I'll be happy again.* Rather, they think, *I am sad and there is no hope for ever being happy again. I might as well give up right now.* This latter tendency is *learned* early in life, and the counselor must help the depression prone person to *unlearn* it. Cognitive therapy provides very powerful techniques for doing this. I would refer the reader to Aaron Beck's book *Cognitive Therapy of Depression* for further suggestions on how to deal with depression-producing thinking.[3]

Early Loss

Closely tied to the experience of sadness early in life is the experience of early losses.[4]

Losses in early childhood predispose the child to later depression in a number of ways. First, it sensitizes the child to the general pain of loss so that in later life little losses create more depression than would normally be appropriate. For instance, a lot of criticism in childhood from a harsh and demanding parent could so sensitize a child that when he or she is an adult even the slightest hint of not meeting the standards of some superior could create a deep depression. Another person, not having experienced this early rejection, would just shrug off the criticism and adopt the attitude: "Well, there are many ways of seeing things, and I see it differently."

Second, the occurrence in adult life of similar losses (real or symbolic) will reactivate the feelings associated with early childhood loss. I recall a patient many years ago who became depressed every time she saw a friend or neighbor in need of something. Sometimes it was a friend who expressed a need for a loan to buy a new car. Sometimes it was a neighbor who needed to borrow a vacuum cleaner because hers was broken. In every instance, my patient felt responsible for the other's need and even felt obligated to meet that need. Obviously, every time someone she knew needed something, she became depressed because she couldn't supply the need.

What was the underlying dynamic of this depression? As we explored her early life, it became clear that she was the little "Cinderella" of her family who always gave up her toys and personal belongings to her older sisters. Whenever a sister needed something that my patient had, her mother would say,

"Now come on, we must share everything. Let your sister borrow your . . ." She came to feel that nothing belonged to her and this created a pervasive sense of ongoing loss. Now, as an adult, every time she perceived that someone else needed something she had, that feeling returned. It took two years of intensive therapy to free her from the sensitizing effects of those early childhood losses.

A third way that early childhood losses can predispose you to later depression is by teaching you to "compound" your losses. *Compounding* is a thought technique in which you pile each loss on top of others. In other words, instead of experiencing losses one at a time and keeping the grief appropriately focused on each individual loss, you learn to pile the losses one on top of the other so as to create a bigger loss. In this way, you "make mountains out of mole hills" and create big depressions out of little ones.

Figure 4 shows how losses are compounded by adding them to previous losses. This is clearly not healthy, and creates more loss than is necessary. Figure 5 shows how losses should be separated so that they can each be dealt with separately. In normally responding to the losses of life, a healthy person should be able to keep each loss as a discrete experience. This keeps each loss

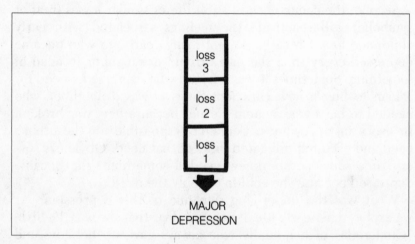

Figure 4
Compounding of Losses

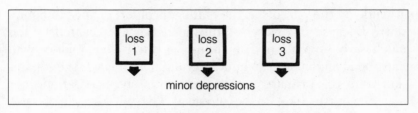

Figure 5
Separation of Losses

in proper perspective, and minimizes the amount of depression that is likely to follow.

This tendency to compound losses is very common, and I suspect we are all prone to it to some extent. I know I am. A few weeks ago I caught myself compounding. The week started with a conflict with some students who wanted something I couldn't give them. That afternoon I had a flat tire going home. That evening our hot water heater developed a leak, so I spent half the night making a temporary repair so we wouldn't be scalded alive by hot water. The next day the alternator on my wife's car went out. I bought a new one and installed it. Later that afternoon she called me at the office to say that the new alternator had burned out. That evening a patient called my emergency telephone service to say that she wished she were dead.

As I sat back late that evening and reflected on how I was feeling, I realized I was significantly depressed and full of self-pity. For two days, everything had seemed to go wrong, and each loss was being piled on top of the others in my head. I carefully unpacked them, mentally kept them apart and focused my thinking on each of them. My depression rapidly subsided. This is not always so easy to do, especially if compounding has become a lifelong habit.

Early Anxieties

Childhood is an uncertain period of life. It is a period when anxiety of all sorts can be created and entrenched as a way of life.

Some anxieties originate from new and threatening situations: displacement due to the arrival of a new brother; change in attitude by the parents as the child gets older; change in family status because of divorce. Other anxieties are created by too much early separation. The child who is left alone a lot or who must be abandoned to an aunt or grandmother, feels the separation from the primary parent very intensely. Separation does not, of course, have to be physical. The withdrawal of love, approval, and support on the part of parents during the critical developmental stage of early childhood can be just as anxiety producing as abandonment.

Arietti (1978) and many others believe that early childhood experiences of anxiety can predispose to later depression.[5] How does the child try to adjust to these anxieties? The child who later becomes depression prone tends to adopt special defense mechanisms. A common one is to find security (and thus relieve the anxiety) by accepting parental expectations no matter how onerous they are. Children come to accept that they must live up to parental expectations no matter how heavy the burden. Only by complying, obeying, and working hard will they be able to recapture the lost love and respect.

While parental love is still available, it is not a steady flow; it is intermittent and conditional, and therefore doesn't offer security. Children may feel that they will be punished for not doing what is expected. The anxiety then changes into guilt feelings and when children feel guilty they again expect to be punished. Children would rather be punished than lose a parent's love; it is the lesser of two evils. If the child is not punished, he or she then often works harder in order to punish him or herself.

It is here that depression proneness enters the picture, because many experts feel that the most effective self-punishment anyone could possibly devise is depression, when you rob yourself of all good and pleasurable feelings. This can easily become a way of "paying for your sins."

What are the theological implications of this? Clearly self-punishment is a form of self-righteousness. You take upon yourself the act of "paying for your sins" and thus usurp the work of Christ on the Cross. I use the important idea of Christ's substitutionary death quite often with my depressed Christian patients, so as to drive home the point that we cannot earn God's pleasure through self-punishment. I point them to 2 Corinthians 5:21: "For he hath made him to be sin for us, who knew no sin; that we might be made the righteousness of God in him."

A pervasive need to punish oneself creates many obstacles to recovery from depression. For instance, it makes it difficult for a depressed client to do "sorrow work," and this is likely to prolong a depression. *Sorrow work* is what grieving is about. Reactive depressions (those associated with loss) require the sufferer to grieve the loss in such a way as to free the lost object. I will discuss this grieving process in more detail in a later chapter, because the counselor needs to know how to facilitate the process. Equally important, however, is teaching the depression prone person how not to engage in self-punishment. This requires that each incident be carefully explored and the client taught the meaning of Christ's redemptive work. A simple "leap of faith" is often all it takes to free ourselves from such a habit.

THE PREDEPRESSIVE PERSONALITY

In closing this chapter in which I have attempted a brief review of some important aspects of the psychodynamics of depression, I would like to comment on the dimensions of personality of the individual who frequently gets depressed. I will confine myself to a discussion of three personality characteristics: rigidity, goal pursuit, and overdependency.

Rigidity of Personality

Depression prone people are not flexible enough to cope with the vicissitudes of life. They are not resilient; they don't "bounce back" quickly enough from a set-back. This is why the experience of loss, even a minor loss, is hard for them to accept. The loss forces them to make adjustments, and they don't find this easy. They would prefer it if things just kept going on as normal. Related to this rigidity of personality is a limited repertoire of coping skills, and this is where the counselor can be most effective in helping: You can teach the client new and more effective coping mechanisms. These could range from improved assertiveness training to enhanced communication skills. Deficits in the client's functioning normally becomes obvious after the first few counseling sessions.

Goal Pursuit

Many depression prone people become focused on only one (or relatively few) goals in life. They pursue one single ambition to the exclusion of others. It may start out as a fantasy and can be fairly minor, or it may be quite all-encompassing, such as winning a Pulitzer Prize or becoming a famous preacher. Often it is an attempt to attain some grandiose self-image.

While the awareness of this goal directedness is conscious, the sufferer is often not aware of the seriousness of his or her preoccupation with it. The patient may work hard to achieve the goal but might just be a daydreamer. It could be a thirst for glory, but often is only a search for love and acceptance.

What's wrong with this obsession with a single goal? The problem is just that! It is an obsession.

A person with an obsession for success becomes so driven to achieve the fantasized goal that he or she becomes supersensitive to failure and losses of any sort. This spells *depression*. The motives are wrong; the preoccupation is excessive; and even when "success" is achieved, it often is a letdown that brings further depression.

When counseling such a person, you should carefully review and work at clarifying the values that drive him or her, and then help in reeducating a wholistic set of goals. These should include a balancing of spiritual with material values, a balancing of recreational with occupational pursuits, and an enhanced appreciation of people as people and not objects. Clearly, these are the values God calls us to.

Overdependency

All humans are dependent on others. No one can live independently and survive. By *overdependency* I mean a personality with an excessive need to lean on others. Such people can't be alone; they can't do anything by themselves; they can't make decisions without asking for advice; they expect others to meet all their needs. Because they cannot always get their way, they become depressed often and easily.

They also alternate between feeling guilty for their excessive dependency and making others feel guilty for not "being there" when needed. They often focus on one person for their needs, and when this is the spouse it places a tremendous strain on the marriage.

These are difficult patients to counsel, because they readily transfer their dependency needs to the counselor. It takes special training and a lot of good supervision to learn how to counsel such depression prone people. I advise that you refer such persons to experienced psychotherapists. It takes years of time-demanding practice to achieve a balance between allowing the client a degree of dependency (which is normal) and pushing the client to be independent—without destroying the counseling relationship. And there is a further risk: These clients tend to have "hysterical" or "histrionic" personalities and are very prone to making "transferences." In other words, they project onto you (their idealized counselor) all their unfulfilled needs and become even more dependent when you represent yourself as caring and concerned. You need to be a well-trained counselor to be able to help such a person back to health again.

CHAPTER NINE

COUNSELING REACTIVE DEPRESSION

DR. THOMAS HORA SAYS that "mourning is an opportunity to let go of attachments."[1] In the Beatitudes, Jesus gave a special place of comfort to those who grieve: "Blessed are they that mourn: for they shall be comforted" (Matt. 5:4). Mostly we link mourning to only one form of loss—the death of a loved one. However, as I showed in chapter 6, reactive depression is best understood and most effectively counseled when it is perceived as a grieving process that follows loss or deprivation. Mourning is, therefore, a process that must be seen to apply to *all* losses and God's comfort can be claimed for *all* times of grieving.

The loss that causes reactive depression must be seen in its broadest context. It can take many forms. For instance, it can be the separation of one person from another—or from a pet. It can be the theft of belongings, the receiving of a tax demand for past errors, or the criticism of a friend. It can be the loss of self-control when you get angry. These are all losses that can create reactive depressions.

Life is full of losses. Friends come and go; children grow up and leave home; every stage of life demands that we let go of that which is past. My youngest daughter and her husband were recently transferred by his company to Germany for two years. After marrying, they had lived thirty minutes away from my wife and me for about two years, and we frequently socialized together. Their separation from us was a distinct loss—loss of their company at weekends, loss of family fun times together, and loss of fellowship. I became depressed for a while and needed to mourn the loss and adjust to letting go. Such losses are the "bread and butter" of living and we adjust to them quite naturally. It is when we don't make a normal adjustment that reactive depression can become a problem.

TEN COUNSELING STEPS

Through my own counseling experience, I've identified ten distinct steps a counselor should help a client take. Each step can lead to the next as the depressed client works through the grieving process.

Step One: Identify the Losses

Some losses are easy to recognize. They are tangible, measurable, and certainly visible. Others are not. They are hard to pinpoint and grasp. They may only be ideas or vague feelings. But since we can only grieve what we know to be lost, the *first step* in counseling reactive depression is to help the sufferer identify the loss or losses.

Very few losses are simple. Every loss represents many things. A loss is like a diamond with many facets or faces. It is these facets that give a diamond its brilliance. The more facets there are, the more a diamond sparkles. Each facet reflects light and, as the diamond is moved slightly, different facets come into the light and reflect their brilliance.

Losses, also, have many facets. For example, being fired from a job is not a single loss—but many. There is the loss of wages, the loss of status that comes with being a gainfully employed person, the loss of face or the feeling of humiliation at having to tell one's spouse and friends that you've been "fired." There is also a threatened loss of not being able to get another good job, a loss of friendships in the workplace, and a loss of familiar surroundings and pleasurable routine. And this is only the beginning!

Step Two: Understand Every Facet of Each Loss

The *second step*, therefore, is to help the sufferer develop a more complete understanding of the full complexity of each loss. Every facet needs to be brought into focus in such a way that will help our mourning. Each of us will experience the same loss differently. We each have our distinctive emotional fingerprints; we differ in our history of losses, in our values, and in our world views. Some of us might place more emphasis on social values; others on material loss.

Different subcultures emphasize different values also, so that one group will experience a loss differently from another. For instance, an Asian client of mine, whose business had failed and caused him deep depression, placed great emphasis in his grieving on his "loss of face." For him, facing his family and friends with his failure was an insurmountable obstacle and far more significant than the financial loss he had suffered. Another client, also of Asian background but more Americanized, emphasized his loss of self-respect. For him, it was a very personal thing. He didn't care what others were thinking, but felt that he had failed himself.

The main point here is that everyone sees the same loss uniquely because of our different histories. Until the client fully recognizes all that has been lost he or she cannot complete the grieving process.

Let me give one other example of how complex a given loss can be. One of my major tasks as dean of our Graduate School of Psychology is to lead the process of student selections. We get many more applications than we can accept; the ratio can be as high as eight to one. The one duty I do not enjoy is sending the letters of nonacceptance. Many of these applicants are quite suitable for our program. We just don't have enough openings for all of them.

Invariably the nonaccepted students receive my letter as rejection. It represents a loss for them especially, if we are the only school to which they applied.

What does this loss mean to them? As with all losses, it is complex. First, there is the feeling of rejection and the loss of an opportunity. There is also a loss of time, a feeling that all the preparation hitherto was wasted, and a sense of hopelessness at not being able to determine one's future. Many feel that God has failed them and lose hope in the future. Painful! I'd say it is, because I receive many letters afterwards asking, "What's wrong with my application? Tell me so I can fix it." Many also ask, "What's wrong with *me*?"

What can I say? There just aren't enough opportunities to go around! Understand your losses so that you can do your grieving quickly!

Step Three: Separate the Concrete from Abstract Losses

A very effective scheme for helping the counselor and client develop a complete understanding of a depressed person's losses is shown in Figure 6.

All losses and all aspects of a given loss can be divided into two general categories, concrete or abstract. It helps both the counselor and the client to separate concrete from abstract losses.

Concrete losses are of those objects that can be seen, touched, measured, and clearly defined. Loss of people, cars, jobs, pets,

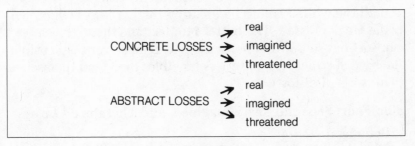

Figure 6
Concrete/Abstract Losses

money, cameras, and special privileges are in this category. They are concrete in the sense that they have a material, perceptible existence.

Abstract losses are of those ideas or concepts that do not have a material existence. They may exist only in the mind, but they nevertheless do exist. Love, self-control, self-respect, ambition, a sense of God's presence, self-mastery, and the respect of others—all are examples of abstract notions that can be lost.

Concrete losses are, surprisingly, the easiest to grieve and get over. Abstract losses can be just as powerful in causing depression but, because they are more difficult to visualize and sometimes understand, they are harder to grieve. The counselor must become skilled in helping a client explore these vague and ethereal losses. In fact, most resistant depressions (those depressions that do not heal) will be found to hover around significant abstract losses. Unfortunately, many concrete losses will *also* have significant abstract losses attached to them, and it is these abstract aspects that will be the more difficult to come to terms with.

Let me illustrate how a concrete loss can be contaminated with many abstract losses. Suppose a manuscript I have submitted to a publisher is rejected. The concrete loss (return of the document with accompanying letter of rejection) is the least significant loss. I can always try another publisher. The more significant loss will be the effect of the rejection on my feelings about myself. I will probably tell myself that I'm no good. I will question my competence and irrationally (I hope) think that I'll never ever again be able to write a book. I will conjure up in my mind's eye visions of all sorts of rejections, and all the while I would be creating further losses which will make me depressed. The better I understand them, the easier I can sort out sense from nonsense and grieve over the sensible. Because abstract losses are less tangible, they lend themselves to all sorts of distortions.

Step Four: Separate Real, Imagined, and Threatened Losses

Refer again to figure 6.

Besides each of the categories of concrete and abstract losses, there are three subcategories: real, imagined, and threatened losses. These subcategories are important to identify because one can complete the grieving process for only *real* losses. In other words, one cannot grieve imagined losses nor can you complete the grieving of threatened losses, whether they are concrete or abstract.

Step four in the counseling process, therefore, is to help the client determine what aspects of the loss are real (sensible and rational) and what are imagined (the figment of imagination). If there are imagined components, you then attempt to convert imagined losses to real losses. If you cannot, you encourage the client to discard them.

The reason you cannot grieve imagined losses is simple: Your mind knows that no real loss has taken place and that there is nothing to mourn. You only go on being depressed. This is how a great deal of depression is perpetuated. Similarly, threatened losses begin the grieving process but, since no actual loss has taken place, you cannot complete your mourning.

What are the differences between real, imagined, and threatened losses?

Both concrete and abstract losses are "real" when there is no doubt that something has been lost. Receiving a supplementary tax notice, having your car break down, or hearing that your best friend is being transferred to another city are *real* losses. Some of them are *concrete* (there may be monetary or other physical deprivations involved), and some are *abstract* (you may feel that you are losing significant emotional support or that you are being blamed for someone else's mistakes).

Real losses are the easiest to grieve when compared to other losses. Your mind understands the limits of the loss and, while there may be quite a lot of pain involved in major losses, sooner or later hope returns, sadness abates, and life resumes. This adjustment process is quite natural and built into all of us. With help this healing process can be facilitated.

Step Five: Convert Imagined Losses into Real Losses

Imagined losses are the product of exaggeration and distortion. Fed by fear and anxiety, we can "imagine" all sorts of terrible consequences. We can take a very little real loss and turn it into a huge imagined loss, all in our minds.

A client of mine recently discovered that he had developed a lump under his arm. He made an appointment to see his doctor, but in the intervening two days his imagination went to work. He couldn't sleep the first night. For hours he lay tossing and turning, suspecting the worst. His imagination told him that the lump could be cancerous. He imagined that when he got to his doctor's office, his doctor panicked, called an ambulance, rushed him straight to the hospital, and so on. The second night his fears fed even more bizarre imagined consequences. He feared he had cancer all over his body, that there was no cure for him, and that his life was quickly coming to an end. It is amazing how we can distort reality in the early hours of the morning when sleep eludes us.

Needless to say, my client became deeply depressed during those two days of waiting. He had created a host of losses in his mind, and together they had started a massive depressive reaction. As it turned out, my client's lump was benign, easily removed, and today he is hail and hearty. His losses turned out to be simple figments of his imagination.

Imagined abstract losses are more common. We imagine that people don't like us; we imagine that someone has betrayed our trust, and we become depressed. Imagination knows no boundaries so there are no limits to the losses we can create. Some people have developed this tendency as a habit and use it to develop or intensify their depressions. It is a wonderful weapon for self-punishment.

The counselor should explore the imagined components of every loss and help the depressed person "test the reality" of each imagined loss. Wherever possible, help the client to convert an imagined loss to a real one, because real losses, no matter how devastating, are the only ones we can grieve. For instance, if a client fears that he is to get fired because of certain rumors he has heard, ask him to "test reality." I did this once with a policeman. For two or three months he had imagined he might get fired. He felt he had slackened off and feared his supervisor was dissatisfied with his work. He became deeply depressed and this only made his work performance worse.

I sent him to talk with his superior. "Find out what your supervisor thinks about your work performance," I told him.

Short interviews they were, but it turned out that his job was quite secure. His fears were all in his head.

If an imagined loss cannot be converted to a real loss through reality testing, it should be discarded. Counseling should then be focused on correcting any overactive, negative, or suspicious patterns of thinking that may be present. Prayer can be directed specifically at this problem and may even be more effective. God can help us deal with our distorted thought habits and his spirit can help us transform our minds (Rom. 12:2).

Step Six: Convert Threatened Losses into Real Losses

In some cases the impending loss or the potential loss may be real, but it is too early to know when or if the loss will occur. These threatened losses are very common. Life is full of potential for these losses: changed life plans; children growing up and leaving home; sudden illness and world catastrophes—they all hold certain "threats." These threats of loss start the depression process, but since there is no finality to the loss, there can be no closure on the depression. The grieving process cannot be completed so that the depression could go on for as long as the threat lasts.

As in the case of imagined losses, the counselor should help the client convert as much threatened loss to real loss as possible, and if this cannot be done then the loss must be abandoned. For instance, suppose you discover a lump in your body. Tests prove it is cancerous and you must undergo treatment. The doctor gives the treatment a 50 percent chance of succeeding and suddenly you find yourself faced with a "threatened" loss of your life. You cannot complete an adjustment to a threatened loss. It must either become real (the treatment has failed) or be abandoned as a loss (forcing yourself to await the outcome).

Forcing threatened losses into real losses is sometimes possible by the appropriate use of confrontation. The client is confronted with certain realities and encouraged to "look at the facts." This may feel cruel at times to the counselor, but no healing can take place while reality is being ignored.

Some threatened losses must be tolerated for a while because they cannot be resolved right away. There is no way of knowing whether a seriously sick parent will "pull through" or not. One hovers on the brink of loss, one moment believing it is "all over," and the next seeing hope restored. There is nothing to do but wait. The only help we can offer as counselors in these situations is to pray for courage and endurance while the client waits for the threat to be resolved. God has promised comfort for these difficult times because he is the Author of all comfort (2 Cor. 7:6). When Jesus foretold his impending departure, he warned his disciples that they would experience a period of sorrow. He then promised them that joy would follow that sorrow. "And ye now therefore have sorrow: but I will see you again, and your heart shall rejoice, and your joy no man taketh from you" (John 16:22).

No matter how bleak a situation may be, this is the comfort we can offer as Christian counselors to those who must bear the burden of painful loss—real or threatened.

On a practical level, we need to give people experiencing prolonged threatened loss permission to "be kind to themselves." They should avoid stressful demands and heavy work schedules, although distractions such as a hobby or travel can be beneficial. We should also remind them of the larger perspective on life and encourage them to review their goals, clarify their values, and see God's larger plan in every experience of life.

Step Seven: Facilitate the Grieving Process

One of the consequences of exploring the full implications of a loss is to intensify the feeling of depression. This facilitates the grieving process. It may seem paradoxical, but, in reactive depression, the more effectively we experience our "low" the quicker we will recover. Fighting off depression or trying to minimize the pain of it only serves to prolong it.

Step seven, therefore, is to facilitate the grieving process by allowing the feelings of depression to intensify. Give your clients permission to feel the pain. Stop them from running away from it. Help them talk about it. No one else is going to give them this opportunity; others will try to cut it off. This step should be carried out in conjunction with the next, but don't move too quickly through this stage. Healing takes place when we allow grieving to run its course.

I find it helpful to explain to the client that there is an appropriate depth and period of depression that corresponds to all losses. Small losses only need small depressions, but large losses need more! I play a game in which I attribute maybe a twenty-minute depression to my coffee being spilled over my favorite suit, a one-hour depression to having a flat tire, a twenty-four-hour depression to receiving a traffic ticket, and a forty-eight-hour depression to a fallout with my boss. I then present a hypothetical loss and ask the client to "choose a depression" that is appropriate. The point here is to teach the client that every loss has its "appropriate" depression and that they should allow themselves that period of despondency. When the period is up—snap out of the depression.

In practice, what happens is quite fascinating. Since this game gives the client permission to choose to be depressed for an appropriate amount of time, they "give in" to the depression, allow a deeper experience of it, and then snap out of it *sooner*. It removes the guilt and many other feelings that feed depression and it stops the compounding of losses. Reactive depressions get shorter when you accept them as normal and don't fight them. Try it for yourself, and see how effectively this technique works.

Step Eight: Face the Reality of the Loss

The ultimate outcome of reactive depression is to "let the lost object go." The sooner we accept the reality of the loss, assuming that there is a real loss, the sooner we will recover from the depression.

Step eight, therefore, is help the client face the reality of the loss. Denial is common at the start of a depression. Wishful thinking tries to restore or delay the loss. Both need to be prevented by the counselor.

In bereavement counseling we understand this principle very well. The grief-stricken family is confronted with the reality of the loss in many ways: the open coffin, the memorial service or graveside service, and so on, all serve to drive home the reality of the death. But we tend to hide from other losses and don't have readily accessible rituals to help us confront reality. In Africa, where I grew up, funerals meant a lot of wailing and open demonstration of grief. There is great freedom to express one's pain openly. But then grieving is over! We could learn a lot from less emotionally restricted cultures on how to come to terms with reality.

Dynamically, facing the reality of the loss facilitates the process of "letting go." Cognitively there is a readjustment of thinking about the lost object, and the development of a new attitude to it.

Step Nine: Develop a Perspective on the Loss

Step nine follows naturally from the previous two steps: help the client develop a "perspective" on the loss. The loss has to be placed in the context of the larger perspective on life. It is here that knowing God through Christ *must make a difference* to the way we adjust to loss. It give us a vantage point from which to evaluate our losses and interpret our future. This essentially spiritual step should be facilitated through prayer and the power of God's Spirit.

One important process every Christian must go through is to learn how to separate the essentials of life from the nonessentials. By this I mean that our attitude toward money, possessions, careers, ambitions, dreams, loved ones, and even ourselves, should be shaped by our belief about the ultimate value of our life and how this fits into God's greater scheme.

There are some aspects to life that are eternally valuable. They are the essentials of life. Other aspects are temporal. They are convenient while we have them but nonessentials when judged by eternity. It may be a bonus to have a job with a high salary, but never think of this as being an essential part of your total life.

By developing such a perspective, and often this can only be done when one is coping with the depression accompanying a significant loss, the pain can be eased and recovery speeded up. It is also the best way to protect yourself against future depressions.

Allow me once again to point you to the apostle Paul's prescription for reactive depression:

"But what things were gain to me, those I counted loss for Christ. Yea doubtless, and I count all things but loss for the excellency of the knowledge of Christ Jesus my Lord: for whom

I have suffered the loss of all things, and do count them but dung, that I may win Christ" (Phil. 3:7–8).

Notice how Paul had dealt with his losses. He had done his grieving ahead of time. He could differentiate the essentials from the nonessentials of life; he had invested his energy in that which was eternal. There was no loss he could suffer at this stage of his life that could devastate him; he had already "counted" his gains as losses. No wonder he could say in the next chapter of his epistle: "And the peace of God, which passeth all understanding, shall keep your hearts and minds through Christ Jesus" (4:7).

Step Ten: Avoid Negative Cognitive Set

While the grieving process I have described thus far is essentially a "normal" process in the sense that we all have the capacity to mourn and adjust to our losses, there are ways in which this process can be sabotaged. When this happens, normal depression becomes clinical depression and needs help. What people "tell themselves" can often be a catalyst for deep and resistant depression. The counselor should understand how such thinking processes can cause depression (often in the creation of "imagined" losses) and prolong it unnecessarily.

Every psychologist knows that emotions affect thinking. This has never been questioned. In recent years, however, the converse has become more prominent: Thinking affects the emotions. In fact, some cognitive psychologists would insist that thinking *always* precedes emotions and our feelings are the product of our thoughts. The truth is probably that both are inextricably bound to each other. For our purpose here, we can say that negative thinking can be the cause of depression as well as one of its consequences.

Cognitive psychologists tend to see depressed persons as being depressed because of a particular *style of thinking*. There is a lot of truth to this idea. It adds a lot of power to Paul's themes for thought outlined in Philippians 4:8–9:

Finally, brethren, whatsoever things are true, whatsoever things are honest, whatsoever things are just, whatsoever things are pure, whatsoever things are lovely, whatsoever things are of good report; if there be any virtue, and if there be any praise, think on these things. Those things, which ye have both learned, and received, and heard, and seen in me, do: and the God of peace shall be with you.

Aaron Beck, one of the major proponents of this cognitive theory, contends that a "negative cognitive set" is primary and that the *depressive emotion* is secondary.[2] In other words, the fact that we feel sad is not as important as the way in which our thoughts *keep* us feeling sad. I don't believe this is true for all depression, but it may be true of some so we need to explore the idea a little further.

Errors in thinking about the self, the world, and the future can cause and maintain some depressions, Beck says. These thinking errors, called "cognitive sets," are invariably negative, causing the depressed person to interpret events in the world in a bleak manner.

This negative thinking style leads to self-depreciation and self-blame, which are taken as truth by the depressed individual. Errors of logic then follow. A person may engage in any or all of the following styles of thinking. They all have the potential to create loss, and therefore can both cause and prolong depression:

1. Arbitrary inference. The client draws conclusions without adequate evidence. "My parents don't love me" or "My work is not valued" are arbitrary inferences, unless of course, there is evidence to the contrary.

2. Selective abstraction. The client draws conclusions based on a single element among many possibilities. "I am a failure in life" is selective abstraction, when one publisher returns a manuscript with a rejection note.

3. Overgeneralization. This describes how sweeping conclusions based upon a single event can be made. "All men are unfaithful," says a rejected wife when only her husband has failed.

4. Magnification and minimizations. These are gross evaluation errors with little or no basis in reality. "What's the use of trying, no one ever succeeds by effort. Success is pure luck."

Depressed persons are victims of these distortions of thinking and treatment should be focused on teaching the client to reverse and realign his or her thinking with reality. A valuable resource for learning the techniques of this approach is Aaron Beck's book *Cognitive Therapy of Depression.* Helping depressed people to avoid perpetuating their depression often requires that their negative thinking patterns be challenged and changed.

LEARNED HELPLESSNESS

One other unique form of loss also requires mention. It is what is known as "learned helplessness," a concept developed by Martin Seligman. Through experiments, mainly with dogs but more recently with humans, he has shown that traumatic events that cannot be controlled lead to hopelessness and depression.[3] It is the emotional state that occurs when you feel that "it is the end."

When you cannot control the outcome of a life event and nothing you do seems to make any difference, this feeling of helplessness causes the body to give up and puts it into depression. One becomes passive, unresponsive, and will often repeat the same mistake over and over again in an endeavor to cope with the helplessness. Feelings of worthlessness and abandonment also occur.

For self-esteem to survive and for a sense of competence, one must feel in control of one's life. Without this control, helplessness and hopelessness set in. To some extent, this accounts for the fact that loss generally leads to depression: One does not have control over the loss. Something was taken away and one cannot bring it back.

The notion that this helplessness is "learned" is interesting in that it emphasizes the point that we did not inherit this tendency. Some people are more prone to it than others, because they have learned it more than others. For instance, learned helplessness has been used to describe the passive way some women repeatedly go back to abusive family environments. They get beaten up again and again and never escape the violence. They feel, or have learned, helplessness, and they believe their only escape is to become depressed.

The counselor should address these states of helplessness and try to establish some small element of control, no matter how helpless the situation. Once some element of control, no matter how small, is established, the depression begins to lift and control over the remaining elements of the problem can be restored.

I had a client once who felt panicked and depressed every time he had to wait anywhere. It could be in line at the supermarket, the bank, or in the waiting room of his doctor. If he had to wait, he felt totally helpless.

We devised a game he would play during these anxiety-producing waiting times. His wrist watch was a complex calculator (almost a minicomputer). I asked him to involve himself in some complex calculation on his super wrist watch, while he waited. Being an engineer, he could calculate areas and volumes of spaces, or figure out how many seconds he had lived to that point. These exercises gave him some control over his waiting time. Just having control over some small element of his life at that moment prevented him from feeling helpless and going into a panic attack.

Every client with a helplessness problem is different, so it is left to the ingenuity of the counselor to devise ways of restoring control, be it ever so small, in the client's life situation.

Believing that God is ultimately in control of everything, and that we can surrender control of all to him, can keep us from states of helplessness. The client can be taught to exercise more faith in God's control, and thus feel that he or she is a part of that larger control.

"But God is faithful, who will not suffer you to be tempted above that ye are able; but will with the temptation also make a way to escape, that ye may be able to bear it" (1 Cor. 10:13).

PART THREE

COUNSELING AGE-RELATED PROBLEMS

THE FOCUS THUS FAR has been on the counseling of depressions in general without regard to age, sex, or other specific life events. My attention will now turn to these special groups. The chapters of the next two sections will be briefer, focusing specifically and as concisely as possible on the main points to be borne in mind by the counselor.

When my daughters graduated from high school, each went through a period of depression. The resolutions of these depressions (with a little bit of help from Daddy) came when they finally realized that the loss of one stage of life gives way to a whole new set of challenges and opportunities in the next.

From the outset, life is a losing of one thing to gain another, and we must learn to adjust by letting go of the old and moving on to that which is to come. The apostle Paul understood this well. He writes, "Forgetting those things which are behind, and reaching forth unto those things which are before, I press toward the mark for the prize of the high calling of God in Christ Jesus" (Phil. 3:13–14).

Such a process goes on at every stage, and especially at important transition points between phases of life. But are there life problems that produce depressions that are specific to a particular age stage? These are the concerns of the chapters in this next section. Again, the best I can do is give you, the reader, an overview of the important issues from a counselor's point of view and then leave you to explore in greater depth any specific topic of interest.

CHAPTER TEN

DEPRESSION IN CHILDHOOD

"I THINK I AM THE stupidest kid in school," says an eleven-year-old boy between sobs. "Sometimes I feel the world would be better off if I drowned myself."

"I'm the goat in our family," says another boy, ten years of age. "They all think I'm weird because I don't like having friends."

A dejected nine-year-old girl cries, "I feel ugly and lopsided. No one likes me. The boys laugh at me and think I'm a geek."

These are statements by depressed children—those who would talk. Many others just sit in my consulting room refusing to say anything. They'll either sit staring at the wall or out of the window. They just don't want to talk. They prefer silence and being alone.

The Greek philosophers (Plato, for example) knew about and described the depression of childhood. Yet until fairly recently, this label was considered inappropriate.[1] It was believed that depression could only occur after the age of adolescence.

Research into childhood depression is only in its infancy. Earlier research reported low rates of incidence because the researchers did not realize that the symptoms of childhood depression might be less marked than for adults or different from adult symptoms.[2] The incidence of "masked" depression, where the main affective disorder is concealed behind anger or behavioral problems, is much more common in children than in adulthood. The identification of depression in children is, therefore, much more difficult. Fortunately, recent research has helped a great deal in clarifying the nature of childhood depression and in helping us recognize it.

How common is childhood depression? Much more common than previously supposed. It is very clear that depression can occur as early as the first few months after birth.

Two syndromes similar to adult depression have been identified: one in infancy, another in prepubertal children.[3] Yet it is believed that other types, different from adult depression, may constitute special kinds of childhood depression.

One study showed that at any one time as many as twenty children in one hundred, or one in five, may be suffering from symptoms of depression.[4] This seems an alarmingly high figure. Not all these children were depressed enough to require special care, but they just existed, day after day, living unhappy lives.

Other studies of prevalence have differed widely. One study of six thousand children showed that 1.8 percent suffered from severe depression, while another reported 3 percent.[5] In a psychiatric setting, as high as 25 percent of preschool children displayed some depressive signs. Differences in the definition of childhood depression are the main reasons for these wide variations in rates of incidence. One thing is clear however: children *do* get depressed.

Though depression has always been thought of as increasing in incidence as one gets older, a recent report points out that "the growing rate of depression in the young has brought about a peak period in youth that outstrips middle age and is exceeded only by the elderly."[6]

What does this say about the risk of children in our Christian homes and churches being depressed? They are probably at as much risk as any other children, and the incidence is likely to be as great. It is a problem, therefore, that Christian counselors ought to pay close attention to and that pastors ought to be aware of. I will examine the problem as it appears in each of the major stages of childhood, from infancy to prepuberty.

SYMPTOMS OF DEPRESSION IN CHILDHOOD

Despite the disparity in diagnostic criteria and differences of opinion that exist between various researchers about the nature of childhood depression, there are important symptoms that can be used to identify the disorder: The child appears sad and unhappy; social withdrawal is very common; there is withdrawal from regular activities or interests and loss of energy; the child has little capacity for pleasure; physical complaints are frequent; expressions of being unloved or rejected are frequent; the child refuses to receive comfort or love—despite protestations of not being loved; increase in aggressive behavior; sleep disturbances become obvious—mostly insomnia; change in appetite—either overeating or refusal to eat foods usually favored.

The features of adult depression that are normally *absent* from childhood depression are: There is no dread of the future; children respond quickly to external changes or distractions (unlike adults).

Since depression is often "masked" or hidden by other symptoms, the counselor should be aware of these indirect indications: Extreme forms of anxiety: nail biting, hair pulling, or muscle tics; irritability, snappishness, and temper tantrums; sulky, quiet, moody, and withdrawn; difficult to please, excessive negativity; self-mutilation; disobedience and deliberately destructive behaviors.

Hyperactivity can be a form of depression. Certainly, hyperactivity is very common in childhood depression, accompanied by school problems, delinquency, and other behavioral or psychosomatic problems. These are seen to be ways the child tries to escape from depression.

Sometimes when the depression is not obvious on the surface it is manifested in dreams and fantasies. The counselor should, therefore, explore these when depression is suspected. Themes of frustration, despair, and hopelessness may emerge.

The assessment of depression in children may involve a very different process than that used in adults. Since children are often brought to counseling by concerned parents, the counselor may make the mistake of only interviewing the parents. Care should be taken to interview the child alone and obtain as accurate a symptom picture from the child, rather than the parent. This builds more effective rapport.

DEPRESSION IN INFANCY

The most serious form of depression in the infant (up to one year of age) is called the "nonorganic failure to thrive" syndrome. Babies with this disorder are unresponsive to external movements or stimulation. There is no eye contact; they cry weakly, refuse food, sleep excessively, and are apathetic. It seems that the disorder is associated with inadequate care from the mother or mother substitute, although some forms of the disorder could have a biological cause.

Rene Spitz first published a paper on the reaction of infants to maternal separation in 1946.[7] He described how children who had developed normal attachment to their mothers and who were subsequently separated at about six months became weepy, withdrawn, and lethargic. The fact that the first six months was normal demonstrates that the separation was the cause of the problem. The infants would lie on their cots, ignoring their surroundings. When approached by strangers, they would cry and scream.

If the infant was not returned to the mother, it gradually developed a severe depression characterized by weight loss, insomnia, a frozen facial expression with a far-away gaze. If the mother was reunited within five months of the separation, the syndrome was reversed. If the delay was longer than five months, the symptoms were not reversible and these children

later showed developmental defects as well as a greater suscep-
tibility to disease.

Bowlby, a later researcher, was able to document the steps
that follow abnormal separation from the mother.[8] First, there
is a stage of *protest.* The infant is very upset and tries to reini-
tiate contact with the mother by crying, screaming, and thrash-
ing about. Second, there is a stage of *despair* where the crying is
softer and less constant. The infant becomes silent and appears
to be acutely depressed. Third, the child may overcome the loss
and may even become sociable again. At this stage it may even
ignore the mother if she returns.

What are the counseling implications for the pastor or counselor of parents caught up in such a syndrome? Obviously,
the first step is to try and restore the mother to the infant. The
separation may be due to ignorance, as is often the case with
lower socioeconomic parents or where the mother is very
young. Parenting has to be taught; it is not instinctual in the
human. The counselor may have to do this teaching or refer
the client to someone who can.

Sometimes the separation is due to illness—physical or psychological. Postpartum depressions, where young mothers become extremely depressed after the birth of a child, may lead to
rejection of the infant. This form of depression may require
antidepressant medication or intense psychotherapy. In such
instances, substitute mothers may need to be provided, to ensure that the child is cuddled and given physical comfort.
Fathers, grandmothers, aunts, and close friends can be mobi-
lized for this task. The counselor needs to be very creative in
dealing empathically with the mother and building a happy
environment for the child.

The problem of infant rejection is increasingly becoming a
problem with young, especially unmarried, mothers. If a problem is anticipated, preventative counseling, in which the young
mother-to-be is prepared for motherhood, may be called for.
Pastors are often the first to become aware of such incipient
problems and should be assertive in offering help or referring
the problem to a counselor.

Infant rejection is as old as human existence. God reminds us of this in Isaiah 49:15 and assures us that he will never forsake us: "Can a woman forget her suckling child . . . yea, they may forget, yet will I not forget thee."

DEPRESSION IN EARLY CHILDHOOD

As a rule, children from age two to around five, are less prone to depression than those who are older or younger. Children at this age have a little more control and gradually become more able to verbalize what they feel. Biologically, children are more exuberant and hyperactive at this stage, but many researchers have warned that experiences may occur that could predispose these children to depression in later life.[9] These predisposed children display excessive separation and grief reactions, temper tantrums, low tolerance for frustration, and manipulative tendencies that try to coerce parents into giving them what they want.

The counselor's attention, at this stage, should be focused on guiding the parents to construct healthy rules for behavior that will help the child cope with depression at a later stage.

Here are some guidelines:

1. Parents should build their children's self-respect with unconditional love. Too easily, parents use the withdrawal of their love as a way of punishing their child for misbehavior. This can be very damaging and depression producing. There ought to be clear guidelines for behavior and discipline for misbehavior, but they should not affect the love-bond.

2. Parents should teach children how to tolerate the frustration of delayed gratification. In life we cannot always get what we want, when we want it. We must all learn to wait for things.

When my three daughters were small, I often taught this lesson in little ways. For instance, if they wanted me to play with them "just for a little while," I would say, "Let me work for another half hour, and then I'll play with you the rest of the afternoon!" In other words, if they could tolerate the frustration of a little delay, they'd get something better. At first there were loud protests, but when I proved that I was faithful to my word (and if you are not, *don't* try this), they learned the benefits of delayed gratification.

On other occasions they would rush in and say, "The ice

cream cart is coming down the road. Can we please have a cone?" I would respond, "If you'll wait until I've finished what I'm doing, I'll take you to the ice cream store and we'll get something better." Sometimes they would choose the immediate over the delayed pleasure, but often they would choose to wait. (The store had a much better selection.) The point is: They learned that delays do not have to be frustrating and depression producing. You can sometimes (one hopes often) get a better deal if you wait.

3. Parents should be careful not to communicate, even unintentionally, standards that their children cannot meet. We live in a culture that places a high premium on success. Mistakenly, parents believe they can motivate children to do bigger and better things—if they challenge them with expectations that are beyond their present abilities. This may work for a few kids, but mostly the expectations are unrealistic and children constantly feel inadequate, even useless. Certainly, they quickly develop the belief: "Nothing I do can please my parents. I might as well not try." Later, this leads to helplessness and depression.

4. Parents should teach children how to deal with failure. Because we are so hung-up on the elusive idea of "success," most Americans have exaggerated fears of failure. Failure devastates most of us; failure demoralizes; failure brings depression. But children should be taught that failure is for growing; failure in one thing doesn't mean failure in all things; failure is always "relative." What may appear to be failure now, may turn out to be a blessing later; in God's economy, there is really no such thing as failure—only forced growth.

DEPRESSION IN MIDDLE AND LATE CHILDHOOD

Several authors have provided groupings of symptoms that categorize types of childhood depression. One such grouping suggests that there are basically three types of childhood depression:

1. The *affectual* depression group. These children are characterized by expressions of sadness, helplessness, and hopelessness. They tend to be between six and eight years of age.

2. The *negative self-esteem* group. These are characterized

by "thought-feelings" based on worthlessness, being unloved, and being used by people. They tend to be eight year olds or older.

3. The *guilt* group. These children feel "wicked," guilty, and wish that they were dead. They tend to be older than eleven.[10]

The nearer children get to puberty, the more prone they become to depression. This is partly due to hormonal changes that begin to take place, but also to the children's increased awareness of environmental problems and losses.

Causes are numerous and varied and can include loss of a parent, sibling, or friends; divorce; a move to a new neighborhood; close friends moving away; excessive teasing by peers; conflicts with authority figures, such as teachers; lack of friends or bad experiences with peers; skin problems or fears of being overweight; emotional immaturity.

Divorce is a particularly devastating experience for children. Divorce is second only to the death of a parent as a traumatic life experience. Bear in mind that divorce represents many losses for the child: loss of the presence of one parent; loss of the "ideal" home; loss of financial resources; loss of security and hope for the future.

The counselor needs to be able to help the child to separate real from imagined losses and to grieve those that are real.

The acute stress of shock, intense fears, feelings of insecurity and uncertainty will cause the child much misery. The child's experience of a divorce is particularly devastating, and since there is so much of it going on, I want to take a moment to focus on this problem. At the time of divorce, and for quite a period afterwards, parents have a diminished capacity to parent. They are preoccupied with their own emotions and survival during the critical months following.

Divorce also creates a conflict of loyalty in children. Whose side should they take? Mommy says it's Daddy's fault. Daddy says it's Mommy's. Each parent tries to win the children over to his or her side—but the children must remain loyal to both. The anger and resentment between the parents only intensifies the children's fears and brings out insecurity feelings.

The impact of a divorce on children can be very profound and long-lasting. Depression can be a problem for many years afterwards, especially if children (and their divorced parents) do not receive counseling. Remarriage and the creation of a "blended" family poses additional problems for children who now find that they have "instant" brothers and sisters and two homes between which they must shuffle and adjust.

Whether the depression is the consequence of divorcing parents, or any other form of loss, the counselor must:

1. Attempt to see the loss from the child's perspective. As an adult, it is too easy for the counselor to minimize the impact of childhood losses, and this cuts you off from the child.

2. Accept the child's depression as a normal reaction, as you would with an adult, and facilitate the grieving experience where appropriate. This means helping the child to verbalize how it feels, what he or she is thinking, and how the loss or losses are perceived.

3. Avoid perpetuating the child's depression. Angry parents can unknowingly prolong a child's depression. They may use excessive or inappropriate punishment and create further fear and insecurity.

Parents should be encouraged to allow their children to grieve, when necessary. Divorcing parents often don't like to see the sadness that their actions create in children. It intensifies their own guilt and sadness. Many divorced children are not allowed to show their unhappiness to their parents and this robs the children of the comfort and freedom they need to do their grieving and "let go."

Children also tend to perpetuate their own depressions. Their imaginations, fed by fear, can exaggerate losses and cause deeper depressions. The counselor can provide reassurance and accurate information to restore reality to the child's thinking.

4. Help the child accept the reality of the loss or losses. The same principle applies to children as to adults: You can only grieve those losses that you know to be real. Vagueness feeds imagined fears, so be open and honest. This is especially true of divorce. Without being cruel, and at a pace that the child can tolerate, lead him or her to face the reality of the loss. The depression may temporarily intensify, but the child will adjust more quickly.

My own parents divorced (I was twelve at the time), and my greatest pain came from not knowing enough about what was going on. We fear the unknown more than the known, but my parents didn't realize this truth. When finally I got up the guts to ask very specific questions, such as "When are we moving?" "Where are we moving to?" "When will I see Daddy again?" my fears subsided, despite the unsatisfactory nature of the answers. I didn't like all I heard, but at least I knew what was happening.

5. Build hope. Build a new perspective on the loss. Pray with the child for God to be the Comforter and Restorer of joy. Encouraging a child to talk about his or her emotions can help to build this perspective. This is not always easy as children will not express their thoughts or emotions unless encouraged. Often one has to suggest words to describe the feelings, and have the child merely say yes or no to the suggestions. At other times it is helpful to have them write a story or engage in play therapy (especially for younger children). This provides them a way to express their feelings.

THE TREATMENT OF SERIOUS CHILDHOOD DEPRESSION

Serious forms of childhood depression are evidenced by extreme sadness, lethargy, or destructive behaviors. Such a depression should be referred to a competent specialist without delay. In fact, as a general rule, a counselor should make a referral to a specialist child-psychologist or child-psychiatrist whenever he or she feels that no progress is being made through conventional counseling. Specific treatments, such as psychotherapy, antidepressants, or other medication, have been shown to be effective in severe cases of childhood depression. Psychotherapy is focused on changing the child's environment, increasing self-esteem, promoting friendships, and resolving school difficulties. Medicating with antidepressants is quite common, but usually only follows a more thorough physical evaluation of the child for hormonal or other health problems that could be causing depression. Since more girls are diagnosed as depressed than boys, the hormonal changes of puberty must be carefully evaluated and monitored by a physician when depression occurs at this stage of life. Correct treatment can save a child from a lot of unnecessary emotional strain.

Since adult patterns of depression proneness are laid early in life, attention should be given to every child who is depressed. A lifetime of melancholic misery can be prevented if parents, pastors and counselors cooperate to provide effective help for children who are beginning to discover that "life is not a bed of roses."

CHAPTER ELEVEN

DEPRESSION IN ADOLESCENCE

MOOD DISORDERS OFTEN OCCUR during normal adolescence. This age is a complex one from a developmental point of view and fraught with difficult adjustments that must be made. Adolescence is probably the most difficult stage of life to negotiate. Most adults remember it with lots of pain and regret!

Adolescents quite often fear they might be going crazy. Parents of adolescents probably fear it of themselves. Considerable emotional distress, including depression, is, more often than not, the norm and not the exception. A lot of this distress is due to the psychological demands of this stage of transition, but sexual maturation, regulated by massive hormonal changes, also plays a significant part.

Adolescence is also a period in which one is particularly vulnerable to stress. You have an adult body, but only a child's mind. Because of improved health and living conditions we grow up faster these days in our physique than we do in our psyches, and this gap causes many problems. Also, our culture has never quite come to terms with this stage of life. Adolescents are not helped greatly in their transition to adulthood; they constantly receive double messages. More primitive cultures generally do a better job than we do of transitioning children to adulthood. They provide a "rite of passage" that gives clear guidelines on how to grow up and a definite transition point between childhood and adulthood. We prolong the transition period and pay the price for this in adolescent turmoil.

How common is adolescent depression? In contrast to a history of debate about whether or not depression exists in childhood, there has been little doubt about its presence in adolescence. The difficulty with this stage of development is that depression may be too omnipresent. More than in any other stage of life, a clearer distinction needs to be made here between what is a "normal" mood swing and true clinical depression. Unfortunately, these normal mood swings can often prepare the way for adult depression. This means that even normal mood depressions ought to be given some help at this stage, if only to avoid their entrenchment as later lifestyles.

Let me illustrate. I worked recently with a boy whose father had walked out on the family when Billy was 14. The father had fallen in love with a younger woman, and one day when Billy came home from school, he found his father packing a suitcase and moving out. Briefly, the father told Billy he was "going to live with another woman." Billy was devastated. In the days following, he went into a deep depression, which is quite normal in such cases. These depressions usually resolve themselves in a short while as soon as the adolescent gets over his grieving. In Billy's case, however, things were not quite normal and the mother was astute enough to notice this and seek help.

Billy had begun to be cruel to the family cat. He kicked it once and discovered that it felt good to take out his rage on another living object. Then he kicked it again—and again. A normal depression was opening the door on a destructive habit, and this needed to be stopped. Fortunately we were able to intervene. Sadly, I know of some situations in which there was no intervention and those adolescents are now adults and do a lot more than just kick the cat!

DEPRESSION IN EARLY ADOLESCENCE

Since adolescence is such a protracted period in our culture, stretching from puberty to almost twenty, consideration of depression at this stage of life needs to be divided into two stages: early and late adolescence.

Early adolescence is characterized by major hormonal changes and the need to gain an ego identity. There is also a withdrawal from parents. Later adolescence is dominated by concerns about entry into adulthood, the role one is expected to play in society, love, and courtship.

Sex hormones, acting in concert with growth hormones, are responsible for the adolescent growth spurt. Puberty ushers in adolescence with a complex series of glandular changes that profoundly impacts the emotions. Since the age of puberty has consistently been getting lower over the past one hundred years (it was about sixteen or seventeen at the turn of the century and now tends to be around eleven or twelve and is still dropping) and the age of marriage is going up, the adolescent faces a long period of "waiting" before sexual and other fulfillments can be achieved. Much depression is associated with this prolonged "in between" stage of life.

A major psychological task for the early adolescent is to withdraw from parents and develop a separate identity. One of the factors that makes adolescence a painful period is that only by rejecting customary family patterns does the adolescent become a "separate" person.[1] This often means that the adolescent must learn to venture out from the family matrix but without severing family ties and support. For the parents, it means a gradual relinquishing of control.

With increased activity outside the home and increased need for independence comes decreased dependence upon the adult world. This withdrawal can cause a kind of "mourning" reaction, similar to the actual loss of a loved person. Since no real loss has taken place, the depression is obscure to both the adolescent and the parents, so the child is likely to be labeled as *moody.*

Accompanying this withdrawal are also feelings of loneliness and isolation, brought on by the embarrassment that accompanies sexual development. This may stir up an intense desire for self-gratification. It can take the form of increased eating or excessive masturbation. These activities, in turn, generate feelings of guilt and self-condemnation and can produce depression.

The making and breaking of relationships is also quite common during this period. In reality or in fantasy, the adolescent may form transient but intense attachments (often they are infatuations) with a variety of adults. These include teachers, coaches, ministers, and camp counselors. With some, the adolescent may have genuine relationships; with others, it's at a distance and only in fantasy.

All this is part of the "letting go" of childhood dependence on the parent and launching out into adulthood. Initially attachments are made to other older persons; later to those of closer age. All relationships with adults are perceived as potentially harmful, however, in that there is a fear of once again losing individuality. Adults are still love objects, but they can be dropped from the adolescent's favor as easily and suddenly as they were "idolized." Ambivalence is the name of the game.

The adolescent's withdrawal from his or her parents is initially facilitated by criticizing them and showing disrespect. Love turns to hate and admiration into contempt, as many parents discover! The children find fault, criticize, and complain about everything a parent does. They may even, temporarily, become ashamed of them. All this is depression producing for all the parties concerned.

Parents should be taught to accept this, but without condoning the criticism or rejection. Adolescents must break the idols they have made out of their parents. This is normal.[2]

Disobedience is also a common way of achieving independence, and this is likely to set up conditions for depression. Childlike obedience to every parental wish is at odds with the establishment of adolescent individuality. Parents who don't allow a measure of freedom (while setting appropriate limits) will create rebellious reactions. But the adolescent also needs love and wants to be cared for. This makes for turbulent behavior, with recurring periods of negativism and rebellion, followed by pleasantness and cooperation. A daughter who is not being allowed to go out on a date may provoke a violent family argument in the afternoon and that same evening want her father to tuck her in bed and be loving. All very confusing! But these are the joys and pains of growing up!

DEPRESSION IN LATER ADOLESCENCE

After the age of about sixteen, the adolescent moves into a distinctly different stage.[3]

Adults begin to expect increasing maturity and assume that the adolescent will move into a definite role in society. Without any rite of passage in our society, this leads to problems, especially losses, that can be depression producing.

There are many limitations imposed on adolescents as they emerge into adulthood. They have to "grow up," yet not too fast. There is a minimum driving age and restrictions in some activities, yet in others they are considered to be adult. Adolescents are enormously aware of and sensitive to these realities. At the college stage they may use extreme behaviors to claim their adulthood: Boys grow beards and girls may display their sexual appeal. For some, the exploration of sex and drugs and other antisocial and nonconforming activities is an attempt to hasten their growing up.

Whether the adolescent is of the conforming or nonconforming type, he or she is responding to the same social pressures as all the others: He or she wants to beat the establishment at its own game.

Sources for depression are many at this stage. Losses abound—real, imagined, and threatened. The adolescent has appetites, but not all the skills needed to satisfy these appetites.

Appearance is a major factor in the adolescent's search for identity. It affects success at courting and acceptance by others; it can determine whether or not you get employment; any physical blemish (and skin problems are common at this stage) can impact the development of self-esteem in a negative and long-lasting way.

One of the hazards that can produce depression is a feeling of alienation. Here adolescents feel that they are "on the outside looking in." Nobody, it seems, wants or needs them. There is no niche to fill and no world waiting to welcome them. The church meets this great and fundamental need in a very effective way. Youth programs and groups, centered in Christ, can provide meaning just at a time when the feeling of alienation is greatest. Many adults, myself included, came to know Christ through a youth group just at this time of alienation.

I recall, with much appreciation, what our small youth group meant to me in my late adolescence. They showed that they cared for me. They went out of their way to love me and make me feel that I was part of a group to which I could unconditionally belong. I made a commitment to Christ as a direct result of their caring. Without that group being there right at the time I needed them most, I may not have become a Christian.

In late adolescence, seeking and finding one's sexual identity becomes the major developmental task. Falling in love, feeling love, and reading about love become preoccupations. There is a strong desire to share sexual feelings with those around. For Christian groups, this is a difficult time to deal with. The pressure towards sexual fulfillment, driven by the biological urge for sex, is very strong. Many tensions are created, rejections experienced, and morals tested at this time—resulting in much depression. Problems with masturbation and with premarital sex dominate the mind of the late adolescent, especially the male. Helping Christian adolescents to successfully negotiate this stage is a great challenge for the church. Clear guidelines need to be established and communicated if teenagers are to have a sense of direction yet not feel rejected.

The adolescent, particularly from a Christian home environment, faces many struggles in trying to restrain sexual impulses. Often this is a great test of commitment and gives rise to many feelings of failure, even when the extent of a sexual indulgence is confined to fantasy. Our society sends double messages. Sexually explicit magazines, movies, and novels promote the idea that sex is for everyone, yet we also expect a certain degree of constraint and faithfulness. Adolescents become confused when there are no clear guidelines. As Christian counselors and pastors, you need to understand the struggle of this stage of life from the adolescent's point of view—if you are going to be effective in guiding him or her through this stage of life.

In counseling adolescents, therapists should be very aware of how psychological adjustment at each stage of life is built upon successful adjustment at preceding stages. Hope for the future well-being of all of us is built upon making the necessary changes now. At each stage of life we have the opportunity to correct the faults of a previous stage and thus prepare us for the future. There is always room for change. It is never too late to modify what has been built into one's personality.

This is particularly important for adolescents to grasp, because they are at that stage of life when they have the resources to change but have not yet created a habit out of that which needs changing. The best time to change is always now.

FORMS OF ADOLESCENT DEPRESSION

Clearly, more adolescent girls than boys experience depression—or at least are so diagnosed.[4] More girls attempt suicide but a greater number of boys actually commit suicide. Research on understanding these sex differences is still in its infancy, so there are no clear guidelines for counseling. Even at the adult level, women are more prone than men to attempt suicide.

Anorexia nervosa (self-starvation and extreme weight loss) is a condition found almost exclusively among females. It is often first seen in the teenage years and has been associated with depression by some researchers.[5]

The depression of adolescence can take three forms: acute, chronic, and masked.

Acute Depression

Here there seems to be clear cause, usually a loss of some significance to the adolescent. The loss could be rejection by peers, a close friend moving away or failure to achieve some goal. Many losses at this stage are related to school and peers, but the family can also contribute its share of these experiences. Often adolescent depression is a reaction to a particular developmental stress: either they cannot master a stage of transition

166

or they feel that they have failed. Fortunately, many of these acute depressions are very brief in duration although they may be very intense. They are deep, but resolve themselves quickly.

Symptoms include: change in mood; usually the adolescent is withdrawn, dejected, and quiet; loss of interest in normal activities; increased irritability and intolerance for frustration or delays; increased sleeping, lethargy, and low energy; weepiness and self-debasing talk; rejection of friends; loss of capacity to love; psychosomatic complaints: stomachaches, physical discomfort, or generalized pain.

Chronic Depression

Depressions that don't abate after a few weeks tend to be more chronic. Adolescents here present adultlike symptoms.

The counselor must be particularly alert to signs of endogenous depression. Whereas even prolonged depressions at this stage can have psychological causes (rejection, insecurity, fear of failing, divorce, etc.), hormonal and other biological factors, including prolonged stress, can cause a variety of chronic depressions.

Symptoms include: lack of response to "distractions" that previously could lift the depression; a significantly worse depression in the morning, as compared to the evening; sneaking off and sleeping a large part of the day, even after a night of good sleep; no ambition or drive to accomplish any task; extreme forms of sadness: unprovoked or continuous crying; significant changes in eating habits: either self-starvation or overeating; inability to enjoy anything pleasurable (anhedonia); significant increase in irritability and hostility.

Masked Depression

As with adults, adolescents may try to defend against depression by using age-specific defenses. For the adolescent, these defenses include: extreme restlessness; use of drugs and alcohol to escape the pain of depression; affiliation with undesirable groups, often getting into delinquent behavior for "kicks"—to relieve the pain; sexual promiscuity and the pursuit of other pleasures—to relieve sadness; aggressive and destructive acts as a way of venting the anger associated with the depression.

COUNSELING THE DEPRESSED ADOLESCENT

Since adolescence is characterized by wide swings of mood, from elation to dejection and back to elation often in just a few hours, the counselor must decide whether or not a particular low mood is a clinical depression and whether or not it needs counseling.

Before You Begin

There is great danger at this stage in "overdiagnosing" and forcing a teenager to undergo counseling when it is not needed. This can send a message to the adolescent that he or she is "no good" or "sick" and serve as a form of rejection that may scar the teenager or make effective therapy impossible. For instance, a loss of interest in the outside world may not be a symptom of depression but rather a sign of apathy or boredom. A loss of capacity for love, an adult symptom of depression, may, in the adolescent, merely be an expression of fear of intimacy, cynicism, or ambivalence. Changes in appetite or sleep may be quite normal for the growing adolescent. A great many adolescents overeat and sleep for long periods of time, without it being a symptom of depression. Great care, therefore, should be exercised in evaluating an adolescent for depression. Often this should be done in conversations with only the parents so as to avoid the teenager prematurely labeling him- or herself as "a problem." Only after you are satisfied that a clear-cut case of depression is present should you ask to see the teenager.

For *mild* adolescent depressions, the treatment should be to counsel with the parents only. Often all that is needed is a change in any parental attitudes or practices that could be causing the depression. Many parents use unsatisfactory methods of discipline or are overly restrictive. They can be shown how their actions produce losses that cause depressive reactions.

Many adolescent depressions are of brief duration (lasting just a few weeks) and often the best advice you can give the parents is "Ignore it." This helps to deescalate their feelings and avoids the creation of further losses. Brief depressive episodes arise as a result of social polarizations, developmental stresses (such as those arising from sexual role definitions), separation from friends, intolerance of temporary frustration, and an inability to maintain their self-esteem. These are common pressures for adolescents, and the emotional conflicts and pain that accompany these growth stressors should be viewed as normal. What the adolescent needs more than anything else is affirmation, encouragement, and the message "It's okay to be feeling this way." They certainly do not need to hear, "I think you've got a problem. Let's go see a counselor!" When you pathologize normal behavior, you can lead to a situation in which you begin to create the very pathology you think you see. Adolescents are at a very sensitive stage of life and can be easily imprinted with fears of being crazy, odd, or different. Teach parents, therefore, that what their teenagers need is an unambiguous environment with lots of unconditional love, so that their transition from childhood to adulthood can be honorably realized.

When an adolescent's depression reaches clinical proportions, especially if it is severe and prolonged (say for more than three or four weeks) or if it is interfering with school or development, the adolescent clearly needs professional help. This help should be provided firmly and quickly. Delays, especially in the severe depressions, may be life threatening.

Some Guidelines for Adolescent Counseling

The scope of adolescent counseling is vast. It is a highly developed specialty all of its own. For my purposes here, I must focus on only a few specific areas of counseling, especially those that impact depression problems.

1. Self-esteem. Many adolescent depressions (both normal and clinical) are tied to self-esteem problems. The self-image, built on childhood needs for praise, approval, and acceptance from the outside world, now becomes tested and threatened. Because feedback is unpredictable and not always positive, much self-rejection emerges. The "body image" is also changing and may deplete self-esteem.

The counselor should, therefore, explore distortions that may exist in the self-image and help the adolescent be more realistic in his or her self-evaluation. Self-acceptance is very important in developing self-esteem, and this should be encouraged by showing your acceptance of and value for the adolescent—just as he or she is. Rather than calling for changes, it may be preferable to push for self-acceptance, especially in less critical areas of life. So much of what our society holds out to be important for self-esteem (appearance, performance, or status) is *not essential* to a happy life. Teach the adolescent that if we overvalue particular physiques or become obsessed about being great athletes, we may only be creating "loss complexes" that can leave us feeling inadequate (and depressed) much of our lives.

2. Coming down to their level. Again and again I have heard an adolescent report on a previous counseling experience by saying, "He didn't understand what I was trying to say," or "She talked just like all adults."

I suppose young counselors have an advantage, as age gap between them and their clients then doesn't appear to be too great. However, the generation gap that can so often be a barrier to counseling an adolescent is more a "gap of attitude" than of age. When I was twenty-two, I knew a couple who were in their seventies. I felt they understood me better than my own peers. Attitudinally, they could think like me and anticipate my feelings. This built tremendous rapport between us. I also know counselors in their late twenties who think like the stereotype of a very "old" person. (By *old* I really mean "adult" in the perjorative sense.) They are rigid, inflexible, judgmental, and unforgiving. Counselors with this attitude will set up so much resistance that counseling will be impossible.

Counselors of adolescents should, rather, come down to their level and try to show understanding—but without condoning their behavior. For instance, a young man may let out a stream of swear words while telling you about a recent conflict with a parent. It doesn't help to respond with "I'd appreciate it if you didn't use such foul language here." Rather, the response should be to the feeling behind the words and an approach that says, "You are using strong language but I can see it is because you are hurting very deeply." This communicates real understanding but doesn't condone the behavior. The counselor should develop a repertoire of such responses so as not to be "on the spot" when your adult sensitivities are pushed to the limit.

3. Resolving conflicts by contracting. A useful therapeutic tool often used with adolescents is called *contracting*. Here the

counselor helps the teenager to negotiate a contract with his or her parents. Contracting is a way of helping a child gain control over his or her environment but it is also a way to facilitate communication. This helps to avoid states of helplessness that can lead to depression.

The counselor begins by helping the teenager write out a list of those freedoms, things, or social changes that are highly desired. These can be written in list form and then ranked in order of importance. Similarly, the parents are asked to prepare such a list. Given these two lists, the counselor facilitates a "dialogue of negotiation," the goal of which is to find ways to trade what is desired by the teenager for something one or the other parent wants. For instance, being allowed to stay out with friends until midnight on a Friday night may be "traded" for additional time spent on studies on some other night. Chores can be traded for chores, privileges for privileges, and kind words for respect.

A formal contract can be drawn up. This helps to entrench the seriousness of any agreement entered into and avoids either the parents or the teenager claiming some unofficial change to the contract. Penalties can be devised (for both sides) as well as ways of redeeming lost privileges. Considerable improvement in communication can be effected through this technique of negotiation. The final benefit is that it teaches the adolescent how to negotiate in other life situations also.

4. Facilitate "creative" rebelliousness. Every adolescent *has* to go through a period of rebellion. But the rebellion does not have to be painful nor does it have to be a negative experience.

Rebellion can be "creative" when *all* the parties involved are fully aware of *what* is going on, understand *why* it is a necessary stage of growing up, and then cooperate in such a way as to facilitate the process. If the parent really understands that a developing teenager *must* begin to break with family ties and develop a separate identity, that parent should be able to help rather than hinder the process. If an adolescent really understands why he or she has a need to rebel, criticize, reject, and push family away, the teen can cooperate in such a way that the process is constructive, not destructive. This mutual understanding and cooperation can be creatively facilitated by the astute counselor.

It is much like inventing a game and then getting the players to make up their own rules. In most families, the adolescent-break-away game is played with no understanding of the rules and even as if there were no game. The counselor has great freedom in devising a set of rules to guide the creative rebellion process. Spend time alone with both the parents and the teenager, and find out what they understand about individuation and separation.[6] Teach all the parties concerned about the teenager's need to "equalize" him- or herself in the company of adults. Devise ways and situations in which the teenager can be treated as an adult, with all the privileges attached thereto. Perhaps some family decisions can be given over to the adolescent to make or responsibilities of a true adult nature assigned to him or her.

One family who was having trouble with a teenage daughter's rebellion told her that for one week she was going to make all the family decisions. They would abide by whatever decision she made on any family matter. What a revelation for the teenager. Instead of being reckless, she was cautious. Instead of being carefree, she was conservative. She came to realize just how much she was fighting against the family system just so she could feel independent. Acting as the decision maker for a week helped her to appreciate the value of a family pulling together.

The generation gap is not the problem. The problem is parents who don't trust the process of growing up. Growing pains can be considerably reduced if parents would get in touch with their own inner turmoil and resolve their own unfinished business from their own adolescence.

THERE'S HOPE

In spite of the many stresses of adolescence, the vast majority of young people ultimately make an adequate adjustment. They become responsible citizens, get married, have children, and then totally forget (it seems) what it was like to be an adolescent. As parents, they, in turn, become the source of conflicts for their adolescent children as they project their own unresolved sexual impulses, fears, and guilt upon them. Parent–youth conflicts have always and probably always will exist. Note what one parent wrote, "I see no hope for the future of our people if they are dependent on the frivolous youth of today, for certainly all youth are reckless beyond words."[7]

The parent? His name was Herod, he lived in the eighth century *before* Christ! There's hope for us all yet!

CHAPTER TWELVE

DEPRESSION IN THE ELDERLY

AMERICANS ARE GROWING OLDER faster than at any other time in history. I don't mean we're aging faster, but that more and more Americans are in the older age groups. This burgeoning aging population poses enormous challenges to the church and our political and social structures.

As much as any other factor, the "graying of America," as it has been called, has and is forcing dramatic changes in our society.

Improved health care is the reason for the increased longevity, and, coupled with a declining birthrate, the ratio of people sixty years old and older to the total population is increasing beyond that of any other age group. By the year 2020, one out of every four Californians will be over sixty years of age. In some other states the proportion will be even higher.

Minority groups show an even greater increase in the percentage of the elderly. In the next twenty-five years, the number of blacks over eighty-five years of age will increase by more than 117 percent. If this surprises you, look at what is happening in other minority groups: Hispanics over eighty-five years of age will increase by more than 1,300 percent, and Asians by 1,500 percent.[1] While these figures relate primarily to California, they give an indication of the dramatic shift that is taking place in society.

Growth of this magnitude in the elderly population requires a new vision of helping and counseling. As our society becomes dominated by older individuals, so does the need for increased physical, psychological, and spiritual care for these people. At the beginning of this century, adults generally died from acute diseases. Influenza and pneumonia were the primary killers. Few adults survived episodes of these diseases. Today, death from either of these diseases is rare. What is more common now is the suffering of depression. In the elderly, this is the most painful of all the emotional disturbances.

Seniors want to remain independent, to live in their own homes rather than be placed in institutions, to continue to feel as if they are accomplishing goals, and to be associated with a community of like-minded older people. But meeting these needs is a struggle for many. Growing old isn't easy. I don't know anyone who relishes the idea of aging! Fortunately the frontiers of knowledge about aging are continually expanding and there are promising signs that our society's attitude to the elderly is improving. There's hope for some of us yet—if only we could keep away from becoming depressed!

It has been almost two thousand years since the great Roman poet, Ovid, described the sadness, frustrations, and losses that typify old age. In *Metamorphosis*, he told of Milo, the great and powerful athlete who in his youth could kill a bull with the blow of his fist. He described Helen of Troy, whose beauty is legendary. Then Ovid wrote:

Milo, now grown old, weeps when he sees his arms hang weak and exhausted, and Helen weeps too when she beholds in her mirror the wrinkles of old age. *Tempus Edox Rerum* —Time, you who devour all things, and you, hateful of old age, together you destroy everything.

In two thousand years, things haven't much changed. This well describes how we feel about growing old! The experience can easily become an unending series of losses that can produce chronic depression. For the pastor, counselor, in fact all of us, this age group is a special challenge. There is much we can do, in Christ's name, to make life better for our aged.

CAUSES OF DEPRESSION IN THE ELDERLY

The elderly have an increased incidence of both physical and mental disorders, with depression being particularly prevalent.[2] There are many reasons for this increase: decline of physical abilities (over 80 percent have chronic, recurring health problems); financial problems and loss in earning ability; societal discrimination against older persons; loss of intellectual and physical adeptness; loss of friends and family through death; fear of one's own impending demise; role changes, such as retirement; isolation (one in three women over sixty-five lives alone); biological factors and chemical changes accompanying aging.

Depressive symptoms are reported by almost 20 percent of elderly Americans.[3] But the true incidence and prevalence of clinical depression is not known with any degree of certainty.

While physical health and illness are significant factors in the elderly, multiple losses and role changes are major causes of depression. In other cultures (for example in China and Africa) the aged are highly valued. They serve as counselors and their wisdom guides their people. What they lose in vigor they gain in respect and old age is often welcomed as the culmination of existence. Western cultures, by contrast, regard aging as a "disease" in itself and reject older people at many levels. To some extent this is changing, but old habits die hard so that it will probably take many generations to raise the level of appreciation for aging to that which it deserves. The prayer of Psalm 71:9 will continue to be on the lips of many: "Cast me not off in the time of old age; forsake me not when my strength faileth."

Interpersonal losses increase significantly with aging as loved ones and friends die and children move away. It is easy at this stage of life to compound losses by allowing each new one to rekindle old ones and form a larger loss package. Incremental losses, that is losses that follow in quick succession one after the other, are common. Social supports fall away very rapidly at this stage. If an elderly person has not made healthy adjustments at earlier stages of life or has experienced much previous depression, the final stage will only be more painful. Old age is likely to bring out the worst of the "left-overs" from earlier life stages.

Close to one-third of the suicides in the United States are committed by people over age fifty-five.[4] This is an alarming statistic and reflects the depth of feelings of hopelessness of the elderly depressed. The typical "high-risk" profile of an elderly successful suicide is a white male, aged fifty-five to seventy, who is retired, widowed or single, and who lives alone and has a history of physical illness and alcohol abuse. A sorry picture, but there are scores of people like this in every city.

DIAGNOSING DEPRESSION IN THE ELDERLY

The signs of depression in the elderly are very similar to those in the larger adult population. But depressives often first present to a physician many physical complaints. They usually don't speak of guilt or sadness but appear to be pessimistic, apathetic, and complain of memory loss and sleep difficulties.

Among the important symptoms of depression in the elderly are the following:

Depressed mood and sadness. This can be seen as changes in posture, speech, facial expressions, and neglect of grooming. The elderly quite readily show their depression on their "outsides."

Loss of appetite with weight loss; neglecting to prepare food or eating one type of food only.

Insomnia of either the onset (difficulty falling asleep) or terminal (early morning awakening) type.

Increased agitation and restlessness at times; at other times increased lethargy.

Many elderly depressed report anxiety, dread, fear, or anticipation of harm.

Depression in the elderly is often confused with senile dementia, which is the loss of mental powers due to advanced age, vascular degeneration (diminished blood flow to the brain), or a disease such as Alzheimer's (a presenile disorder in which there is progressive deterioration of brain functioning). These organic disorders all give evidence of confusion, uncooperativeness, and unsociability with memory loss and confusion. Disorientation, suspiciousness, frightened behavior, and even hallucinations can also occur.

Not only can depression coexist with senile dementia, but it can cause many of these symptoms. The counselor needs to consult the elderly person's physician so as to have a clear understanding of what symptoms are psychological, what are organic, and what are perhaps an interaction of the two. For instance, fears can be produced by the despair of depression or by the disorganization of a diseased brain. Counseling may need to be tailored to the specific cause of the fears if it is going to be maximally effective. Reassurance may be helpful in fears caused by depression, but not in those caused by organic conditions, where a more structured environment may need to be created. For example, an elderly person's kitchen might be rearranged so that foods and utensils can easily be found without relying too much on memory. The same can be done for many aspects of the confused elderly person's environment.

The following pointers can help to differentiate true depression from senile-produced problems:

1. True depression is characterized more by sadness, while dementia is characterized by confusion and disorientation.

2. In depression the elderly person complains more about memory loss but simple tests show that the memory is normal. In dementia there is poorer performance on memory tests and clearer evidence from the recent history that there are memory problems.

3. The depressed elderly are cooperative and desire help.

Demented elderly are uncooperative, unsociable, and tend to reject help.

4. With depression, deterioration is fairly static but it is progressive with dementia.

Some depressed elderly persons develop a pseudodementia and deteriorate rapidly. One of these pseudodementias, the tea-and-toast syndrome, occurs when an elderly person becomes depressed, withdraws, neglects him- or herself, and lives on very little nourishment (literally tea and toast). Malnutrition follows and the nutritionally deprived brain can mimic dementia. This is why supplementary food services are so vitally important to lonely elderly persons. Every church ought to have such a service for the elderly in their community.

There are other biological factors that can cause depression in the elderly. Treatment is primarily medical or psychiatric but counseling can provide support and help to maintain the patient on appropriate treatment. Here are some examples of biological factors that can cause depression: High levels of MAO (monoamine oxidase) are often present in the aged. (The MAO destroys the neurotransmitter norepinephrine. Treatment is with an MAO inhibitor.) Changes in thyroid and pituitary function, often aggravated by increased levels of stress, are common. Diabetes and other disorders of metabolism also become more common as one ages.

In addition to psychotherapy, antidepressant drugs and ECT provide effective techniques for treating depression in the elderly. Often the most effective form of treatment is that which combines drug therapy with counseling. Counseling provides for stress reduction and life management and this facilitates the treatment of the underlying organic causes.

COUNSELING THE DEPRESSED ELDERLY PERSON

More than in any other age group, the depressed elderly client must receive care that is comprehensive. Attention must be given to meeting physical needs, changing environmental structures, improving family systems and communication, and providing proper health care. I cannot address all these needs here, except to remind counselors to look at the total life situation of the elderly and mobilize help at all levels.

Important Issues

Here are some suggestions for issues to be addressed during the early sessions:

1. If the depressed client hasn't had a physical check-up in recent years, insist on one. There is an interaction between early psychological changes, especially the onset of depression, and acute or chronic medical illness.[5] Toxic states secondary to infection, malnutrition, or the misuse of drugs or alcohol can produce depressive symptoms.

2. Prepare an inventory of "losses" experienced over the past twelve months. This will help to differentiate reactive elements from endogenous in the depression. Have any children left the area? Has a spouse died? Has there been a financial setback? These losses can easily accumulate and be compounded in the elderly person's mind.

3. Involve family members whenever possible. It is such a pity that we see illness as an individual problem in our culture. Africans (and I suppose other cultures also) can teach us a lesson here. They see illness as a family, or even a community, responsibility. If a son is sick, the whole family will go to the doctor. It is as if everyone acknowledges their contribution to the genesis of sickness. In the case of the depressed elderly person it *is* a family problem, and everyone ought to become involved. Family members can provide encouragement, support, and the resources needed to relieve the depression and make life more tolerable for the aged.

Family members can also provide important information on losses, past functioning, changes, and solutions to problems. Their importance in facilitating the grieving process accompanying changing relationships is well documented.[6]

4. Because of suspicion, cognitive changes, and diminished learning capacity, the elderly client may be confused, frustrated, and even paranoid about being counseled. The counselor should provide adequate one-on-one counseling time to build trust and overcome suspicion. Good listening skills are essential here. Hold off on advice giving for a while and show that you are interested in his or her past, pets, and preferences. As we get older, we like to reminisce. Take advantage of this in building rapport.

5. Counseling with depressed elderly persons may demand a more active role than with other adults. Because the client may have gaps in memory and reduced ability to reflect on what is happening, you may need to take greater initiative in delineating and clarifying problems. Some dependency should be accepted but create a balance by pushing as much responsibility back on the aged client as you can.

6. "Threatening" losses and events are more damaging to the elderly than to younger adults. Fears of desertion, suffering, and death dominate their thinking. Try to communicate hope. In this regard, point them back to spiritual resources. Many will have become disillusioned and full of doubts about their spiritual walk. They may even feel that God has abandoned them. Many great saints of God have weakened in faith as they have become old. It's not a sign of weakness—but the reality of declining mental abilities taking their toll. God knows this!

I pray with them often in therapy, helping them rekindle their earlier trust and faith in God. I try to show them that even at this stage in their life, God has a plan and a purpose for every moment of their day. I reassure them that I will be with them until they find a new sense of God's presence.

7. In the depression of old age, guilt over real or imagined past sins can intensify. This can be a difficult problem to deal with because, for many of them, the need to feel guilty serves as a form of self-punishment that relieves their pain. Dynamically, I suppose we ought to leave them feeling guilty since this does serve some useful psychological function. Unfortunately, however, the guilt often becomes neurotic, intensifies, and can feed back into and perpetuate the depression. Concerted efforts should be made to convince the client that God *has* provided forgiveness; despite the feelings of guilt "You are forgiven." Teach clients *not to trust their feelings*—to ignore them. After a while they will go away. Faith is a matter of belief, not of feeling!

Cognitive Counseling in Depression

In my counseling experience, excessive focusing on the feelings of depression has not been productive in effecting therapeutic change. This is especially true in the elderly. Awareness of feelings is helpful, of course, in many other areas of psychological health, but in depression it often only exacerbates the pain. You don't give water to a drowning man!

Cognitive therapy, as I have previously mentioned, has emerged in recent years as a time-limited, structured, psychosocial approach for the treatment of depression. It has special value in counseling the elderly so I will take a moment to explain a few of its concepts.[7] It is left to the reader to pursue further understanding of this approach. The techniques of cognitive therapy can be applied to any age group.

Cognitive therapy postulates three specific concepts to explain depression: the negative triad; underlying beliefs or schemas; cognitive errors, such as errors of logic and information processing.

1. The negative triad. This is an interactive set of negative views the depressed person has about him- or herself, present experiences, and the future. No matter how unpleasant life has been, depression only results when our perceptions are distorted and we see ourselves as deficient, inadequate, and unworthy.

2. Schemas. The negative triad ("I am defeated." "Nothing I do works out right." "I have nothing to look forward to.") forms a framework of beliefs, or a schema. These schemas are sets of beliefs that dominate thinking. For instance, a schema could be the belief: "Unless I do everything perfectly, I'm a failure." This schema, in turn, sets up unrealistic expectations which create or exaggerate losses and cause depression.

3. Cognitive errors. Both the triad and schemas mentioned above, arise out of and lead to errors of thinking that distort our perception of life and make us depression prone.

Common examples of these thinking distortions include: *selective filtering*—where we pay attention only to the negative things that happen to us; *overgeneralizing*—where we take one incident and make general and grossly exaggerated conclusions about our world; *catastrophizing*—where we blow little events out of all proportion.

Let me illustrate how these three thinking distortions operate in the life of a typical elderly person. Suppose you are an older person taking the written driving test to renew your license. For you, this is a threat, whereas most of us take it in our stride. You pass the written test—but fail to answer four items correctly. Instead of feeling relief at having passed the test, you say to yourself, *I nearly failed the test.* This is *selective filtering.* Next you think, *I clearly have problems with my memory. I must be going senile. Perhaps there are other things I'm forgetting that I don't know about.* This is *overgeneralizing.* Then you think to yourself: *This is it! I'm going to pieces. Everything is going wrong with me. Perhaps it would be better if I were dead.* This is *catastrophizing* and you will probably react by becoming depressed. Each of these steps, with increasing power, creates imagined losses—and more depression.

As we get older, we become more prone to these thinking distortions simply because our brains decline and leave us with less thinking ability. If you previously have had some tendency towards these patterns of thinking, they only get worse as you get older. This is why it is so important to make healthy adjustments earlier in life.

The main aim of cognitive counseling is to reverse the negative thinking patterns that create imagined losses. This is done in four ways:

1. The depressed person learns to *monitor* his or her thinking. (My book *The Success Factor* gives suggestions for doing this so I will not repeat the ideas here.)[8]

2. The depressed person is taught to *recognize* the connection between negative thinking and feelings of depression.

3. The depressed person is taught to *think more honestly* and be more reality-oriented.

4. The depressed person learns to *develop healthier schemas* that produce a more positive outlook. Here again, being a Christian ought to have a major influence on how we think. God is in control of our lives and Christ is our Savior. This ought to create a hopeful outlook, so that we can say with Paul, "For I have learned in whatsoever state I am, therewith to be content" (Phil. 4:11).

Often this contentment is not so much learned, but *poured* into us by a loving and caring God. Hallelujah!

Thinking Distortions in the Elderly

As we get older, we all become more prone to "thinking distortions." There are, however, some common distortions that depressed older people tend to exhibit. They are clearly irrational and need to be challenged and corrected wherever they are encountered. Here are a few suggestions for countering them. The counselor can easily develop additions to the list, once you grasp the essence of these distortions.

"I'm too old to change." This reflects a passive giving up. Respond by asking: "But is it possible for you to learn a new way?" The dysfunctional assumption ("I cannot change") needs to be moved to "We can all learn something new." Emphasize also that we don't know we can't learn something unless we try first.

"If only this hadn't happened to me, I wouldn't be so depressed." Here the tendency is to blame the external event or life in general for one's depression. Variations include "If only he (or she) would change," or "If only I had more money." We all tend to attribute our depression to some external cause. Counter it by emphasizing that we change the way we react to what happens to us.

"You're too young to help me." Younger counselors must often deal with the problem of age differences. Youthfulness can sometimes be a disadvantage especially at the start of counseling. Respond, if you sense this attitude or if the depressed person says as much, by pointing out that counseling is a skill we learn, and age has little to do with effectiveness. Encourage the client to temporarily suspend judgment and give assurance that you will provide an opportunity to evaluate progress at a later stage.

"No one has any respect for old people." Point out that this is more a fear than a fact. For one, you are demonstrating your respect for the elderly. In any case, true age is more an attitude than the count of one's years. We are as old (or as young) as we believe ourselves to be. Others will respect us more if we maintain a youthful optimism and enthusiasm for life.

"There is nothing more to live for. I might as well give up life now." Feelings of hopelessness predominate in the depressions of the elderly. They don't respond directly to occasional reassurances. It takes repeated and persistent phrases, such as "That's not true. That's just the way your depression makes you feel," to finally make a dent in these hopeless attitudes. Encourage the aged client to pray for hope and a revitalizing of his or her spirit.

Remember that older individuals don't like taking risks. They avoid failure by adopting a cautious attitude. Start with small risk-taking suggestions like encouraging a widower to sit in public places to be around lots of people before attempting to introduce himself to strangers or going to meetings for older singles. Don't force them into taking big plunges; failure will only demoralize them further.

OTHER TREATMENT CONSIDERATIONS

Above all else, the counselor of elderly depressed persons should be flexible and willing to try a variety of treatment approaches including antidepressant drugs. The most rapid alleviation of depression is still the use of electroconvulsive therapy (ECT).[9] This highly effective treatment is relatively harmless, especially when compared with the prolonged use of drug therapy. Failure to be flexible only prolongs the misery and disability of many severely depressed older people. In the case of high risk for suicide, ECT should definitely be tried.

The adjunctive use of minor tranquilizers for anxiety and hypochondriasis, and sedatives for insomnia, should also be encouraged.

Often the greatest resistance to treatment with drugs or ECT comes not so much from the depressed aged person as from family members. Due to ignorance or just plain prejudice, they prefer to prolong the suffering than to accept that these physical forms of treatment are safe and God-given, in competent hands. Encourage family members to talk to others who have benefited from these treatments. One testimony from a recovered depressive can be worth more than many hours of persuasive counseling.

PART FOUR

COUNSELING SPECIFIC LIFE PROBLEMS

Of the ten to fourteen million people in the United States who have a diagnosable depression, only 50 percent actually seek treatment. At this moment, therefore, about seven million people are clinically depressed and are not seeking help. Many of these sufferers are members of our Christian churches.

Why is this? In my first chapter I showed that there is still much prejudice against depression, especially in certain sections of the church. But this doesn't entirely account for so many neglecting to get help. In some, the disorder is confused with other conditions. Also, there are those who cannot afford to get professional help. But by far the greatest number of people who will remain untreated are those caught up in specific life situations where they typically don't view their problem as serious enough to warrant professional help.

This section will discuss three life situations that often cause depression that goes untreated: depression in women, in the mid-life crisis, and in bereavement.

CHAPTER THIRTEEN

DEPRESSION IN WOMEN

STUDIES OF BOTH PSYCHIATRIC patients and the general U.S. population report that depression is more common among women than men.[1] This is true for many other cultures also. Explanations are conflicting, but if the sex difference is real, some of the biological factors such as genetic predispositions and hormonal influences may be the contributing factors. So also would psychosocial explanations such as social status, learned helplessness, role conflicts, and the like.

Another explanation could be that there is little difference in the incidence of depression but that women seek help more often than men. Women are less defensive, more open to admitting and expressing feelings, and not so hung up on the need to be "strong." This certainly has been my experience as a psycho-therapist. Whereas I see more female than male clients, my impression is that males are much more defensive and overpro-tected. Sorry fellas!

But differences in help seeking cannot account for all the dif-ferences between male and female depression rates. Some depressions are clearly biological. Among these are the premen-strual syndrome (PMS) and postpartum depression (following childbirth). Other depressions are due to social-status discrimi-nation against women. Learned social helplessness, impover-ished socialization, dating inhibitions that prevent women from taking the initiative, the impact of the housewife's role, failure to maintain self-esteem when a marriage fails, difficulty in de-veloping a career after divorce, and difficulties in being a work-ing mother (both married and single) are all factors which contribute to special risks for depression in the female. *No single factor* accounts for depression being more common in women. Together, however, they place all women at greater risk.

The conflicting and multitudinous causes of depression in the female are illustrated by the story of one of my clients. I will call her Penelope.

When she was a nurse in training, she married a young doc-tor. It seemed the right thing to do! They were both in the same profession, could share "doctor talk," and had a deep under-standing of each other's call to serve humanity. Also, but Penelope plays this down, being married to a doctor provided financial security.

After a few years, a son was born. Penelope became en-grossed in the mothering task and never really noticed that her doctor husband was growing more distant. In fact, it wasn't until fourteen years had passed that she suddenly discovered, quite by accident, that her husband had had a string of affairs and was now deeply involved with another woman.

Penelope was devastated—and infuriated. At first she de-manded a divorce. On reflection, however, and counting the cost of it, she changed her mind and switched to pleading for her husband to give up the affair and return to "the nest." But it was too late; shortly afterwards he moved out and then began Penelope's painful experience with depression.

Soon she discovered the first of many sex discriminations in our culture that can cause depression in women. Her husband's friends had done the typical "male" thing in encouraging him to move out and become more independent. Male stereotypes predominate in many worldly circles and they all send the same message: "Be free"; "be yourself"; "live while you still have a chance." Female stereotypes try to perpetuate the "home and family" priorities, whereas male stereotypes perpetuate independence and nonresponsibility.

Penelope then sought legal advice and encountered her second sex discrimination. The male attorney was so chauvinistic that he tried to persuade her to settle quickly by letting some of the family assets go. Then she found that friends maintained their ties with her husband, but cut her off—that years of being a homemaker were not valued when she tried to reenter the job market; that obtaining credit as a single mother was near impossible; that even in church circles (or perhaps even more so) a divorced woman is received with great suspicion by other wives.

The net result? Penelope got depressed—while her husband thrived.

THE SOCIAL CHANGES AFFECTING WOMEN

All counselors must be cognizant of the cultural and social factors that influence the development of emotional dysfunctions. Counselors, especially males, should be aware of their own sex biases and prejudices. These are just as damaging as racial prejudices. Power has been in the hands of men for centuries and women have been kept in a state of dependency while men have determined women's fate. Our world is still male dominated, and sex biases, while they are changing, die hard. The counselor who is not sensitive to these issues should refer a female client to someone who is sensitive.

In our society, girls are taught to be dependent and submissive. A unique state of helplessness is created and when girls become women, this dependency creates vulnerability to those events that become precipitating factors in depression.

When women go into counseling or psychotherapy, many therapists persist in encouraging them to "take the blame" for

191

their unhappiness. Sexual stereotypes abound in all cultures, but in ours, *femininity* is clearly defined as being dependent, passive, submissive, and compliant. But these are also the characteristics of childhood! Unfortunately, many well-meaning Christian leaders and writers have assumed that this is a biblical understanding of the role of women. In the name of Christ we continue to maintain a subtle form of bondage that is further from the truth than any modern day heresy.

I realize I may be "pushing some buttons" here, but if we are going to help women out of depression, all stereotypes in the mind of the counselor must be set aside.

Much has been written about the so-called "women's question." There surely is a lot of confusion about what it means to be a Christian woman in this day and age. Having brought up three girls and successfully delivered them into adulthood as the most beautiful (and I mean this in the total sense of the word) persons I could have hoped for, my wife and I know something of the struggles young Christian women must go through to attain some identity and not feel like second-class citizens.

Allow me to make three assertions on this matter: 1. We are *all* (men and women) created in the image of God (Gen. 1:27). 2. Neither sex is superior or inferior to the other. Differences do *not* imply superiority or inferiority (1 Peter 3:7). 3. The happiest couples I know are those who live in true and equal partnership with each other, with God as their "superior" or head. (Eph. 5:21).

Many changes are taking place today that have an effect on women. Women are increasingly assuming leadership positions in government, industry, business, and the church. On the other hand, many women are also finding it appropriate to seek fulfillment as homemakers or to suspend their career ambitions for the period of child rearing. Greater flexibility of roles and how to fulfill them is the order of the day. Gone is the notion that a woman can only be fulfilled if she conquers the world. Many wives and mothers no longer feel intimidated by notions that unless they are receiving a paycheck, they will never feel worthwhile. By the same token, those who seek either to give priority to a career or to combine a career with homemaking no longer need feel guilty about such choices. The counselor should not prejudge any life situation or try to impose a model of his or her own bias. Try, rather, to determine what roles would bring out the best qualities of the client—as seen by the client.

RISK FACTORS FOR WOMEN

Despite the improvement in acceptance of role diversity for women, there are many risk factors that have been identified as contributing to great vulnerability for depression. The significant role changes that are taking place are themselves a risk factor. Social change is stressful, confusing, and unsettling. It is bound to give rise to many losses that can be depression producing. But are there other factors that place women more at risk than men? I believe there are.

Living Alone

According to the 1980 census, almost eleven million women over fourteen years of age live alone. Within these numbers are over eight million single mothers and their eleven million children. Many of these women are courageous, skillful, flexible, and resourceful. They handle a multiplicity of responsibilities, problems and crises, often all by themselves. But only a few are content to be alone and are free of depression. Singleness is not always their first choice, and depression is greatest in those who don't want to be single or have most recently become single.

Fortunately, despite the double standards in our culture that favor males, older single women tend to become happier than their male counterparts.[2] The plight of the single male is not as encouraging. They have more difficulty, over time, adjusting to divorce and widowhood.

For the counselor, help for the single female should focus on forging a nurturing environment. Self-caring should go hand in hand with self-responsibility and taking control of one's life circumstances.

Sexual Desirability

Another risk factor that has been identified is that of sexual desirability. One study of events preceding the onset of clinical depression showed that any experience that led to a questioning of a woman's sexual desirability was devastating.[3] The depression usually developed slowly over weeks or months following such a rejection.

The precise loss here is not clear. It could be the feelings of rejection, diminished self-worth, or the loss of a sexual outlet. Sexual roles are changing, and sexual desirability, even in marriage, can be variable. The counselor needs to be aware of how complex a loss it is to have one's partner no longer find you sexually desirable.

Children

The management of day-to-day problems in the home, particularly as they relate to children, is a source of frustration and depression in women who are mothers. Very young children and adolescents are particularly depression producing. Young children are a cause presumably because of the greater physical demands they impose on the mother. Adolescents are a cause because of their greater potential for disruption and the mother's decreased ability to control. Such a woman often feels that she is failing as a parent. The counselor should try to convince her otherwise, and help her see that mothering is an emotionally demanding task. Children, also, should be shown that their mothers are only human, with limits of endurance for both physical and psychological stress. Adolescents, particularly, should be encouraged to lend a helping hand when necessary. The overall happiness of the family can be enhanced if all the parties involved will only cooperate.

Body Chemistry

I have tried not to overly blame the female body's biochemistry for depression, but it is a well-studied fact, born out by my own clinical experience, that some (perhaps many) women experience feelings of depression and irritability that are clearly biologically triggered. Such depressions are significantly higher before menstruation. It has been found that feelings of helplessness, hostility, anxiety, and yearning for love characterize the premenstrual phase.[4] The underlying assumption of many researchers is that the endocrine cycle does affect mood. Estrogen and progesterone levels influence the central nervous system's monoamine oxidase (MAO) levels. MAO is known to deplete neurotransmitter levels and cause depression.

This phenomenon of the premenstrual syndrome (PMS) is now widely accepted as affecting many women. Clearly, the drop in estrogen levels coincides with the onset of the low mood. The mechanism is purely biological and one should not attribute any neurotic or maladjustment characteristics to women who suffer from it. They often need reassurance that they are not crazy or psychological misfits.

Many men don't understand or accept the PMS phenomenon. This only increases tension and exacerbates the depression of wives or daughters by creating additional losses.

Diagnosing PMS is relatively straight forward. The client should be encouraged to keep a mood chart, in which she rates her mood at the end of each day on a ten-point scale for several months. Zero can mean "no depression." Four or five can mean "mild depression" and a nine or ten, "severely depressed." Typically, the symptoms begin seven to ten days before menstruation, becoming progressively worse until the period begins, when there is relief. There are many variations to the pattern, but the distinguishing feature of the syndrome is the regular cyclical nature and timing of the symptoms.

It is important to distinguish PMS from dysmenorrhea or painful menstruation. PMS occurs *before* and during menstruation with three clusters of symptoms: 1. pain symptoms: cramps, headache, backache, and muscle spasms; 2. psychological symptoms: tension, irritability, anxiety, and depression; 3. physical symptoms: breast tenderness, swollen joints, and weight gain.

Dysmenorrhea is the pain and cramping *during* menstruation. Sometimes it occurs in the same women who suffer from PMS.

Treatment of PMS should be undertaken by a physician or clinic that specializes in this disorder, with the counselor providing support. Often a diet low in carbohydrates and salt is recommended, as is a mild diuretic a week before menstruation to get rid of body fluid. Caffeine drinks, such as coffee, tea, and colas should be avoided. Progesterone is also administered in various forms (usually as suppository) to some PMS sufferers.

The counselor can assist by providing encouragement and

teaching the client a relaxation technique. Generally, stress-management techniques help PMS sufferers considerably. Instead of blaming themselves for responding so badly to their environment, women who find ways to minimize their stress don't experience as much depression.

OTHER SOURCES OF DEPRESSION IN WOMEN

In addition to the risk factors discussed above, there are a number of additional sources of depression for women. Many of these are stereotypic ideas or irrational beliefs about what women should be or do. Here are some examples:

Addiction to Romantic Love

The poet Lord Byron wrote "Man's love is of man's life a thing apart, 'tis a woman's whole existence," and "In her first passion woman loves her lover, in all others, all she loves is love."

Unfortunately, it still holds true for many women: Love is their whole existence. Men are not so hung up on love. Our culture teaches them that other things are also important—sport, work fulfillment, hobbies, etc. But, sadly, our culture still inculcates "romantic" love (which is often overromanticized) as the major emotional value. Without being "in love," without a relationship with a man, women often feel diminished, unhappy, and unlovable.

I once counseled an unmarried woman who had just turned fifty and became deeply depressed. The reason for her depression was clearly her belief that she had never been fulfilled in love. She had developed a morbid obsession about finding a partner, but the more she searched the harder it became to find someone. She sincerely believed (or more accurately had programmed herself to believe) that she could never be a whole person apart from a man. Because she believed this, it became a self-fulfilling prophecy. She had developed what we can only call a "neurotic addiction to love." True, we all need love. But the overly romanticized view of love taught in romantic novels and soap operas and with which our age is obsessed is a distortion of true love. Such a love-addicted woman is bound to be depression prone. The unrealistic expectations of such a person are bound to create many disappointments—and losses.

"Why does God give a life partner to some and not to others?" How often do we counselors, pastors, and psychotherapists hear this rhetorical lament! The answer I have ready is a simple one: I don't know. I remember a lonely man asking this question twenty years ago, when he had just turned forty. I had a female client ask it last week. "I don't know why God doesn't send us all a perfect partner," I tell them. I am thankful for his having sent me someone very precious (we've been married for thirty years), but I also know this: It doesn't help to be bitter and unhappy if he hasn't sent you a perfect life partner, let alone any sort of partner.

To avoid depression the counselor must teach the client with an addiction to romantic love that she must learn not to be morbidly dependent on other relationships. Don't let her settle for secondary living through a man. A woman must *first* be her own person, establish her own security, and be autonomous. Then, if a man does come into her life, she can see this blessing as a bonus. It is not the sole reason for her existence.

The woman who is not pursuing the fulfillment of her own person often has feelings of emptiness. Even when marriage does occur, such a woman can easily go on creating unrealistic needs for further romance and not be content with the marriage she has. Boredom and disappointment can be her lot, whether she is married or not.

Marriage Anger

Anne has been married for twenty-two years to a school teacher named David. The marriage is not in jeopardy, at least not if Anne comes to terms with her feelings. You see, Anne is very angry at her marriage. David is forty-four years of age, deeply engrossed in his work, and while he is vaguely unhappy he doesn't think he has a marital problem nor that it's necessary to take care of his two teenaged sons. David spends his spare time, except for church on Sundays, in front of the television set watching sports programs. He seldom wants to go out or have friends over to visit. He leaves Anne to do all the "kid's stuff" and gets pretty mad if she imposes any demands or requests that he take care of chores.

Slowly, insidiously, Anne has become depressed. Underlying

her depression is a lot of anger. "Is this what I got married for?" she wails. Slowly they have stopped talking to each other and fighting is about the only communicating they do. Sex is infrequent and not satisfying to either of them. David is more impulsive and explodes periodically to vent his feelings. Anne keeps it all in, withdraws, and internalizes her pain as a deep-seated rage.

When they first married, Anne and David had lots of "shoulds" in their beliefs. Anne felt David *should* behave in a certain way. Because he didn't, Anne became angry, cold, and distant. David did the same and slowly a pervasive and persistent "marriage anger" has set in.

Marriage anger is a significant cause of depression in couples, affecting the wife more than the husband, though both can get depressed. The depression then disturbs the marriage relationship further, so it becomes a self-perpetuating cycle. David is able to escape to his work to relieve his anger and depression by becoming engrossed in distractions, but Anne is pretty much stuck with it and sees no way out.

"I knew I was depressed," says Anne in therapy one day, "because I cried so much. I couldn't explain why I was crying, but later I realized that we were both depressed and angry. That's when I decided we would get help." Fortunately, David agreed to get counseling also.

David and Anne worked hard in therapy—and were able to salvage their marriage. Their depression was mutually contagious—infecting both of them. But the root problem was the marriage anger—anger that each felt toward the other over unfulfilled expectations.

Counselors will encounter many of these "angry marriages." The approach I find most helpful is to emphasize to both partners that in order to get happiness *out* of a marriage, you have got to put something *in*. Nothing in, nothing out. It's a simple law, but always works. Also, if we behave towards someone *as if* we love them, the feeling of love will follow. Love feelings *follow* love behaviors, not vice versa (see 1 Cor. 13).

Defusing anger feelings is a matter of openly talking about the *causes* of the anger and finding ways to meet one partner's real needs while not sacrificing the other's. Some sacrifice and compromise is inevitable, but when given freely and received with appreciation, sacrifice is seldom resented. Of course, the final antidote for all anger that is produced by hurt is forgiveness. Teach your clients how to give and receive forgiveness.[5]

Fulfillment of Motherhood

There is something special about being a mother—as there is something special about mothers. I have greatly respected my wife as a mother and homemaker. I would not have wanted it any other way. There were times when she felt like she would have felt better about herself if she had accomplished some career goal outside of homemaking, but as we see our three daughters move towards motherhood themselves, we can see the value of good modeling. Mothering is not instinctive—it must be learned, and a good mother teaches it from the beginning.

But not all mothers feel that homemaking is a privilege. They protest vehemently, demean their role as nurturers, and long for more glamorous careers. Many women have difficulty balancing the demands of time and the necessity of having to work. They have the worst of both worlds and invariably are overstressed.

Depression can result from role confusion or the demeaning of certain roles. The counselor must avoid trying to impose role definitions on a given client, yet attempt to both affirm the roles chosen by a mother while helping her explore new and alternative outlets for her skills.

Some years ago, my wife developed a book of Scripture cards on a variety of themes. Feeling the need for some self-expression outside of homemaking, she tackled the task of publishing the cards herself. From printing to collating to packaging, she engaged and coordinated the work of a dozen or so specialists and published her own creation. She felt wonderful. She demonstrated that she was competent to tackle most things she chose, and she improved her self-image immensely. Many homemakers need to demonstrate to themselves that they can accomplish a meaningful goal outside of mothering. They should be encouraged to do this. Completing a college degree, writing a book, or learning some new skill can significantly alter a woman's self-image.

The Menopause

The first severe depression of many women's lives occurs at the time of menopause or shortly thereafter (the involutional period). This is not coincidental, but is often the *consequence* of a major biological change. Despite much research on this subject, there seems to be no clear-cut *causal* connection between the cessation of estrogen production from the ovaries and depression. The depression is probably caused by a mixture of factors. Most women don't experience this "involutional melancholia" at the time of menopause. Life goes on as normal; in fact it might even take a turn for the better because of the diminished endocrine disruption of the menses.

If menopause is responsible for depression, it probably can be attributed to the psychological meanings attached to the phenomenon of menopause as much as it can be to the biological changes taking place. The toll of losses at this stage are quite enormous, but many of these are only imagined losses. The counselor can reassure the client on many of the imagined losses by pointing out the following:

1. While child bearing ability is lost, postmenopausal women retain sexual desire and may continue to have satisfactory sexual relations for the rest of their lives. For some, sexual desire increases.

2. The age of menopause has dropped over the past seventy or eighty years and continues to drop, just as the age of puberty has come down. To experience menopause before age forty is not so uncommon now. Some women feel that a premature menopause is a sign of weakness. Have the client consult a physician for treatment of estrogen deficiency, if she is concerned.

3. The menopause is not a sign of old age or that aging will be accelerated and one can continue to be attractive, vital, energetic, and successful. It's all a matter of attitude and acceptance of this inevitable stage of life. Adjustment to this stage will ensure a happy continuance into the next stage of life.

4. Many imagined losses are created by irrational thoughts. Notions such as "Life will now offer less and less; I will begin to

look older; nobody has loved me in the past and they won't love me more now; youth has ended, old age is approaching" are all ridiculous and need to be challenged for what they are: lies. Menopause is only a milestone and it can be the time to rededicate oneself to a more purposeful and productive life in Christ. It is not the time for self-pity and masochistic self-punishment. Turn the affliction into an opportunity for growth (Ps. 119:71).

Loneliness and Shyness

Many women feel lonely, even when they are married and have families. Single women feel even lonelier.

Loneliness is a fact of existence for many. We all have feelings of isolation now and again. It is also normal to want to be alone for a while. My wife calls it her "need for aloneness." I resented her wanting it at first—but have come to see how important it is for her to be alone, if only to "sort out her head." Jesus needed aloneness. In Gethsemane he told the disciples to sit in one place, while he went alone to "pray yonder" (Matt. 26:36). It was nothing for him to feel ashamed about.

While we need time to be alone on occasion, we also need friendships and support. And being married or going to work day after day doesn't necessarily satisfy these friendship needs either.

Everyone needs a "true friend." Jesus is this friend, but we also need people. A friend is someone with whom we can be ourselves, honestly and transparently. Such a friendship can help us survive life's worst disappointments and ordeals. Friendship can preserve us from much depression.

Some depressions are due to "friendship deprivation." Holiday depressions are quite common, and usually follow estrangement from families and friends. You might suggest that a "substitute family" be developed or another lonely or needy group served. I had one client who frequently suffered depression at holiday time. When she took my advice and visited some homes for the elderly, she discovered many wonderful and appreciative hearts. Now she looks forward to holidays, so she can be a joyful witness to those less fortunate than she.

The hardest case for the counselor to deal with is the perpetually lonely and shy woman. She may need to be encouraged to take classes at the local college or join a women's group at church, where friendship is a little more structured. If you have several such shy and lonely women, or for that matter men also, why not try forming a therapy group with them? You can mix ages and marital status—in fact, "anything goes" when it comes to forming groups. With perseverance you can transform many lonely lives into happy ones, just by linking their hands in friendship together.

CHAPTER FOURTEEN

DEPRESSION IN THE MID-LIFE CRISIS

THERE COMES A TIME in life when all of us stop to reassess our past and, by virtue of this reassessment, envision the remaining years of our life. We may do it many times. A colleague of mine turned thirty years of age last week, and from his conversation with me it was obvious that he was reassessing his life. A few months ago another friend turned forty, and he did the same. But these periods of reevaluation and "shock" (because that's what it turns out to be) pale into insignificance when we get to the forties, fifties and for some even the sixties. It is at these times that we experience what has become known as the "mid-life crisis." Invariably, whatever else one feels or does, this period evokes some depression.

I'm sure some readers are saying: "Not again! If I hear the term *mid-life crisis* once again I'm likely to scream." So let me hasten to add that I believe we have overdone our emphasis on mid-life problems. I agree with Harry Cheney that we have a "tyranny of psychological determinism" spreading like a plague through our churches.[1] Too many are excusing their sin as a "mid-life crisis" and believing that just because they are unhappy they have an excuse to do anything they like. As I will show, we must guard against such deterministic thinking. A crisis can come at any stage of life, not just in the middle.

Mark, a recent client of mine, says he "never knew what hit him." A prominent minister of a large evangelical church, he had always felt confident and secure. God had blessed his ministry, people had responded to his message, and his church had grown far beyond his expectations. By all accounts he was successful. Many were pleading with him to "go national" and add a television broadcast to his ministry. Publishers were asking him to write books. What more could he possibly want?

Shortly after his fiftieth birthday he was sitting at his desk when he was overcome by a sudden and intense fear. He went and stood in front of a mirror and stared at himself. For a long time, he just stood there, motionless, as if frozen in body and mind.

Frightened by this episode, he tried to avoid being alone the rest of the day. That night he dreaded going to sleep, so he lay for many hours thinking about his anguish and fear. Many ideas kept flashing into his mind. Why was life so short? Why had so much of what he aspired to be not come to pass? His success as a minister, he felt, was of little import. What about his deepest longings? He felt hungry inside—hungry for some new experience, some new love, some relief from the pressures of all the demands made upon him. He was sure nobody really cared for him; they just wanted him for what he could do for them. While his marriage was not the greatest, he felt satisfied sexually. Even so, there was this urge to throw all morals overboard and experience an abandon in other sexual relationships. He was both scared and ashamed of these thoughts, yet they gripped him—for many weeks. He slipped into a deep depression. At the insistence of his wife, he sought help.

This picture is characteristic of a mid-life crisis. Without excusing it, let us acknowledge that many men experience it to some degree or other. Sometimes they only wake up to it when they are already involved in an affair. At other times they delude themselves into believing that the changes they are making in their lives are "for the best." Most times it is a state of panic and depression.

Some psychologists describe it as a "symbolic death," others as a "roof falling in."[2] It seems that never before have so many people had to deal with this "gap" in the life cycle. Of course, never before have there been so many older people to experience a mid-life transition.

For a few, the crisis of the mid-life period is not so much a symbolic death as it is an opportunity for a new birth and a revitalizing of one's life. One must, of necessity, come to terms with one's mortality. To do so "in Christ," and to realize that maturity provides many benefits of wisdom, courage, and clear sense of God's calling, is to find middle age to be a fruitful and deeply satisfying period.

There is still much to be conquered after the mid-life period, and we can be victorious in it because we have the mastery that comes with experience. It is a time when we can begin to reap the fruits of our labors. It is not a time for regrets, recriminations, or stagnation. The Christian counselor has a unique opportunity to help the person (male or female) who becomes bogged down at this crossroad; you can point these people to the power of Christ, available for just such a crisis.

THE NATURE OF THE MID-LIFE CRISIS

The contemporary overemphasis on mid-life crisis is a little misleading since every stage of life has its crisis potential. Adolescents often experience it when they move into adulthood. They don't want the responsibilities of being an adult, but want all the benefits. Leaving college can precipitate a crisis. So can having a baby, getting a new job, being fired from an old one, or having to move from one place to another. After my youngest daughter and her husband arrived at their new home in Germany, reality hit home, and a crisis of adjustment was forced upon them. So every stage of life has its changes that force us to make adjustments, and the consequence can be a crisis of some sort. Fortunately, we weather these well and go on with the business of life without too much disruption, if we walk with Christ.

There seems to be something special about the mid-life period, however. Many go "overboard" at this time. They explore new behaviors and make changes that are too drastic, too impulsive, and too damaging to the lives of others. It is mostly males who catastrophize this experience, although the mid-life crisis is by no means an exclusively male phenomenon. It frequently involves extramarital sexual activity and a giving up of marriages to search for some new excitement and stimulation. It is always a search for reassurance. It is a time of great temptation—and the potential for sin is enormous!

Before I delve too deeply into the causes of the mid-life crisis, let me add a word of warning. I have worked with many Christian men in the mid-life crisis period. I have no illusions about how only the "weak" or those "lacking in spiritual commitment" succumb to the temptations of this phase of life. It can hit any of us, no matter how spiritual we may be. I have seen men strong in their faith throw overboard everything in which they believed—in an attempt to recapture some youthful aspect of their being. I have come to believe that none of us is without price; we all can be "bought" by the right set of conditions. This may sound pessimistic, but it is only because I think it is foolish to believe you are beyond the realm of temptation. It is better to be "on guard" than too confident. Or, as the apostle Paul so wisely says, "Wherefore let him that thinketh he standeth take heed lest he fall" (1 Cor. 10:12).

There is another side to this caution as well. I have also heard well-meaning men say, "Well I am at that stage of life when it is necessary to throw away old hangups and explore the new. You see, this is my mid-life crisis period, so I can do what I like." It is an attitude of "it's okay to be questioning my old values at this stage because everybody does." It's as if they are using the phenomenon of the mid-life crisis to give them permission to experiment with something new.

This is dangerous! Having labeled something like the mid-life crisis, we may have created a monster. Instead of it being a label to help us understand the phenomenon of forced change at the involutional period, it is becoming an excuse to throw everything sacred and precious away, causing pain and sorrow to many. I actually sat with a client last week who had just thrown away twenty-five years of marriage and three children. He willingly described his marriage as "very satisfying," but he wanted to try something new because a friend was doing the same. He could not pinpoint any significant defect in his marriage or home life and admitted that his wife was a very competent, flexible, and adaptable person. He even went so far as to say he still loved his wife. Yet he was leaving her to court another woman, fifteen years his junior, simply because she represented another "era" of life, and he wanted to "stop growing old in his mind." He was abandoning his marriage, even though he had no assurance that the other woman would marry him. He was willing to "take his chances," he said, and then added: "You see, I am at the mid-life crisis stage. If I don't do it now, I never will make the change."

He's quite right of course. It is only at this mid-life crisis stage that you make such impulsive and unwise decisions. But this does not make it legitimate.

CAUSES OF MID-LIFE CRISIS

In its essence, the mid-life crisis is both a period of life and a process of reassessment in which one explores and tests new choices, generally evoked by a deep pessimism about one's existence.[3] This pessimism emerges in full force when youth is over and maturity starts to take its place. One becomes discontented about one's lot in life and begins to believe that what is left is not going to be much better. There may also be a need to recapture one's youthfulness by "going back" either to earlier models of behaving or, for the male, by becoming romantically and sexually involved with a younger woman.

To make the psychodynamics of the mid-life crisis even more complicated, the thought processes that underlie the discontentment and negative appraisal of one's life remain on the periphery of consciousness or may be fully repressed. People who suffer from such a crisis are usually *unaware* of it being a crisis at all. They think they are just making a natural change. The only mood they may feel is one of depression.

Not all mid-life crises are to be characterized as a search for sexual freedom or a running away from family responsibilities. There are many quiet and highly moral mid-life crises. Here, spiritual commitments remain strong and there is no desire to give up any moral ties. Marriages remain intact and love remains alive and vital. All that may happen is that people become disillusioned with their work, question whether or not they have accomplished any significant goal, and simply become depressed. In a nutshell, this is probably how most Christian men would experience their own mid-life period of reappraisal. This, also, could be the drama of the involutional melancholia of middle-aged women.

Besides a fear of getting older and a desire to recapture youth or sexual pleasures, there are a number of other causes of the mid-life crisis. Here are some of the more important.

A Crisis of Values

During the early part of adulthood, many adults suspend their critical judgments on matters of money, love, and other important values. They put them "on hold." During their adolescent years they may have questioned and even kicked against some of these values, but as they settle down into adult life, they "go along with the crowd." William Hulme notes that questions about the meaning of life and the satisfaction of material things, which might have been troublesome in adolescence, now return. One again begins to ask the teenage questions of identity (who am I really?) and become intensely aware of one's individuality and aloneness. It can be a frightening experience and Hulme rightly points out that this crisis is really spiritual in nature.[4] It is sometimes called a type of neo-adolescence in which one has to rework many of the same issues of the teenage years all over again. If someone was not successful in resolving important adolescent conflicts, those questions are likely to raise their heads again at this stage.

A Crisis with Spouse

Another factor that may precipitate a mid-life crisis is the change in relationship with one's spouse. After the years of child rearing, it is easy for a couple to grow apart. They live under the same roof, but closeness and intimacy is eroded by familiarity. I believe that there comes a time in every marriage, and it happens for most at the mid-life stage, when a person must rediscover his or her spouse. Perhaps it is a rekindling of love or it may be falling in love all over again. Something has to happen. If not, or if people begin to believe that how they feel toward their spouse is how they will always feel, a marital crisis could begin.

A Crisis over Children

A change in relationships to children can also precipitate a mid-life crisis. At this stage in life parents can pretty well see how the kids are turning out. Dreams may turn to fears and a significant disillusionment can set in. For the mother who has spent all her adult life taking care of children, there is suddenly a big, gaping hole in her sense of purpose. As children get older, they leave home and might even refuse to have anything further to do with their parents. Power over them is gone—for many parents, so is any real purpose for their lives.

A Crisis with Work

Work provides most adults with more than just financial security; it is the means by which they derive meaning and purpose in life. Observe older men when the time comes for retirement. Few of them "let go" easily. They experience it as a deep sense of loss of their identity.

At the time of mid-life, the vocational goals and dreams are reevaluated more harshly than at any previous time. Our success-driven culture forces us to confront our worth, our value, and our prospects for the future. What I have observed in many men and women is that success is very relative. I sit with one man in therapy and he tells me that he would be satisfied if he had achieved a certain rank in his promotion at work. I then counsel another man, who is at such a rank, and he says that he's not satisfied because he would prefer another rank. And so it goes on. One person would be satisfied with a certain bank balance, but another, who may have twice that amount, is also dissatisfied. No matter how much success one has achieved, there's always room for dissatisfaction. It can be helpful to remember this.

Mid-life may, for a significant group, be the appropriate time to effect change. Nothing I have said is intended to imply that one should be content with one's lot, no matter how bad it is. The counselor may need to evaluate a mid-life-crisis client to determine whether or not he or she is achieving at an optimum level of performance and whether or not significant opportunities are being missed. I have had the joy of helping many men, and a few women, explore their unrealized potentials and open up new careers at the mid-life stage of their lives.

A Crisis with Aging Parents

For a small but growing group, the period of the mid-life invariably brings a role reversal: becoming the guardians of aging parents. Just about the time when one feels a new-found freedom from not having to take care of children, a new set of responsibilities may emerge. With advancing age, parents begin to decline physically and gradually move back to the helplessness of childhood. Some aging parents deteriorate faster than others, but for most a dependency on someone younger finally emerges. The effect on the mid-life adult, especially the male, is a feeling of constrictedness and control. There is a loss of freedom as the responsibility load gets heavier. More regular visits to the aging parents, taking care of their financial matters, organizing social outlets, providing transportation to the doctor and dentist—all begin to feel like a horrendous burden that can precipitate a crisis of wanting to "run away." It can certainly cause quite a bit of depression.

A Crisis of Letting Go

It is quite clear that one of the developmental tasks of the mid-life period is to let go of the feeling of youthfulness. Carl Jung, an early pioneer of our understanding of the mid-life crisis, saw life as occurring in four stages: childhood, youth, mid-life, and old age.[5] The transitions between childhood and youth and mid-life and old age are not as radical as the one from youth to mid-life. We turn from being outwardly oriented to being inwardly set. It is a stage we are totally unprepared for— no colleges to help and no abundance of parental guidance and support. It is a lonely transition, full of potential for loss.

A successful transition from the exuberance, abundance, and opportunity of youth to the realities and harshness of the middle-life requires that one stop clinging to unrealistic expectations.

Mid-life offers a most appropriate time and opportunity for altering the attachments of childhood and youth.[6] One now knows one's limitations and that time is not "on our side." One is ready for serious transformations or "conversions of the heart." For the first time, clients stand at a place where they can see where they have come from. They can view the long, torturous road of youth from some vantage point. They can also see the road ahead—full of opportunity and the fruits to be reaped. If they turn, however, and try to go back from where they've come, attempting to hold onto or recapture their youth, they will create a "mid-life crisis" and plenty of depression.

If they are successful in letting go here, later life will be much easier to handle. They will have begun the cycle of many "letting gos" that must, inevitably, characterize the latter part of life. There is much to be gained by the ability to let go. Deeper and more abiding values take over and become the ideals for elderhood.

A Crisis of Faith

Mid-life crises are also crises of meaning.[7] In this sense it also becomes a crisis of faith. Everything one has ever believed, every value and standard one has ever stood for, is opened for scrutiny. I have known strong and secure elder ministers who have wakened one morning and said, "What's the use of my going on? Why bother with all the struggle? I don't think it is worth it!" They've then left their families and gone off to marry a younger woman. I have seen Christian mothers look into their children's eyes and say, "I want more excitement in life than you can give me," and then run off with a no-good, dead-beat, ne'er-do-well. As I so often say these days, "Nothing surprises me anymore."

But not everyone is going to do something so drastic. For the majority, going through the mid-life period may mean a crisis of faith of lesser proportions. It may be a questioning of values, often concealed behind smiling faces, but there is no risk of abandoning one's faith or family. They may struggle to ignore these disillusionments and continue with their normal routine of existence. They may be full of doubts but they continue going to church, or preaching, with a deep sense that "this too shall pass." Their spirituality may suffer a little, but they plod on hoping that it will all come right in the end, and it does. There will be some depression. For some it will be mild and easy to bear. For others it will be deep and painful. The loss of faith, temporary or permanent, will need to be grieved just as any other losses.

COUNSELING THE MID-LIFE CRISIS

Every pastor or counselor sooner or later has to deal with someone in the mid-life crisis period. Men seem to be worse at handling this period and avoid seeking help until they are either very depressed or have "blown it" by some outrageous behavior or affair.

I have occasionally counseled a person in Christian service who wants to get a divorce but fears the consequences of this in terms of employment or rejection. This person doesn't want help for the crisis but reassurance that what he or she is doing is acceptable. These clients want you to say "It's quite normal for you to do what you're doing. No one can point a finger at you because you deserve to get the most out of life." I tend to avoid getting involved in such cases. The motive for counseling is wrong; the client wants to be relieved of guilt feelings over being irresponsible and doesn't really want help! If you confront the selfish motives, and often you have to do this, such a person abandons therapy.

Educating the Client

The first step in counseling a mid-life crisis client is to educate him or her on the nature and causes of the mid-life crisis. Explore earlier life conflicts that may have remained unresolved and thereby contributed to the present crisis. Of course, you may need to persuade the client that what he or she is experiencing is *not* a crisis so much as it is just a giving in to the flesh. Explain that the mid-life period is for reevaluation, and this is where the energy should be focused, not on running away. Explain, also, that this transition period comes as a series of changes and not as one dramatic event. Only at a later stage does one look back and see how the journey fits together and how a new life structure has emerged.

Dealing with the Losses

Talk about what is being "lost" and what must be let go of. If necessary, allow clients to reminisce about their youth. What regrets do they have? What opportunities have they lost? How does this affect the future?

Allow a grieving period. Give permission for clients to feel sad. Point out how appropriate it is to feel the loss of opportunities and to realize life has its limitations. Point out that some injustices must just be accepted. Jesus said, "Blessed are the peacemakers," so they should make peace with all their hurts and those who did the hurting. As with other reactive depressions, the more one understands his or her losses, the sooner healing takes place.

Finding Self-Understanding

Help your clients develop a deeper understanding of values—their meanings and purposes. As we get older, we ought to become more "transparent" to ourselves. We should come to know our motives better and be able to recognize those that are unwholesome. Sadly, most people don't develop this self-insight outside of therapy and counseling. The structure of normal relationships, including deep friendships, seems to mitigate against it. We put up barriers and hide behind facades and this is not conducive to the exploration of our inner selves. This lack of self-understanding is a significant cause of depression in later life.

Improved self-understanding can be facilitated by the following techniques:

1. Keeping a meditative journal. Encourage clients to keep a journal of thoughts and feelings. This is a useful therapeutic technique in general counseling, but here it is particularly valuable. It helps clients confront their emotions, and it very concretely pinpoints those issues that are troublesome and need exploration.

A meditative journal is an important variant for Christian clients. A time needs to be set aside each day for this exercise. The client first spends a little while in Scripture reading and prayer, asking God to be present, and then takes the journal (which can be any sort of notebook) and begins to write down thoughts and feelings just as they occur. Thoughts don't have to make sense or be expressed in complete or grammatically correct sentences. Simply have the client write down everything that comes to mind. At first, people are reluctant to do this because they don't believe there is anything to write about. But as clients *start* to write, the process is stimulated and becomes self-sustaining. All one has to do is *begin.*

After an appropriate period of writing, which depends both on the degree of inspiration and available time for the exercise, the client should once again pray and read a portion of inspirational Scripture. Each day's entry should be dated and then reviewed during the counseling session.

The ability of such a journal to get at deep issues is quite remarkable. I keep a journal, and prefer to do the exercise in the early morning. I find that it helps me prepare for the day in quite a wonderful way. God's presence is very real at these times. I believe he does want us to know ourselves, our sins, weak spots, wrong motives, and secret hates. But he also wants us to know our strengths and potential for his service. King David knew the value of such self-understanding, as it is given by God. He wrote: "Search me, O God, and know my heart: try me and know my thoughts: And see if there be any wicked way in me, And lead me in the way everlasting" (Ps. 139:23, 24).

2. Resolving value conflicts. At the mid-life stage, a conflict of values inevitably arises. For years, one might have suppressed certain desires, but now they suddenly take on new force. Avarice, lust, and envy may suddenly become obsessional. Pressures from family and society have kept unholy desires under control, but this control may be externally imposed and therefore resented, not something that comes from the heart. At the mid-life stage, this control weakens and is likely to precipitate a period of experimentation.

Whether or not a client has acted out these conflicts or given in to the suppressed desires, it is important to get them out into the open. The man who secretly longs for an affair in order to experience some new sexual thrill needs to talk about this urge. Keeping it covered or secret doesn't take it away. Like a sore, it continues to fester if it is not opened to the light.

I recently counseled a devout middle-aged man who had convinced himself that if he did not think about his sexual fantasies, they would go away. He declined, at first, even to talk about them in therapy. However, the more he tried to suppress his unclean thoughts, the more bothersome they became and the more he became depressed. Finally he consented to share these deep inner secrets and, to his surprise, their hold on him weakened. This is the wonderful thing about sharing your burdens with someone else: the obsession subsides because the element of neurotic guilt is reduced. When someone else also knows about these hidden desires, it doesn't feel quite so bad and a system of accountability is established that makes one feel a little less threatened. It is because we deep down don't want to surrender to these urges, that they bother us so much. Christian counseling helps to strengthen the side of righteousness, but it does so not by denying the presence of the bad but by exposing it to the full daylight of a shared encounter. God is then able to free us from our obsessions in a new and victorious way.

3. Finding resources for strengthening faith. I think that faith is tested more at the mid-life transition than at any other time of life. Not only does depression negate faith, but the loss of ideals, confrontation with reality, and the realization that life is rapidly passing by place strains on one's beliefs that will be quite intense.

When things are going well, faith is easy. In times of crisis, it is not so easy. But only faith can sustain us in these times. Faith in God can provide us with "evidence of things not seen" (Heb. 11:1), but when we are despondent, we tend not to trust this evidence; we then want more concrete proof. At these times, the Spirit of God calls us to take the "leap of faith" and move closer to God, not further away.

Trusting God in moments of catastrophic trauma is probably easier than trusting him in the vague crises of the mid-life transition. In the former, you have nothing else to rely upon. In the latter, things don't seem so critical.

The counselor has to help the client strengthen his or her faith at these times. This is vital, because in moments of this vague crisis one needs the vitality of the very resource that natural tendency wants to throw away. How can you do this? Here are a few suggestions:

Always pray with the client. Demonstrate the practice of your own faith.

Teach the client that the good news of Christ is that God's intentions toward us are always *good,* no matter what we may feel about our circumstances (Rom. 8:32).

Point out that if the crisis feels bad with Christ in it, how much worse it would be without him.

Emphasize that God is in the refining business more than he is in the miracle business. The mid-life is a time for purifying, not a time anyone should bypass. Unfortunately this is not a message we hear much these days. True, God works miracles and can take us out of unpleasant life circumstances. But he also refines or purifies us by requiring us to go through troublesome circumstances.

One of my hobbies is making gold and silver jewelry. Hand-made rings make wonderful gifts for daughters, secretaries, and spouses. I know how to remove impurities from precious metal. It takes lots of heat. Again and again, Scripture uses the same image with respect to the believer:

> But he knoweth the way that I take: when he hath tried me, I shall come forth as gold (Job 23:10).

> Behold, I have refined thee, but not with silver: I have chosen thee in the furnace of affliction (Isa. 48:10).

> That the trial of your faith, being much more precious than of gold that perisheth, though it be tried with fire, might be found unto praise and honor and glory at the appearing of Jesus Christ (1 Peter 1:7).

CONCLUSION

God can use the pain of a mid-life crisis to remove the dross of selfishness, personal ambition, and dirtiness. But it takes our cooperation. He calls us to participate with him at this stage of life, perhaps more so than at any other, in doing the work of sanctification! Though the way through this fire may be hurtful and unsettling, as in all of life's crises, his covenant with us is to be present and help "in every time of need."

When, one day, the mid-life crisis is over and all commitments are restored, when the anxiety produced by unholy desires is relieved and the pain of "kicking against the pricks" subdued, we will find that instead of fearing that life is nearly over, we will find that a whole new day has dawned. Life after the mid-life crisis can be more meaningful than it ever was before. I know, because that's where I am now!

CHAPTER FIFTEEN

DEPRESSION IN BEREAVEMENT

MUCH HAS BEEN WRITTEN about bereavement. Overall, ministers and counselors are quite competent to deal with most mourning experiences because normal bereavement is a self-limiting reaction. Given time and a supportive environment, most people recover without needing any special counseling.

Even though normal bereavement is a self-healing process, significant depression still follows the loss through death of someone close. Bereavement, in fact, is considered to be a very common precipitating factor of reactive depression.[1] Death is the most significant loss any person can experience. But because people accept the inevitability of death more easily than they do other losses, the process of grieving in bereavement goes on quite normally. Except in a few instances where a mourning individual does not adjust to the loss within a reasonable period of time, bereavement is seldom the cause of long-term clinical depression. In fact, some experts would even go so far as to say that the depression of bereavement is not in the same class as other clinical depressions. I disagree because I think that *all* reactive depressions are the same—the differences in degree being due only to the meaning of the loss and the ease or difficulty with which the sufferer grieves the loss. In all cases of mourning, I believe that counseling can be beneficial.

NORMAL VERSUS ABNORMAL GRIEF

The counselor, then, must be able to distinguish between a grief reaction that is in all respects normal, and one that is abnormal. A normal reaction, though intense, is at least headed in the direction of adjustment to the loss. The process of grieving, as described in chapter 5, is following a course that will lead to the ultimate lifting of the depression.

Abnormal Grief

The following characteristics will help the counselor distinguish abnormal grief from a normal reaction:

Abnormal grief reactions may take the form of inability to grieve immediately after the loss. This is evidenced by an absence of weeping or an outward appearance that is too cheerful. At the other extreme is a prolonged hysterical grieving manifested by crying, shouting, and swooning. (In some cultures such behavior is expected and is therefore normal.)

Overactivity, without a sense of loss, is an early sign of distorted grieving. Normal grieving creates a "slowing down" and a reduction of activity and lessening of interest in other activities. Abnormal grieving often creates excessive energy as a way of escaping from the pain of the loss. The sufferer may start all sorts of new projects, may refuse to go to bed at a normal time, and generally becomes hyperactive.

Furious hostility against specific persons, for example the doctor and hospital, may assume paranoid proportions and be abnormal. The sufferer dwells on the rage to the exclusion of the other concerns of normal grief.

An oversuppression of hostility can also be abnormal. This shows itself in emotion and conduct as a "frozen" masklike appearance or formal, stilted robotlike movements. Lack of any emotional expressiveness may be a sign of abnormal grief.

Self-destructive behaviors, such as giving away belongings, making foolish business deals, or engaging in other self-punitive actions, especially without guilt feelings, are early indications of an abnormal grieving response.

If social isolation continues unaltered or becomes progressively worse after three or four months, the prognosis is not good. Similarly, if the depression continues to get worse after three or four months, an abnormal grief reaction must be suspected.

Other more general signs of an abnormal grief reaction include: portraying the dead person as a total saint with no shortcomings, being too positive about someone who clearly had imperfections or who may have done harm to the survivor; deterioration of health, weight loss, and other psychosomatic symptoms that persist.

Normal Grief

Several features prominent in normal grieving have been identified by Parkes, Lindemann, Kubler-Ross and others.[2] Most of these are well-known so I will merely touch on them briefly here:

1. *Somatic symptoms* are prominent in the early stages of grieving: sighing respiration, exhaustion, stomach disturbances, restlessness, yawning, and choking.

2. *Psychological symptoms* follow quickly: feelings of guilt with thoughts like *What more could I have done?* or concerns over unresolved emotional conflicts.

3. A deep sense of loss over the absence of the loved one is prominent. There may be preoccupation with the image of the deceased person; hearing his or her voice, seeing a glimpse of the face in the distance. This may even seem bizarre to the griever. This is a sure sign that normal grieving is under way.

The sense of the dead person's presence can be so vivid, especially at night, that the griever hears, sees, or feels touched by the person. At the same time there is a simultaneous feeling that all other persons are emotionally distant.

The counselor should discourage any belief that the dead loved one is physically present in spirit. Not only is this theologically incorrect, it feeds the psychopathology of abnormal grieving. It may also predispose the griever to pursue spiritualism or forms of it, so as to communicate with the departed loved one.

I vividly recall when I was thirteen years of age, just after my grandmother had died, hearing my grandfather in the next room "conversing" with my grandmother nearly every evening. It saddened me, even then, to realize that his imagining of her being physically present was not helping his grieving. "Let her go," I wanted to say to him, but never got up the courage. He never recovered from his loss of her and lived another twenty years longing to go to be with her. When it came, his death was a great relief to me. I knew he was at peace.

4. Some hostile reactions and irritability are normal. There is also disruption of normal patterns of conduct and relationships. There is a desire to be alone, indecisiveness, and erratic memory. It is even normal for the griever to feel that a part of the self has been destroyed or mutilated.

How Long Does Normal Grief Last?

Contrary to what most people expect, one never completely gives up ties to a deeply loved person who dies.[3] There is always a residual bond that can trigger episodes of grief long afterwards, especially on special occasions such as birthdays and holidays. The more practical question, then, is how long does it take for the acute symptomology following bereavement to subside? A common estimate says it takes up to three months for the more severe aspects of the reaction to pass. But many other factors can combine to either lengthen or shorten this period:

The number of remaining relationships (the more there are, the easier it is to adjust).

The strength of these relationships (the stronger, the better).

The intensity and length of association with the deceased person (the more intense, the longer it will take).

The number and severity of unresolved conflicts (many unresolved conflicts will lengthen the grieving period).

The degree of dependence on the deceased person (a lot of dependence will lengthen the grieving period).

The circumstances of the deceased's death (sudden or traumatic deaths are harder to accept, and grieving is prolonged).

The mental healthiness of the survivor (severe neurotic tendencies will prolong grieving).

You can see that grievers are recovering when the depression begins to lift and they appear to be functioning normally again. They also are able to experience pleasure—as they once could.

THE STAGES OF GRIEVING

The following framework may be useful in determining how far a mourner has progressed in the grieving process.

Both child and adult separation reactions have been used to provide five generally recognized stages.

1. Denial. This first reaction occurs before grieving has really begun. The mourner denies that the death has actually occurred and expects the deceased to suddenly reappear.

2. Searching and protest. Here the survivor is preoccupied with the lost person and quietly "searches" for him or her. Prolonged conversations with the dead person and wearing items of clothing identified with the dead person may be typical at this stage. Direct expressions of hostility against the deceased may also occur.

3. Despair and depression. This is the main emotion of the readjustment period, as the realization of the loss sets in.

4. Disorganization follows this despair. Turmoil, emptiness, pointlessness of life, and even thoughts of suicide may be present.

5. Reorganization and acceptance finally occurs in which normal functioning is resumed. Some periodic regressions to earlier stages of grieving may occur from time to time, but the mourner quickly recovers from these repeated grieving episodes.[4]

DEALING WITH THE SHOCK OF SUDDEN DEATH

When a loved and cherished person is suddenly and traumatically taken away in death, as in a car accident, cardiac arrest, or after surgery, a unique "shock" is experienced that is superimposed on the normal grieving process. Pastors and counselors often have to be the ones to impart the news of sudden death.

Here are some suggestions for counseling the survivors of such an unfortunate occurrence.

1. Patience and gentleness are essential. Remember that the immediate family is likely to be in a state of shock.

2. Immediately after imparting the news of death, try to get the family together and seated in a quiet area where they cannot be disturbed. Provide some beverage and other comforts, as appropriate.

3. Have the physician or other involved persons give as detailed an account as possible of the circumstances surrounding the death. Survivors may benefit from being allowed to ask questions about the last hours of the deceased. Don't push families who don't want this information.

4. Develop any issues that may arise, draw out unanswered questions, and point to ways these might be resolved.

5. Physical acts of kindness may, at first, be the only way of showing support or comfort, so focus on these more than on spoken words.

6. Don't shut off silence too readily. Survivors need a little time to think and process their shock.

7. Make sure family members know how to reach help in the hours or days following. Give them a telephone number or refer them to an appropriate counseling agency if necessary. The need to talk may be delayed in some of the survivors.

COUNSELING THE BEREAVED

Immediately after the death and through the funeral or memorial service, the grieving person is usually adequately supported by friends and other family members. Grieving only really begins after the loved one is placed to rest. When all the family has gone and friends have returned to their normal business, the mourner feels the loneliness of the loss the most. Support should therefore be provided, through counseling, immediately after the formalities have ended.[5]

The process of grieving described in chapters 5 and 9 should generally be followed. The griever should be allowed to express feelings and reminisce about "old times." This may mean allowing the bereaved person gradually to retrace the whole life story, from the recent events surrounding the death, back through the years, recounting happy and sad times. Allow grief to be expressed. *Never* allow your own sadness that might sympathetically resonate with the griever's to get in the way.

The most important rule to remember is: Never short-circuit the grieving process.

Avoid statements that could be interpreted by the mourner as indicating that he or she is weak, sick, or lacking in faith or feeling. Never negate a person's right to feel sad and despondent; let him or her cry.

The Value of Tears

In many forms of depression, but especially in mourning, crying may be both common and necessary. There's a lot of therapeutic healing to be derived from an occasional "crying spell." Unfortunately, our culture doesn't value it very much. Our mores allow women more freedom to express their emotions in tears than men—who are taught to control themselves.

Crying is a complex physiologic and psychological reaction. The watery saline solution produced by the lachrymal glands is so complex that even the chemical configuration of tears varies from time to time. But despite its complexity, the positive effects to be derived from crying are well documented. I'm sure each reader could vouch for this also. What does crying do? Crying occurs in response to complex social situations, usually in response to loss. Tears from peeling an onion are not chemically the same as the tears of sadness. Crying helps the body to neutralize conflict and maintain its chemical balance. Crying serves as a psychological release for pent-up emotions. It decreases tension and frustration. Crying serves as a way of expressing very deep feelings, for which we cannot find words.

There is a danger in encouraging a very depressed person to cry all the time, but this is seldom a problem for the counselor. The more common difficulty is getting someone to cry who won't. Irrational fears, a sense of embarrassment, and a fear of losing control causes some people to block their crying ability. The counselor can prepare the way for weeping by providing an accepting, understanding environment into which the hurting person can pour his or her tears.

Avoid Clichés

Clichés such as "It's God's will that this has happened," even though well meant, are unfeeling and unnecessary in the early stage. Because the sufferer may be angry at God for the death, a statement such as this doesn't build faith, but erodes it. Other clichés, such as "Think about what you've still got left" or "After all, you've got three other children," are equally unfeeling. This doesn't restore perspective at this stage, but may only intensify the pain. It tells the sufferer you don't understand the first thing about bereavement.

Also avoid outright exhortations to stop grieving ("Cheer up; life must go on.") They create guilt and intensify the depression by adding further losses.

Most experienced counselors feel that "Your presence means more than words." If you can remain calm, composed, and accepting in the presence of a weeping, bitter, angry mourner, you are doing your job well. Patience is essential. "Self-help" groups can be extremely helpful for demonstrating that grief is universal and that there is life after bereavement.

In the event that the grieving process does not proceed normally, counseling must continue and be focused on the issue of reactive depression. Referral to a psychotherapist for more intensive psychotherapy or to a psychiatrist for antidepressants or other medication may be necessary.

Facilitating the Grieving Process

As with all reactive depressions, the primary therapeutic intention is to facilitate the grieving process. The following points should be followed where appropriate.

1. Focus on the reality of the loss. Many people don't have the courage to help a bereaved person confront the loss realistically. They cloud the issues by diminishing the importance of the loss. The counselor should be courageous, though not callous or brutal, in pointing out the realities of the postdeath life.

2. Increase the depression. Don't be afraid to allow a bereaved person to be more depressed. Allowing this, without feeling guilty, facilitates the process. The exception is, of course, in those situations where there is a risk of suicide. Here,

225

medication should be used to reduce the risk of self-destructive actions. Antidepressants won't help much in the early stages, but a tranquilizer might.

3. Develop perspective on the loss. There comes a time in the grieving process when it is appropriate to say "I think you should pull back and put your loss in the perspective of your faith, or in the context of other life circumstances." At the right time, and it usually comes much later in the grieving process than most of us think, such a discussion can help to speed up the final stages of mourning. To determine if the time is right, simply ask the client. If the client says "I'm not ready yet," it probably means that he or she isn't!

4. Focus on eternal things. The final solution to all death is life in Christ and the eternal life that this brings. This is the hope we all have: "that there shall be a resurrection of the dead, both of the just and the unjust" (Acts 24:15).

It's a great help for the bereaved family to receive reassurance that the deceased is "with the Lord." This can be of tremendous comfort to the mourners of someone who clearly was a believer. If the deceased was not a believer, there can be an additional loss to be grieved: the loss of the soul. Questions such as "How can I know he was saved?" or "What will happen to her? I know she didn't believe in God" can cause an agony of broken-heartedness in addition to the acute grief. These fears can haunt the bereavers of someone who was not a committed Christian.

I usually deal with those fears by pointing out that it is not for us to judge the eternal destiny of any deceased person. I try to help the bereaved client set aside extravagant fears of damnation until after a period of grieving has been allowed; I promise them we will discuss it at a later stage. It may require a separate grieving process. I encourage them to *focus on their lives* with God in Christ.

Christ's care for us, as demonstrated in his earthly life, affirms the blessedness of mourning. Christ always enters when loss is absolute. You will recall that as he approached the dead daughter of Jairus, ruler of a synagogue, Jesus sent the professional mourners away (Matt. 9:23–25). Christ dispensed with them, not just because he was to raise her from the dead (he could have left them there to witness his miracle), but because paid wailers are often just a "cover" for genuine mourning and a distraction from the true source of blessedness in times of grief. He was offering himself, filled with the Spirit of God, as the sole Source of comfort to those who are bereaved. As Christian counselors and pastors, we do well to keep this in mind: He is still the sole Source of all comfort. God foretold that Christ was "anointed . . . and sent . . . to bind up the broken-hearted, to proclaim liberty to the captives . . . to comfort all that mourn . . . to give them beauty for ashes, the oil of joy for mourning, the garment of praise for the spirit of heaviness" (Isa. 61:1–3).

PART FIVE

COUNSELING PITFALLS

Counseling can be hazardous to your health; it can also devastate your pocketbook.

Our culture is becoming increasingly litigious. A recent spate of lawsuits against ministers and churches brings into focus the fact that allegations of malpractice are rapidly expanding to all helping professionals, and that religiously related counseling is no longer protected under the notion of separation of church and state. While the extent to which the clergy are legally responsible to the state for their actions is debatable, those in counseling situations where the activity is primarily "non-religious" can be held accountable for negligence or failure to act responsibly.

Whether their backgrounds are in ministry, marriage and family counseling, or psychology, those who undertake the complex task of counseling the depressed have a special obligation to protect their clients from harm. Introducing religious concepts into such counseling cannot be construed as a "religious activity," and no counselor who acts negligently will be able to hide behind such protection.

Whereas counseling does involve some risk (especially when counseling someone who is suicidal), there are ways of preventing or reducing vulnerability to allegations of negligence and lawsuits. In this closing section we will examine one major area of risk, namely counseling the suicidal person, and two important aspects of counseling: how to avoid legal problems, and when to get help when you need it. We will examine the pitfalls and highlight what you should know about the law to protect yourself.

Knowing *your* rights as a counselor is important. Knowing the rights of the person you counsel is more important!

CHAPTER SIXTEEN

COUNSELING THE SUICIDAL PERSON

I WILL NEVER FORGET my first experience with a suicide. It wasn't anyone I was treating in therapy, but a close friend. It happened before I became a psychologist, while I worked as an engineer. I sometimes wonder if my friend's suicide influenced me to give up engineering to become a clinical psychologist.

I was in South Africa, newly graduated as a civil engineer when I met him. He was about ten years older than myself and taught me many of the practical engineering skills I acquired in the first few years of practice. He was a loner, never married, with little desire to make friends outside of his work. He lived alone, and as far as I knew his only living relative was his older sister who lived in another town. I invited him to go to church on many occasions, but he always declined, saying he didn't believe there was a God.

My friend had tried to take his life at least twice before. Once he tried to gas himself by locking himself in his garage with the automobile engine running. A neighbor saw the smoke and rescued him. On another occasion, he tried to hang himself in his kitchen but, again, he was found in time. He never talked about why he so desperately wanted to die, and none of us asked him. In retrospect, I can see that he was frequently depressed, but he masked his depression so well that most of us who worked closely with him never sensed his despair.

Finally, he took his life with an overdose of sleeping tablets.

Since I've begun practicing as a clinical psychologist, suicide has hung as a constant fear over my professional life. In an average clinician's practice, it seems that there is always someone on the verge of taking his or her life. And that someone is also depressed.

WHO ARE WE TALKING ABOUT?

While suicides are not always committed by those diagnosed as clinically depressed, there is a marked correlation between the two. Researchers estimate that between 30 and 70 percent of suicides are completed by people diagnosed as having major depression and 15 percent of people with major depression commit suicide.[1] In my experience, I have never known anyone to commit suicide who hasn't been depressed.

For many other depressed persons, thoughts of death will become obsessional. In fact, I believe almost everyone who is depressed thinks about wanting to die. It is one of the symptoms of depression. Without it, there probably is no severe depression. While these thoughts are bothersome to both the depressed person as well as those close to him or her, they are quite normal and in most cases should merely be acknowledged and accepted.

Suicide is a major cause of death in the United States. Fifty-five thousand suicides are reported every year, but the rate may be as high as seventy-five thousand because so many are unreported.[2] Many deaths of a suspicious nature, including some single-car accidents, are suspected to be suicides, but are not reported as such unless there is conclusive evidence, such as a suicide note.

Even more alarming is that the suicide rate is on the rise. Over the last twenty-five years, the rate for people between the ages of fifteen and twenty-four has increased threefold. The rate has also increased for those over sixty years of age, due in part to the longer life-span we now enjoy. It is the third killer, after accidents and cancer, among the younger age groups.

Who actually commits suicide? Who only make attempts? Who make threats so as to manipulate and get attention? If a person thinks about suicide, is he or she likely to actually make an attempt? These are some of the major questions that plague every counselor's mind. Since counseling a potential suicide client carries many risks, it is important for the counselor to know something about the phenomenon of self-inflicted death.

Some progress has been made towards answering these questions, but much research is still needed. I doubt if we'll ever have definitive answers to all of them. Here are some tentative answers given by the National Institute of Mental Health (NIMH).

Who commits suicide? Among the clinically depressed, more women try, but men succeed more often.

Who attempts suicide? Most often it is a Caucasian woman who has a history of recent and past stressful events, an unstable childhood, and prior psychiatric illness. She is unmarried, has few social supports and lacks a close friend in which to confide.

Who succeeds? The person to complete the suicide act is, by contrast, a Caucasian man over forty-five who is unemployed, unmarried or widowed, and living alone. There may be a history of medical and psychiatric illness, some humiliating recent experience, and possibly alcohol abuse.[3]

The findings are parallel for adolescents and young adults. Girls under high stress attempt suicide more often, but boys who have been publicly shamed when being disciplined or caught by the law are more likely to succeed.

Several hypotheses have been advanced to explain the purpose of the suicidal act.

1. Suicidal persons want to punish themselves.
2. Suicidal persons want relief from suffering or an end to their "worthless" lives.
3. Suicidal persons want to symbolically kill some other person.
4. The suicidal act has no psychological meaning; it is just an indication of deteriorating biochemical changes in the brain brought on by depression.[4]

Perhaps there is some truth to *all* of these ideas. In some suicides, some of these reasons may predominate over others. Points 1 and 2 are related. Such people do feel that it is better to die than suffer, but they are unlikely to carry out the suicidal act if they don't *also* feel that they deserve to die. Point 3 is a common psychoanalytic interpretation of suicide. Yet in severe psychotic depressions, biochemical disturbances in the brain are the dominant cause of the mental confusion that can lead to suicide. All these ideas, therefore, have validity for different suicides.

THREAT OR REALITY?

Depression produces a deep longing to finish with life and even a morbid preoccupation with death. Many clinically depressed people talk about suicide and never attempt the act. But recent studies by the NIMH indicate that at least two-thirds of those who commit suicide did in fact communicate thoughts about killing themselves to family, friends, and physicians before they acted. Many were under the care of a physician at the time, but no one realized the seriousness of the threat.[5]

Assessing and managing suicidal risk is a challenge for all mental health professionals. For most, it can be a source of extraordinary stress.

A study by Litman (1965) of over two hundred clinicians soon after a client had committed suicide found these counselors' experiences to have a nightmarish quality. They had intense feelings of grief, loss, and depression. Frequently they blamed themselves for the suicide.[6]

For the counselor, the cardinal rule in working with a severely depressed person—or anyone who talks about dying—is: Consult a specialist or refer the client to a professional who can deal with the suicide risk. For the safety of the sufferer, hospitalization may be the only safe way to go.

Not all counselors should undertake the challenge of working with suicidal clients. Extraordinary measures may be called for, including hours of extra counseling sessions, late-night phone calls, and energy-sapping strain. Once you decide to help somebody who is suicidal, you have to take responsibility all the way down the line. Above all, you have to communicate that you care, down to the last drop of blood (yours or theirs).

A recent issue of the *California State Psychologist,* the publication of the California State Psychological Association, featured a vivid example of the lengths to which a counselor must go to help a suicidal patient in order to communicate caring. A young woman, suffering from schizophrenia, had been hospitalized during a psychotic episode. She continuously scolded her therapist saying, "You don't really care about me." One day, without warning, she escaped from the psychiatric ward of the hospital after threatening to take her life.

After hearing of the runaway, the therapist, also a woman, spent a whole evening driving from bar to bar, social club to social club, suspecting that the patient would have returned to some of her old haunts. About midnight, she found her patient in a bar, and lovingly guided her back to the car, returning her to the hospital. The report states that from that day on, the patient began to show rapid improvement and grew less impulsive. Later, after she was fully recovered, she told her therapist that "the night you came and rescued me" had been the turning point in her struggle with mental illness. It had become clear to her that the therapist really cared.

There are *no* infallible rules for assessing suicidal risk. If you are in doubt about a client, then act responsibly and take precautionary measures. Too much is at risk for a counselor to take chances. In many instances, more than one factor may operate, so the *total* picture must be always taken into account. Here are a few helpful suggestions:

1. Direct verbal warnings, in which there is a statement of intention to commit suicide, are one of the most useful predictors. Take the statement seriously, inform the immediate guardian or responsible person, or refer the client immediately

to a professional who can handle the risk, hospitalizing if necessary.

2. Past attempts. Up to 80 percent of completed suicides are preceded by a previous attempt.[7] Take a careful history of every client and obtain as much information as possible about previous suicidal threats or attempts. Relatives, previous counselors, and other involved persons should be approached for information. Don't rely only on the word of the client.

3. Alcohol abuse or other drug usage increases the risk of suicide. Between one-quarter and one-third of suicides are associated with the presence of alcohol. Find out if the client drinks alcohol or uses drugs.

4. Depression. Since depression is a significant cause of suicide, its presence should always be investigated. A sense of hopelessness, with depression, increases the risk of self-inflicted death.

5. Bereavement. When there has been a bereavement in the past three years, there is a much greater risk that a depressed person will take death as a way of escape. This is especially true where the deceased is "very close" to the suicidal person, and where inadequate adjustment to the loss is evident.

6. Health status. Illness, especially severe illness, increases the risk considerably. Check for fears of cancer or the presence of major diseases.

7. Indirect statements and behavioral signs. People planning to commit suicide may communicate their intention indirectly, through words (talking about "going away") or actions (giving away valued possessions or acquiring a gun or knife). Often, though, the presence of a lethal weapon is not known until after it's been used.

An excellent review of other factors identifying suicidal target groups is provided by Dorman Lum, a pastoral counselor, in *Responding to Suicidal Crisis.*[8] Although a little out of date now, this book provides excellent guidance from a Christian perspective.

GUIDELINES FOR COUNSELING THE SUICIDAL

Always assume that it is preferable to prevent suicide than aid or ignore it. Quite apart from moral or spiritual considerations of this complex issue, I don't believe a person is entitled to take his or her life. The law requires counselors and therapists to make every attempt to avoid the culmination of such an act.

Intervention may require that you send the police to a client's home or place of work, deprive the client of the means of suicide, report threats to family members, or hospitalize the client with an involuntary commitment such as the seventy-two-hour "hold" procedure. You need to know that the law allows and requires you to do this in most states. Check out what your particular state permits.

Such drastic action is a deliberate violation of the usual confidentiality limits anticipated in counseling and psychotherapy, but self-destructive behaviors are never held to be in confidence when their disclosure may prevent the death of a client. In fact, the reverse may be true: You could be held liable for not reporting a suicidal risk. For this reason, the counselor (licensed, lay or pastor) should always inform a client of the counselor's responsibilities. These are best spelled out in a written document that can be given to the client.

The following guidelines may be useful in helping you counsel a suicidal client:

1. Always stay within the limits of your training and experience. Never risk new interventions or proceed into a sphere that is unknown to you without supervision from someone who knows what is going on. This is a fundamental rule of practice for all mental health professionals, so it should apply to all counselors. If you are out of your depth, and you don't get appropriate help, you are legally vulnerable.

2. Research and always have available to you the names of competent psychiatrists or clinical psychologists to whom you can refer severe cases for immediate hospitalization. It is too late to be worrying about this when you have a suicidal risk staring you in the face. Do your homework ahead of time, and know what to do in order to get speedy help.

3. During the initial contact screen all depressed clients you counsel for suicide risk. Be frank and open. Ask direct questions: "Do you ever think about dying?" "Do you have a plan for killing yourself?" and so on. Don't be bashful. Clients appreciate a direct approach as it engenders confidence.

4. Send doubtful cases for psychological testing and evaluation. If in doubt, refer out! Standardized scales have been developed to evaluate suicidal risk and these are known to clinical psychologists.

5. Clarify your willingness to care for and be available to the client. When and where are you available? What telephone number should the client call if the impulse to commit suicide is strong? Where can you be reached on weekends or during holidays? Who should be called if you're not available? Be absolutely clear, and anticipate the "worst case scenario" as you plan back-up options.

6. Organize a supportive environment for the client. The support and presence of caring friends and relatives can help reduce the desire to die. Find out the extent to which family, friends, and church resources can be helpful. If he or she lives alone, can the client live with a relative? Can a friend "move in" for a while? Creative thinking, with the client's participation, can also communicate caring.

7. Develop a "contract" with the client, in which he or she says that you will be contacted *before* he or she ever tries to do something. Such a contract should be made in confidence and in writing. Take the contract seriously, and remind the client often that this is your agreement. Many suicides have been prevented this way. It gives the suicidal person permission to call you—right at the moment of impulse. Often, just the knowledge of the agreement is enough to relieve the impulse.

8. Be sensitive to your counterfeelings, especially negative ones. When one deals with suicidal threats over and over again, one just gets plain tired. You get to the point of saying, "Go ahead and get it over with." Such feelings can be picked up by a suicidal person and taken as rejection.

9. If, despite your best efforts, a client does succeed in taking his or her life, get help yourself. The feelings of guilt and self-blame, as well as the depression that inevitably will set in, should be counseled by someone else. You will need the objectivity of another counselor or therapist to prevent you from exaggerating your contribution to the disaster. If you expect others to trust you when they are in trouble, you should be willing to do the same yourself.

THE CHURCH AND SUICIDE PREVENTION

Suicidal behavior has often been described as a "cry for help." To this cry we, as concerned Christian persons, must respond. Not only does the Christian gospel have resources to offer those who are in a desperate, despairing mood, but who else is there to care? Historically, the church's stand on the sinfulness of suicide has given rise to many injustices through a lack of compassion and concern.[9] Today, more and more ministers are taking an active role in organizing the suicide prevention ministry of the church. With proper training and the provision of effective counseling services both by lay and professional counselors, ministers are able to lead the church into its role of servanthood for broken lives.

The church is uniquely equipped to minister to those contemplating suicide. There is a rich and abundant supply of sensitive and caring people; there is a wide spectrum of groups able to give support—from youth groups to adult Bible classes to singles and older groups. No other social organization has this diversity. Couple these resources with the power of the Holy Spirit and the ultimate message of Christ's meaning to life, and lives can be significantly changed.

One obstacle remains: Unnecessary prejudice in complacent church-going Christians against the suicidal person must be eradicated. We need to create in our churches a vital theology that embodies pastoral and church care for those who "cry out for help." Jesus would not have turned a deaf ear to these cries. Why should we?

CHAPTER SEVENTEEN

AVOIDING LEGAL PROBLEMS

WHO SHOULD BE ALLOWED to counsel? Should pastors counsel? Should those who take on the challenge of counseling be free to counsel anyway they choose? There are no easy answers to these questions. A recent clergy malpractice suit in California has certainly "stirred the pot" and opened up a Pandora's box of issues.

I have always considered pastors to be the "general practitioners" of the counseling field. Research has shown that 39 percent of people seeking help for emotional problems first consult a member of the clergy, while only 29 percent go directly to a psychiatrist or psychologist.[1] Some counseling must, therefore, be done by all ministers if only to persuade disturbed people that they need to seek professional help.

Many churches now operate counseling services staffed by trained lay people and/or professional counselors. This has been an exciting development over the past decade. However, malpractice insurance is typically not available to cover these services and this places the counselors, lay and trained, at risk for litigation in the event of something going wrong. If such church-based counseling services were confined to providing spiritual counseling, there is little, if any, risk of running foul of the law. The law that governs the practice of medicine and psychology generally exempts the clergy from any regulation; provided they stick with spiritual matters. For example, the California Business and Professions Code explicitly states that the provisions that deal with the licensing of physicians and surgeons do not "regulate, prohibit, or apply to any kind of treatment by prayer, nor interfere in any way with the practice of religion."[2] Similarly, the section detailing the licensing of psychiatrists and psychiatric personnel exempts the "provision of services . . . when done by the tenets of any well-recognized church or denomination."[3]

But what has happened in recent years is a blurring of the distinction between *spiritual* counseling and *psychotherapy.* Frequently, psychotherapy and not religiously oriented counseling is being offered by ministers and other church-based counselors, and a greater degree of accountability will be invoked by the courts for those who counsel but do not confine their counseling to matters of faith, spiritual development, and penitence. Because of the risk of suicide, no area of counseling is more open to legal pitfalls than the area of depression, which is *not* always the result of spiritual waywardness. Most depressions require more treatment than simple solutions.

HIGH RISK SITUATIONS

What are the potentially high risk situations in counseling? Thomas Needham has provided an excellent list of these. Among the more important are the following:

Using and interpreting psychological tests without adequate training and supervision.

Applying simple spiritual solutions to complex emotional and psychological problems.

Believing that only biblical training is needed to solve severe psychotic disorders or suicidal intentions.

Advising against medical or psychological treatment, when such treatments have clearly been established as effective.

Counseling severely disturbed clients regarding whether or not to take psychiatric medication.

Keeping inadequate records.

Failing to protect records as confidential.

Failing to respond responsibly to threats of violence against others.

Failure to report cases of child abuse to the appropriate authorities.

Labeling as *demon-possession* clear cases of psychotic disorder and thus preventing reasonable access to effective treatment.

Poorly supervising secretarial and lay counseling staff, who then misjudge the seriousness of a situation.

Developing "dual relationships" in which the boundaries of power and influence are blurred. (Taking favors from clients, counseling close friends or relatives, and becoming emotionally involved with a counselee are considered to be *dual relationships*.)

Having sexual relations even with the consent of the counselee, is considered unethical, and in some states illegal.[4]

The greatest risk of all arises because of inadequate training and supervision. Many young pastors are thrust into counseling situations with strong desires to be spiritually effective, but are insufficiently trained and experienced to deal with high-risk situations. Often they are taught to believe that all emotional problems are basically spiritual in nature, and that, as pastors, they therefore have all the answers needed to cure any and all emotional problems. This is absurd and naive, as any experienced minister will tell you. If a pastor and his or her lay or other counseling helpers hold to such a view, they will expose themselves to a great risk of litigation.

Spiritual Healing

This is *not* to say that spiritual healing or biblical resources are not effective in counseling. They certainly are! But they must be reserved for and applied to those problems for which they were intended—problems of sin, unrighteousness, unbelief, and spiritual guilt. When a counselor cannot recognize blatant schizophrenia, myxedma madness, hysterical paralysis or the confused mental state of an organic brain syndrome and applies simplistic spiritual solutions to these problems, valuable time in obtaining effective treatment is being lost, endangering the client's well-being.

When a counselor further advises against the appropriate treatment (which very often happens especially in cases of schizophrenia and severe depression) and the sufferer takes his or her life, that counselor must be held accountable for neglecting to provide appropriate treatment.

Through the establishment of graduate schools of clinical psychology in Christian institutions, Christians are developing professional knowledge and skills and integrating that knowledge with a firm faith in Jesus Christ. Such dual training is not only the best safeguard against legal retribution, it is absolutely necessary if effective help for the church to develop sound counseling services is to be forthcoming.

To those who strongly believe that "faith healing" must be applied in every situation, I say that one should always perform the act of faith healing *together* with whatever help modern medicine or psychology can offer. In other words, prayer for healing must be accompanied by appropriate professional help. This is consistent with what is done in cases of physical illness. Probably the most prominent faith healer of our day, Oral Roberts, has built an exceptionally fine hospital and medical school. Most who believe in faith healing would not deny access of a cancer sufferer to modern medicine. They would pray for such a person while encouraging him or her to go to a doctor and obtain the best available medical advice and treatment. The same should apply in cases of emotional distress, such as depression. The physical or psychological defects producing depression may be unseen, but they are real. Unfortunately, precisely because emotional illnesses are less tangible than physical illnesses, they tend to be given "spiritual" interpretations.

Types of Lawsuits

Most counselors today lack understanding of what constitutes professional liability and are, therefore, at high risk for malpractice litigation. When compared to medicine, psychology has experienced much fewer malpractice suits. Times are changing, however, and there needs to be a greater awareness of the types of suits that can be expected.

What are the types of malpractice suits that are typically brought against psychologists and counselors?

1. Breach of contract. This is a failure to keep a promise of providing effective results. No counselor should ever promise to cure or accomplish anything. If you do, you can be held liable to a "breach of contract."

2. Physical assault. Physical injury is also a major reason for malpractice claims. One well known case is that of Abraham vs. Zaslow (1970) where the therapist "restrained, poked, and abused" a patient as part of "rage reduction therapy." Many therapists use plastic bats for simulated beating. These can easily be misused and lead to malpractice claims.

3. Sexual assault. This includes unauthorized or unreasonable touching and comprises the largest number of lawsuits now against psychologists. In California, a therapist having sex with a client (usually a male therapist) can face *three* legal consequences: He may be prosecuted under criminal law, held liable for malpractice, or have his licenses revoked.

4. Abandonment, which involves failure to continue to counsel when it is still needed and from which the counselor has not been properly relieved. This means that all terminations of counseling should be clearly documented and clients informed accordingly.

5. Suicide. When a client commits suicide a suit for "failure to protect" can be filed. You can be liable if you fail to apply the "usual degree of care" in assessing suicidal potential or fail to provide a reasonable degree of care and skill in preventing the suicide.

6. Negligent infliction of emotional distress. While *intentional* infliction of emotional distress is an old cause for action, there has been a trend recently to sue for *negligent* infliction (where you unwittingly inflict pain on another). For example, in

Cooper vs. Doscher (1984), a suit alleged that a psychologist misdiagnosed a child. The parents contended in the suit that this misdiagnosis resulted in shock and distress for themselves. The court held that the psychologist was negligent in not foreseeing the damaging effect of the diagnosis. For counselors who make public diagnostic labels this should be a warning: Be alert to the consequences that any diagnostic label you might use will have on others who don't have the knowledge to interpret it with appropriate boundaries.

PRECAUTIONS TO BE OBSERVED

It is not appropriate for me to discuss at length the details of the law as it applies to counselors or the rights of pastors and churches to exercise their freedom to practice religion. If the reader would like a more thorough review of these matters, then I recommend that you read the book *Clergy Malpractice,* in which various authors provide a thorough review of issues ranging from "Malpractice in the Ministry" to "What the Law Says" and "Church Discipline: Handle with Care."

Why are risks for counselors, especially pastors and lay-counselors, increasing? The obvious reason is that the culture has become more and more litigious. Everybody wants to make a buck, so people try to take advantage of your negligence or carelessness. But many also want to just "get revenge" and are looking for reasons to vent their frustration and anger against the authority the church has over people.

There are other significant reasons also: Many lay-counselors and pastors are inadequately trained and the public is demanding protection; attitudes and beliefs about the nature of emotional distress are out of date in some churches where any explanation, other than a spiritual one, is resisted; a greater dependence on lay ministries is being encouraged, without adequate supervision being provided.

How can the counselor protect him- or herself against risk? Here are some suggestions:

Know Your Limits

But don't just know them, admit to them also. It is so easy for one's ego to get wrapped up with being successful in every counseling case. The sign of a competent counselor is that he or she knows when to refer a client to someone else who is either more competent or more specialized. Anyone who practices outside of the limits of his or her training and experience is held by law to be negligent.

There is a particularly dangerous situation inherent in the pastoral-counseling field. Some pastors see their ordination as a license to do whatever counseling they feel is necessary. This can easily take them into realms beyond their experience and training. The better trained you are, the more you know your limits and practice within them.

Obtain Supervision

No one should embark on counseling activities, no matter how well trained, without supervision from an experienced counselor. Easily half of what one learns to do in counseling comes from being supervised. Supervision helps you "test the limits" of the theory you've learned; it helps you apply the theory as it was intended to be. Just as you can't learn to fly an airplane just by reading a flying manual, so you cannot learn to counsel just by studying theory, reading a book or taking a correspondence course. A coach or instructor is needed to help you translate theory into practice.

Use Other Professional Resources

The problems that confront the counselor are always complex and require a team approach. You cannot know everything, but you can know what other resources are available to you. Refer clients for "evaluation and testing," if you are in doubt about a diagnosis. Subtle psychotic disorders are not always easy to recognize. Even if you are confident about diagnosing, a referral for a second opinion will help to protect you in the event of something going wrong. This is particularly necessary in the more severe depressions, where anti-depressant medication may be helpful. Don't deny your client his or her rights to a speedy healing just because you don't understand what is going on. While you continue your counseling, call for consultations with other professionals.

Maintain Confidentiality

You have a primary obligation to protect the confidentiality of *everything* that transpires in the counseling room and the violating of a confidence is a very common cause for litigation. Don't discuss cases with anyone but an identified supervisor, and get permission (in writing) from your client even to do that. Don't provide information to *anyone* else, including parents, spouses, doctors, psychologists, or other counselors. You need written permission from your client to release this information to anyone.

Safeguard all records (they should be under lock and key), and be careful not to publicize who you are seeing in counseling. A common mistake here is to display appointment calendars and counseling notes. All information must be protected and treated as if it is confidential.

Often overlooked is the need for adequate sound-proofing. If a secretary next door can hear what is being said in your office, you are violating confidentiality. Office construction, for counseling purposes, must provide adequate insulation and "sound traps" to make clients feel safe.

Report Child Abuse

In many states now, it is mandatory that all cases of suspected child abuse be reported. To delay even a few days to check out the validity of an alleged child abuse complaint is a criminal offense. Obtain a copy of your state's law as it pertains to the reporting of child abuse and study the document carefully. In California, mental health professionals cannot now be licensed or re-licensed without taking formal training in what to do in the case of alleged child abuse.

Your Duty to Warn

You have a clear responsibility to warn anyone of a threat to harm him or her, as well as to take the necessary steps to protect anyone from making a suicidal attempt. Rules of confidentiality do not apply when there is a threat to violate the law.

Avoid Dual Relationships

As mentioned earlier in this chapter, dual relationships are clearly a risk for counselors. In essence, counseling and friendships should not be mixed, because they interfere with each other. Some of the reasons cited for keeping dual relationships to a minimum are: Counselors might not be confrontative with those they know socially; the counselors' own needs to be liked and accepted will interfere with counseling; by the very nature of counseling, counselors develop power over others, increasing the risk that they can be exploited.[5]

The ethical guidelines for psychologists, published by the American Psychological Association, clearly prohibits dual relationships because they impair professional judgment (principle 6(a)). Examples of dual relationships include counseling with employees, close friends, or relatives. Some professional associations would even go so far as to preclude receiving gifts or favors, or even having casual social contact such as going to lunch.

For the pastoral counselor, where other relationships are inevitable, this prescription against dual relationships can be problematic. Often pastors encourage friendships with parishioners who may then need counseling. Too much friendship may disqualify you from being an impartial counselor, in which case you ought to refer the client to another counselor. Every counselor needs to be aware of, and cautious not to exercise, the power he or she holds over counselees. Any attempt to manipulate or exploit this power will place you at great risk for legal action.

Avoid All Erotic and Sexual Conduct

In recent years, sexual contact with clients has clearly become taboo. Erotic contact between a counselor and a client is viewed as unethical at best, and devastating at worst.[6] Apart from moral considerations, which are important to us Christians, secular counselors have banned sexual intimacies because of power differences. Clients may share deeply personal material about their sexual desires and struggles and previous intimate relationships. In this way they expose their vulnerabilities to their counselors, who can then exploit and take advantage of the trust. If a client is sexually provocative, this behavior has to be seen as part of the problem being counseled. To respond to it is to become a part of the problem. The law assumes that you have abused your power even if you've been seduced. You are the one with the power to refuse.

It seems such a pity, doesn't it, that this danger has to be emphasized in a book on counseling from a Christian perspective? Unfortunately, sexual intimacies between pastoral counselors and parishioners (and I don't just mean intercourse, but kissing and other physical touching) can be as common as between nonreligious counselors and clients. In fact, there is evidence to suggest that secular counselors are less likely to engage in erotic behavior than religious counselors. The penalties for the secular counselor are great; they can lose their licenses to practice if they have sex with a client.

A recent study, carried out in collaboration with one of my graduate students, revealed that at least 35 percent of the ministers from four major denominations in California admitted having engaged in behavior toward a parishioner considered to be "inappropriate for a minister."[7]

I consider ministers to be at great risk for "sexual transferences." By *transference* I mean the tendency for clients to transfer feelings to the counselor that really belong somewhere else. These can be feelings of love, affection, and sexual desire, as well as anger and hate. This accounts for clients sometimes falling in love with their pastor/counselor. Such feelings are the product of the unique counseling relationships and should be understood to be brought on more by the *role* of counselor than by his or her *person*. If the counselor responds to this transference, believing it to be meant for him or her, the relationship could get out of hand.

Unfortunately, ministers are not trained to deal with transference in the counseling situation and can easily find themselves involved in a torrid love affair which can destroy their reputation and ministry. In *Leadership* (Fall 1982), I published an article entitled "Transference: Loosening the Tie that Binds" which may be helpful to the reader. Charles Rassieur's book *The Problem Clergymen Don't Talk About* is an excellent treatment of the risks of pastoral counseling in this area, as is *Counseling Christian Workers* by Louis McBurney.[8]

Seek Additional and Ongoing Training

None of us will ever reach the point where there isn't something more to know about counseling. Continuing education needs to become a habit and something we seek without being coerced. New and improved techniques of diagnosing and counseling are being developed all the time; sometimes one must relearn skills that have long since been forgotten; sometimes we just need a spiritual "shot-in-the-arm" to help us through a period of emotional burnout. Whatever your needs are as a counselor, continuing education will certainly be one of the ways in which you can reduce your risk of litigation.

CONCLUSION

This chapter has focused on ways the counselor can be destructive to a client and the many pitfalls that can lay you open to lawsuits or charges of ethical violations.

In a short chapter it is not possible to provide a comprehensive guide to appropriate counseling behavior. Depending on your primary discipline, you must make sure that you know both the legal limits of your freedom to practice and the ethical standards set down by your appropriate professional organization. Psychologists and marriage and family counselors are governed by state laws and by ethical principles, published by their respective associations. The American Association of Pastoral Counselors also has a code of ethics. These are all presented in the appendix of the book *Clergy Malpractice*, to which I have already referred.

The overriding principle of all these documents is that the counselor must *first* safeguard the well-being of the client. If you follow this principle, there's not much you can do to get yourself in trouble!

CHAPTER EIGHTEEN

GETTING HELP WHEN YOU NEED IT

THERE ARE TWO IMPORTANT questions that counselors should periodically ask themselves: 1. When do I need to refer a client to another counselor or specialist? and 2. When do I need to get help for myself?

In the previous chapter, and at other places throughout this book, I strongly advocate that competent counselors know their limitations and refer to a specialist any client whose problem is beyond their level of competence. It is not always easy to discern this "boundary of competence," which is why every counselor should be supervised by a more experienced counselor during the first year or two of practice. Only with experience, gained under the watchful eye of an impartial supervisor, can one become competent to judge one's own limitations.

The focus of this last chapter will be on the second of these two questions: When do I need to get help for myself?

It is a well-established rule that the personal needs of a counselor should not interfere with the therapeutic process or be detrimental to the client.[1] The more counselors are unaware of their personal needs, the more they are likely to project those needs into the counseling relationship. This is why most counselor and psychologist training programs place a high priority on personal counseling.

Naturally, if counselors were expected to have resolved all their personal problems before they begin counseling, most of us would be excluded from practice. But we should place a high priority on increasing our awareness of those biases and personality idiosyncrasies that could interfere with our work.

Counselors expect their clients to examine their own behavior and motives and to explore their inner world so as to understand themselves more fully. To me it seems a reasonable expectation that counselors be equally committed to understanding their own inner lives.

Without a high level of self-understanding, counselors will not be able to help their clients beyond a certain level of healthiness. It's like counseling spiritual matters: You can't expect the person you are helping to go further along the road than you have traveled. You lead the way and invite others to follow. If you are not willing to "go ahead," you might possibly obstruct the progress of the person you're trying to help. This easily happens when the problem you are counseling is one you haven't resolved for yourself. The focus and content of the counseling easily shifts from the counselee to the counselor.

For instance, I knew a psychologist who had never quite resolved his feelings for his father, a large domineering man. As the boy was growing up, his father taunted him with "You'll never amount to anything" and "You'll always be useless." The father was quite adept at fixing or building things—so my friend grew up afraid to attempt any repair himself. He knew his father would criticize it. In short, my friend grew up believing he was a klutz.

Deep down he knew his father never meant his critical remarks. They were supposed to encourage him to try harder, never to be satisfied with what he had accomplished. They were designed to motivate and prod him to attempt greater things. "Never be satisfied with anything you've done," the father would say, "always push yourself to do it better the next time."

Later in life my friend discovered he had developed a lot of resentment towards his father. He had come to internalize his nagging parent, and he carried the "voice of demand" around within himself all the time. Now, whenever he counsels a client with a "strong father," he finds himself getting angry and prodding the client to attack the father, or, worse, spending a lot of the counseling time expressing his own feelings instead of listening to those of the client. This shift of focus to the psychologist's problem instead of the client's should never be allowed in counseling.

To be an effective counselor you should be aware of your own needs, areas of unfinished business, personal conflicts, defenses, and vulnerabilities. More important, you should know how these might intrude on your work and be sufficiently on guard so as to interrupt them and return the focus of counseling to the client. There is only one way to develop this awareness: Get some counseling for yourself.

In the area of depression counseling, it is critical that you be aware of your own "unfinished" business. Without it, you may find yourself becoming depressed along with your client—often for reasons that elude you. This quickly leads to burnout.

Being a counselor has many benefits as well as hazards. Among the benefits is the privilege of growing alongside others. You can develop insights and change your own behaviors as you help others do the same. Among the hazards is the revelation of your own weaknesses, often at times when you least expect or desire this knowledge.

Experienced counselors will tell you that they derive much personal benefit from their work. They feel a deep sense of satisfaction from helping others to achieve greater self-awareness. But that's only part of the story. Therapeutic encounters often serve as mirrors in which counselors see a reflection of their own problems. Much personal gain can be derived from almost every counseling situation.

But counseling is not the same as being counseled, and there is a limit to how much self-awareness can be derived from being a counselor. Counselors should not depend on self-knowledge coming entirely from their counseling. They should strive to minimize the use of clients to fulfill their own therapeutic needs.

VULNERABILITIES OF COUNSELORS

The personal conflicts and unfinished business within counselors are as varied as the counselors themselves, but there are some general vulnerabilities that can be identified. These are common to most pastors and counselors:

A Need for Approval

This is perhaps the greatest hindrance we all have to contend with as counselors. Most of us grow up with a strong need to win the acceptance of others, to gain their admiration, respect, and even their awe. It is a byproduct of the culture we live in. We're taught to be competitive, but there are insufficient rewards for those who don't make it to the top. When we start counseling, the client becomes a "significant other" from whom we attempt to receive confirmation that we are competent.

To illustrate, imagine the following: You are a male counselor who all your life felt that you never quite measured up to your father's idea of masculinity. You played various sports, but never made the top team nor did you receive any outstanding award for any sporting activity. To compensate, you applied yourself to your academic work, studied hard, and developed a sharp intellect. You graduated from college with top honors.

One day a man, just a few years older, comes to see you because he has a depression problem. You recognize him as the top athlete in your high school class. You recall how he was admired by the girls and worshiped by some of your buddies. As you start to talk, you feel a little intimidated. You ask yourself, *Will he accept me? Does he remember me from high school?* Before you realize it, you've launched into a lengthy explanation of some technical detail of depression. You're trying to impress him with your knowledge. You're strongly pushing for admiration by matching your intellect with his physical prowess. In the process, you've made an idiot of yourself, because you can see from his face that he is not impressed. He is probably saying to himself, *What's this fool up to? Why is he trying so hard to prove he is smarter than I? Maybe I should go somewhere else!*

Such encounters—where we try to win approval by proving that we have something the client doesn't—always have a reverse effect. We lose approval.

There are many other ways you can seek approval: giving premature advice; trying to convince a client that you are indispensable; collaborating with a client's distorted view of some event and not being honest with your feedback; agreeing with a client's ideas.

One of the essential ingredients of good counseling is *objectivity*. Excessively needing approval from your client removes you from the place of objective impartiality and truthfulness.

A Need for Power

Closely allied to the need for approval is a need for power. Sometimes it is a need to control others; at other times it is a need to feel powerful.

One expression of this need for power is a need to feel you have all the answers concerning how others should live. This is not just a matter of providing clear moral guidance, but a need to direct another's life down to the last detail. There is also too much personal interest in seeing that the client follows your direction. Slowly, you come to believe that you are indispensable.

A need for power can also express itself in too much interest in seeing that the client gets better. This puts the client in a bind. He or she may not be doing better, yet feels coerced into saying so—by the tone and manner of your voice. If the client doesn't get better, he or she is blamed for not cooperating or taking your advice. After all, you are giving the right treatment; if it fails, it must be because he or she is not following through.

Counselors who overcontrol their clients feel important and powerful because the clients become more and more dependent. Instead of teaching them the *process* of problem solving, you teach them how to depend on you. The cycle of dependency is thus intensified.

A Fear of Deep Emotion

The "blood" of counseling is deep emotion. Just as the surgeon gets used to blood, so must the counselor become accustomed to deep, hurting, wrenching emotional pain. If you don't like the sight and sound of it, you can't do your job properly. I certainly would never let a surgeon operate on me who finds blood distasteful! A counselor who is afraid of deep emotion would never get close enough to see my minor hangups, let alone the major ones.

If you haven't explored your own deep feelings, you are bound to become unseated when you first encounter gut-wrenching sobbing.

Just this last week, a fifty-year-old male patient in a deep depression fell on his knees in front of me, pleading for immediate relief. Sobbing from deep down in his psyche, he implored me to do something to relieve his pain. I assured him that I was doing everything I could, and that it would take another week before his antidepressant medication took effect. "One more week," he cried, "I can't stand this another week." He fell crumpled and beaten to the floor with groans so deep I thought he would die.

I pulled back my thoughts for a moment and reviewed my own feelings. Tears had come to my eyes and my stomach was in a knot. I started to pray over him and a deep peace settled over both of us. I knew that if I was going to be of any help to my patient I could not retreat from the pain of that encounter. I had to stay there and just let him feel all his pain. Five minutes later his emotions were under control and he was able to leave my office feeling that a great burden had lifted. You can learn to "stay" with such pain—if you have been exposed to the deep pain within yourself. You lose the fear of it. After all, Jesus was not afraid of the deepest of deep human emotion. He knew what it was to cry (John 11:35) and could probe without fear the deep emotions of a woman taken in adultery (John 8:3).

Burnout

The counselor is also very prone to *burnout,* a syndrome of emotional exhaustion, depersonalization, and reduced personal accomplishment that can occur among individuals who do "people work" of some kind. But a definition doesn't adequately capture how debilitating the care of others can be. Pastors, counselors, social workers, teachers, psychologists, and many other people helpers, once vibrant with enthusiasm and power, can be reduced to ineffective rubble, emotional exhaustion, and depression, through burnout.

Severe cases of burnout are characterized by emotional turmoil, extreme fatigue, negative feelings, depression, and withdrawal. You just stop caring. No longer do you sense a client's pain. If anything, you resent it. You become detached from all responsibilities and have a pervasive feeling of being "beaten." You give up hope of ever being able to avoid defeat.

Burnout mostly occurs in one or more of the following situations: allowing sympathy to dominate your emotions rather than empathy; having too many emotional demands over too long a period; having set your ideals too high; having set your personal expectations too high, so that failure cannot be tolerated; having inadequate social support to help you accept your limitations; having an overwhelming sense that your resources are not adequate to meet the many demands placed on you.

What is the best way to prevent and cure burnout? Get counseling for yourself. If you feel you have any of these characteristics, seek help for yourself. If you are already on the road to burnout, prevent further deterioration by getting help. Counseling for counselors who are in burnout serves a number of purposes: It helps restore perspective; it provides social support; it identifies problem areas; it provides "accountability"; it provides the very same healing you seek to offer others.

PERSONAL THERAPY FOR COUNSELORS

After training clinical psychologists for many years now, I am convinced that there is no better way to improve your self-awareness than by experiencing counseling. If you have any unfinished business or find yourself particularly vulnerable to emotional pain while counseling another, your own therapy is not just desirable but mandatory.

One reason to undergo personal therapy is to give you first-hand experience, but there are other, more compelling reasons. Here are some of the benefits to be derived from your own therapy:

Your Own Spiritual Growth Will Be Enhanced

Lack of self-understanding is a major obstacle to God's working within us. I work with many Christians. Nearly every one of them reports that the therapy has helped psychologically *and* spiritually. As these people get to know themselves better, they see God's answers for their lives. They are able to cooperate better with his Spirit. It is a false, and I would even say satanic, notion that God doesn't need our cooperation in sanctification. Our growth in Christ is a team task: He will not work in us that which we will not receive from him.

Awareness of Your Defense Mechanisms

Each and every one of us has developed a unique set of defense mechanisms, unique ways of interpreting and reacting to anxiety and stress. Some people deal with anxiety by denying that there is anything to be afraid of. Others tend to intellectualize their anxieties, resorting to pseudologic. Others rationalize, resorting to complex explanations for all their problems. On a more subtle level, we might use less troublesome emotions to cover more painful ones.

During one period of my life, I used anger to cover up my anxieties. Whenever I felt afraid, I became extremely angry. The anger was designed to give me the courage to overcome my fears, but often it would only alienate other people and cause me more anxiety. As a defense mechanism, my anger solved one problem, but created another.

I suppose one could eventually come to some awareness of such a problem, but it is far more efficient to work such problems through with an understanding counselor and save yourself the hurts and disappointments of "trial and error" learning.

Better Recognition of Emotions

The effective counselor must, of necessity, have developed a comprehensive "feeling vocabulary." You need this so as to be able to accurately reflect back *to* clients what it is they feel. You must have the ability to put into words what someone is feeling. Most people you counsel (especially men) will not have this ability. Their "feeling language" will be restricted to "I don't feel so good" or "I just feel lousy." Hardly therapeutic.

Perhaps a few will have developed the language sensitivity of a poet and the ability to capture, in just a few phrases or sentences, the depth and complexity of an emotional state. For most of us this capacity must be learned. We need to identify the right "labels" and learn how subtly they can vary from person to person. It is not enough to say "It seems like you're angry." Anyone can say this. But to be able to communicate what someone feels so that he or she can identify with it at a deep level takes sensitivity. This sensitivity is best developed in your own counseling where you can learn the correct labels and develop a "feeling vocabulary."

CONCLUSION

The work of counseling and psychotherapy is both demanding and satisfying. It has its times of failure and its times of successes. It has its sadnesses and it has its joys. It is *not* the panacea for all human problems. As I have tried to show throughout this book, it is only the servant of the gospel, a tool that Christian pastors and counselors can use to help people to live more satisfying and complete lives.

In the final analysis, emotional health, and especially freedom from depression, is a spiritual endeavor. Only by living the life God has designed for us, with the resources He has provided, will we really be satisfied. It is the great privilege of the Christian pastor, counselor, and psychologist to nudge people along this road to more complete lives. As you join me in this task—with great fear and uncertainty and the acknowledgment of its awesome responsibility—may you always remember that we are merely channels for the "Father of mercies" who is "the God of all comfort; who comforteth us in all our tribulation, that we may be able to comfort them which are in any trouble, by the comfort wherewith we ourselves are comforted of God" (2 Cor. 1:3, 4).

GLOSSARY OF TERMS

ALZHEIMER'S DISEASE. A presenile disorder with progressive dementia and loss of capacity for purposeful movement and speech; symptoms include memory loss, carelessness, and disorientation

AMBIVALENCE. The coexistence of opposite ideas, feelings, or wishes toward a given object or situation

ANHEDONIA. Absence of ability to experience pleasure

ANOREXIA NERVOSA. Self-starvation leading to loss of weight

BLENDED FAMILIES. Separate families united by marriage; stepfamilies

COGNITIVE PSYCHOTHERAPY. Psychotherapy that focuses on how thoughts create and influence feelings

COMPOUNDING. Adding losses to each other so that they create more depression

CONCURRENT THERAPY. Treatment of two or more family members, seen separately, usually by different counselors

CONJOINT THERAPY. Treatment of two or more persons in sessions together

CONTRACTING. A behavioral technique whereby agreements are made between family members to exchange rewards for desired behavior

COUNTERTRANSFERENCE. The transference of feelings from a counselor to a client

DEMENTIA. A reduction or absence of intellectual functions in consequence of organic brain disease

DIFFERENTIATION. Psychological separation and independence from others

DST. Dexamethasone suppression test: used for diagnosing endogenous depression

ECT. Electro–convulsive therapy, a form of treatment for depression

EMOTIONAL CHAINING. Where one emotion triggers another, then another, until the final feeling state is unrelated to the first

HELPLESSNESS. *See* LEARNED HELPLESSNESS

HYPOCHONDRIASIS. Overconcern for the body and its details of functioning; exaggeration of any symptom

INTROJECTION. A process whereby one incorporates a mental image of an external object

INVOLUTIONAL MELANCHOLIA. Depression brought on by the decline of the reproductive system

LEARNED HELPLESSNESS. Seligman's notion of how we learn to believe that we cannot influence the outcome of any event

MAOI. Monoamine oxidase inhibitor: an antidepressant drug

MELANCHOLIA. A morbid mental state characterized by depression, usually with profound and painful dejection

NEUROTRANSMITTER. The chemical in the nervous system that facilitates the transmission of impulses across the gaps called synapses

NUCLEAR FAMILY. Parents and their children

PMS. Premenstrual syndrome: the experience of emotional and other disturbances just before the onset of menstruation

POSTPARTUM DEPRESSION. Depression that follows the birth of a child, often due to disturbances of body chemistry

PROJECTION. The process of "throwing out" upon another the ideas or impulses that belong to oneself

REACTIVE DEPRESSION. Depression following an identifiable happening, usually a loss of significance

REFRAMING. Relabeling a behavior to make it more amenable to change

REGRESSION. Return to a less mature level of functioning

REINFORCEMENT. A reward that increases the rate of a particular response

RESISTANCE. Anything that a client does to retard or oppose the process of counseling

ROLE PLAYING. Acting out the parts of a behavior to practice new ways of behaving

SCAPEGOAT. A person or object on which anger is displaced

SENILE DEMENTIA. A deterioration (more rapid than mere aging) of mental functioning in old age caused by shrinkage and atrophy of the brain

SEPARATION INDIVIDUATION. The process whereby we draw apart from our parents and develop our own autonomous functioning

TRANSFERENCE. The projection of unresolved feelings and needs onto present relationships. Often seen when a client "transfers" unmet needs onto the counselor

UNCONSCIOUS. Psychoanalytic term for memories, feelings, and impulses of which a person is unaware

BIBLIOGRAPHY

The following books are recommended to provide supplementary reading for counselors of the depressed.

Beck, Aaron T., et al. *Cognitive Therapy of Depression,* (New York: The Guilford Press), 1979.
While written from a secular point of view, this book is a classic and extremely helpful manual for the more advanced pastoral counselor. It provides detailed descriptions of the many techniques used by counselors of the "cognitive" approach in the treatment of depression.

Benner, David G. *Baker Encyclopedia of Psychology,* (Grand Rapids: Baker Book House), 1985.
This encyclopedia with its 1,050 entries provides coverage of important concepts and ideas in psychology from a Christian viewpoint. The pastor and counselor will find it to be a rich source of understanding.

Collins, Gary R. *Christian Counseling: A Comprehensive Guide,* (Waco, Tex.: Word Books), 1980.
Organized by individual problems, this guide provides direction in counseling a wide spectrum of psychological problems. The emphasis is on practical solutions from a biblical point of view.

Crabb, Lawrence J. *Effective Biblical Counseling,* (Grand Rapids: Ministry Resources Library), 1977.
Emphasizing that counseling is centrally a relationship between people who care and not a discipline with a lot of dependence on technical knowledge, Crabb shows how it can be integrated into the life and ministry of the church.

Egan, Gerard. *The Skilled Helper,* 3rd ed. (Monterey, Calif.: Brooks/ Cole), 1986.
Together with an excellent training manual entitled "Exercises in Helping Skills," this book is used by many counselor training programs as a basic textbook for systematically developing helping and interpersonal relating skills.

Hart, Archibald D. *Feeling Free,* (Old Tappan, N.J.: Power Books), 1979.

Many Christians are overwhelmed by their emotions, including depression. The theme of this book is to help Christians maintain a balance between controlling their emotions and being free to experience them. It provides help in integrating the more important emotions into a cohesive and healthy whole.

Hart, Archibald D. *Coping with Depression in the Ministry and Other Helping Professions,* (Waco, Tex.: Word Books), 1984.

Focusing on the risk factors inherent in ministry and some of the people-helping professions (including counseling), this book provides a personal resource for understanding and coping with depression. It is supplementary to the material provided here.

Hart, Archibald D. *The Success Factor,* (Old Tappan, N.J.: Power Books), 1984.

This book focuses on the principles of thinking and provides a variety of exercises to "capture" and "redirect" one's thinking. Emphasis is placed on reality thinking as the most appropriate form for Christian believers.

Kirwan, William. *Biblical Concepts for Christian Counseling,* (Grand Rapids: Baker Book House), 1984.

A foundational book which deals with biblical concepts important to the counselor, it also provides a review of four counseling positions while outlining a Christian model.

Malony, H. Newton, et al. *Clergy Malpractice,* (Philadelphia: Westminster Press), 1986.

No counselor, pastoral or professional, should undertake the task of helping others these days without a clear understanding of the legal risks involved. This handbook covers the major issues currently receiving close attention in legal and professional circles as they pertain to clergy malpractice.

McBurney, Louis. *Counseling Christian Workers.* (Waco, Tex.: Word Books), 1986.

Christian workers are just as needy as others. Counseling them presents special problems and this book provides valuable help to those who must be counselors to those who pastor and counsel others.

NOTES

Chapter 1. Popular Misconceptions About Depression

1. John Carter and Bruce Narramore, *The Integration of Psychology and Theology* (Grand Rapids: Zondervan, 1979), p. 20.
2. William Kirwan, *Biblical Concepts for Christian Counseling* (Grand Rapids: Baker Book House, 1984), p. 64.
3. Archibald D. Hart, *Coping with Depression in the Ministry and Other Helping Professions* (Waco, Tex.: Word Books, 1984), pp. 26–30.

Chapter 2. The Problem of Depression

1. Anne H. Rosenfeld, "Depression: Dispelling Despair," *Psychology Today*, June 1985, p. 29.
2. Brana Lobel and Robert M. A. Hirschfeld, *Depression: What We Know*, National Institute of Mental Health, Publication No. ADM 84-1318, 1984, p. 51.
3. J. H. Boyd and M. M. Weisman, "Epidemiology of Affective Disorders," *Archives of General Psychiatry*, Sept. 1982, 39: pp. 35–46.
4. *Diagnostic and Statistical Manual of Mental Disorders (Third Edition)* (Arlington, Va.: American Psychiatric Association, 1980), p. 217.
5. Robert Cancro, "Depression in the Eighties," Report of a symposium held in New York City in November 1980.
6. Frederick F. Flach and Suzanne C. Draghi, eds., *The Nature and Treatment of Depression* (New York: John Wiley, 1975), p. 7.
7. Rosenfeld, "Depression," p. 32.
8. Ibid.

Chapter 3. What Is Clinical Depression?

1. C. H. Spurgeon, *Lectures to My Students* (Grand Rapids: Zondervan, 1954), pp. 154–165.
2. Janice Wood Wetzel, *Clinical Handbook of Depression*, (New York: Gardner Press, 1984), pp. 17–67.
3. Ibid., pp. 179–214.
4. Ibid., pp. 129–178.

265

5. Ibid., pp. 215–240.
6. Ibid., pp. 241–266.
7. Flach and Draghi, *The Nature and Treatment of Depression,* p. 3.
8. John Bowlby, *Attachment and Loss* (London: Hogarth Press, 1980), 3: 245.

Chapter 4. Diagnosing Depression

1. *Diagnostic and Statistical Manual of Mental Disorders,* p. 205.
2. Ibid.
3. Ibid., p. 206.
4. Ibid., p. 218.
5. Ibid., p. 223.
6. Ibid.
7. Lobel and Hirschfeld, *Depression: What We Know,* p. 53.
8. Bassuk, Schoonover, and Gelenberg, *The Practitioner's Guide,* p. 88.
9. Arnold H. Buss, *Psychopathology* (New York: John Wiley, 1966), p. 176.
10. Joseph Mendels, *Concepts of Depression* (New York: John Wiley, 1970), p. 98.
11. Aaron T. Beck et al., *Cognitive Therapy of Depression* (New York: The Guilford Press, 1979), p. 398.

Chapter 5. Understanding Reactive Depression

1. Wetzel, *Clinical Handbook,* p. 44.
2. Ibid.
3. Ibid.
4. Paul Tournier, *The Adventure of Living* (New York: Harper & Row, 1965), pp. 240–241.

Chapter 6. Understanding Biologically Caused Depressions

1. *Special Report on Depression Research,* National Institute of Mental Health, Publication No. ADM 81-1085, 1981.
2. Bassuk, Schoonover, and Gelenberg, *The Practitioner's Guide,* p. 38.

3. Ibid., p. 81.

4. Ibid., p. 27.

5. William Nelson et al., "Hypothalamic–Pituitary–Adrenal Axis Activity and Tricyclic Response in Major Depression" *Archives of General Psychiatry*, September 1982, 39: 1033–1036.

6. Bassuk, Schoonover, and Gelenberg, *The Practitioner's Guide*, p. 26.

7. Archibald D. Hart, *The Hidden Link Between Adrenalin and Stress* (Waco, Tex.: Word Books, 1986), p. 131.

8. Bassuk, Schoonover, and Gelenberg, *The Practitioner's Guide*, p. 88.

9. Sydney Walker, III, *Psychiatric Signs and Symptoms Due to Medical Problems* (Springfield, Ill.: Charles C. Thomas, 1967), p. 112.

10. Robert Berkow, ed., *The Merck Manual of Diagnosis and Therapy* (Rahway, N.J.: Merck & Co., 1982), p. 463.

11. Ibid., p. 339.

12. James Dobson, *What Wives Wish Their Husbands Knew About Women* (Wheaton, Ill.: Tyndale, 1975), pp. 143–156.

Chapter 7.   Preparing to Counsel a Depressed Person

1. Bassuk, Schoonover, and Gelenberg, *The Practitioner's Guide*, p. 31.

2. Lawrence M. Brammer and Everett L. Shostrum, *Therapeutic Psychology* (Englewood Cliffs, N.J.: Prentice–Hall, 1982), p. 161.

3. Frank Lake, *Clinical Theology* (London: Darton Longman and Todd, 1966), p. 57.

4. Gerard Egan, *The Skilled Helper* (Monterey, Calif.: Brooks/ Cole, 1986).

5. Brammer and Shostrum, *Therapeutic Psychology*, p. 299.

Chapter 8.   The Psychodynamics of Depression

1. Silvano Arietti and Jules Bemporad, *Severe and Mild Depression* (New York: Basic Books, 1978), p. 130.

2. Ibid., p. 126.

3. Beck et al., *Cognitive Therapy of Depression*, p. 244.

4. Joseph Mendels, *Concepts of Depression* (New York: John Wiley, 1970), p. 27.

5. Arietti and Bemporad, *Severe and Mild Depression*, p. 132.

Chapter 9. Counseling Reactive Depression

1. Thomas Hora, *Existential Metapsychiatry* (New York: Seabury Press, 1977), p. 206.
2. Beck et al., *Cognitive Therapy of Depression* p. 34.
3. Martin E. P. Seligman, *Helplessness* (San Francisco: W. H. Freeman, 1975), p. 21.

Chapter 10. Depression in Childhood

1. Julian De Ajuriaguerra, *Handbook of Child Psychiatry and Psychology* (New York: Masson Publishing, 1980), p. 460.
2. Herbert Yahraes, *Causes, Detection, and Treatment of Childhood Depression*, U.S. Government Printing Office, 0-265-810, 1978, p. 1.
3. Lobel and Hirschfeld, *Depression: What We Know*, p. 43.
4. Yahraes, *Causes, Detection, and Treatment*, p. 1.
5. Ajuriaguerra, *Handbook of Child*, p. 460.
6. Yahraes, *Causes, Detection, and Treatment*, p. 1.
7. Arietti and Bemporad, *Severe and Mild Depression*, p. 87.
8. John Bowlby, "Separation Anxiety," *International Journal of Psychoanalysis*, 1960, 41:89–113.
9. Arietti and Bemporad, *Severe and Mild Depression*, p. 90.
10. Joy Schulterbrandt and Allen Raskin, *Depression in Childhood: Diagnosis, Treatment, and Conceptual Models* (New York: Raven Press, 1977).

Chapter 11. Depression in Adolescence

1. Michael Nichols, *Family Therapy: Concepts and Models* (New York: Gardner Press, 1984), p. 157.
2. Ibid., p. 158.
3. Group for the Advancement of Psychiatry Committee on Adolescence, *Normal Adolescence*, (New York: Scribner Library, 1968), p. 80.
4. Lobel and Hirschfeld, *Depression: What We Know*, p. 44.
5. Ibid., p. 45.
6. Stanley L. Copel, *Behavior Pathology of Childhood Adolescence*, (New York: Basic Books, 1973), p. 105.

7. Group for the Advancement of Psychiatry, *Normal Adolescence,* p. 7.

Chapter 12. Depression in the Elderly

1. *Star News Report,* (Pasadena, California) May 26, 1986, p. A-4.
2. *Special Report on Depression Research,* p. 93.
3. Lobel and Hirschfeld, *Depression: What We Know,* p. 45.
4. Ibid., p. 46.
5. Lawrence D. Breslau and Marie R. Haug, eds., *Depression and Aging* (New York: Springer Publishing Company, 1983), p. 159.
6. Ibid., p. 160.
7. Ibid., p. 168.
8. Archibald D. Hart, *The Success Factor: Discover God's Potential through Reality Thinking* (Old Tappan, N.J.: Fleming H. Revell, 1984), p. 154.
9. Breslau and Haug, *Depression and Aging,* p. 154.

Chapter 13. Depression in Women

1. *Special Report on Depression Research,* p. 15.
2. Wetzel, *Clinical Handbook,* p. 103.
3. Ibid., p. 105.
4. Helen A. De Rosis and Victoria Y. Pellagrino, *The Book of Hope: How Women Can Overcome Depression* (New York: Bantam Books, 1977), p. 223.
5. Archibald D. Hart, *Feeling Free* (Old Tappan, N.J.: Fleming H. Revell, 1979), p. 85.

Chapter 14. Depression in the Mid-Life Crisis

1. Harry Cheney, "Is the Mid-Life Crisis a Phoney?", *Christianity Today,* September 2, 1983, p. 82.
2. Janice Brewi and Anne Brennan, eds., *Mid-Life: Psychological and Spiritual Perspectives* (New York: Crossroad Publishing, 1985), p. 26.
3. Daniel J. Levinson et al., *The Seasons of a Man's Life* (New York: Ballantine Books, 1978), p. 61.

4. William E. Hulme, *Mid-Life Crises* (Philadelphia: Westminster Press, 1980), p. 11.
5. Brewi and Brennan, *Mid-Life*, p. 29.
6. Eugene C. Bianchi, *On Growing Older* (New York: Crossroad Publishing, 1985), p. 6.
7. Hulme, *Mid-Life*, p. 77.

Chapter 15. Depression in Bereavement

1. Arietti and Bemporad, *Severe and Mild Depression*, p. 65.
2. Wetzel, *Clinical Handbook*, p. 44.
3. Henry E. Adams and Patricia B. Sutker, eds., *Comprehensive Handbook of Psychopathology* (New York: Plenum Press, 1984), p. 98.
4. Wetzel, *Clinical Handbook*, p. 44.
5. Lake, *Clinical Theology*, pp. 290–305.

Chapter 16. Counseling the Suicidal Person

1. Lobel and Hirschfeld, *Depression: What We Know*, p. 49.
2. Ibid.
3. Ibid., p. 50.
4. Ibid.
5. Ibid.
6. Robert E. Litman, "Acutely Suicidal Patients: Management in General Practice," *California Medicine*, 104, no. 3 (1966): 168–174.
7. Lobel and Hirschfeld, *Depression: What We Know*, p. 50.
8. Doman Lum, *Responding to Suicidal Crisis* (Grand Rapids: William B. Eerdmans, 1974), pp. 97–116.
9. Ibid., pp. 29–35.

Chapter 17. Avoiding Legal Problems

1. Howard J. Clinebell, *Basic Types of Pastoral Care and Counseling* (Nashville: Abingdon Press, 1984).
2. H. Newton Malony, Thomas L. Needham and Samuel Southard, *Clergy Malpractice* (Philadelphia: Westminster Press, 1986).
3. Ibid., p. 49.
4. Ibid., p. 89.

5. Gerald Corey, Marianne Corey and Patrick Callanan, *Professional and Ethical Issues in Counseling and Psychotherapy* (Monterey, Calif.: Brooks/Cole Publishing Co., 1979), p. 142.

6. Ibid., p. 144.

7. Richard Blackmon, *The Hazards of Ministry,* Ph.D. Dissertation (Fuller Theological Seminary, Graduate School of Psychology, 1984).

8. Louis McBurney, *Counseling Christian Workers* Vol. 2, Resources for Christian Counseling (Waco, Tex.: Word, 1986). Charles Rassieur, *The Problem Clergymen Don't Talk About* (Philadelphia: The Westminster Press, 1976).

Chapter 18.   Getting Help When You Need It

1. Corey, Schneider, and Callanan, *Professional and Ethical Issues,* p. 28.

INDEX

Archibald D. Hart

Archibald D. Hart is dean of the Graduate School of Psychology and Professor of Psychology at Fuller Theological Seminary. He graduated from the University of South Africa and earned the Master of Science and Ph.D. degrees from the University of Natal. Additionally, he has done postdoctoral studies at Fuller Theological Seminary.

He has had a private practice as a clinical psychologist. His books include *Children and Divorce, Depression: Coping and Caring, Coping With Depression in the Ministry and Other Helping Professions,* and *The Hidden Link Between Adrenalin and Stress.*

Dr. Hart and his wife Kathleen reside in Arcadia, California and have three married daughters, Catherine, Sharon, and Sylvia.